Must Canada Fail?

With the compliments
of the Canada Council

Avec les hommages
du Conseil des Arts
du Canada

Must Canada Fail?

Edited by
RICHARD SIMEON

McGill–Queen's University Press
MONTREAL AND LONDON 1977

© McGill-Queen's University Press 1977
International Standard Book Number 0-7735-0314-5 (cloth)
International Standard Book Number 0-7735-0313-7 (paper)
Legal deposit fourth quarter 1977
Bibliothèque nationale du Québec
Reprinted 1978

Design by Anthony Crouch MGDC
Printed in Canada by
Imprimerie Gagne Ltée
Phototypeset by
Eastern Typesetting Company

Contents

Preface

This book is an attempt to grapple with the most immediate of all
Canadian issues, yet its roots go back almost ten years. In 1969 Leslie
Frost, the retired premier of Ontario, felt that the secession of Quebec
was a distinct possibility, for which Canadians had done nothing to
prepare themselves. To fail to do so was to risk being overtaken by
events. He also recognized that governments, for many reasons, could
not be seen to undertake such thinking of the unthinkable. At his
request, the late John Deutsch, then principal of Queen's University,
assembled a group of academics to explore some of the issues posed by
the challenge of national fragmentation. The result was *One Country or
Two?*, edited by R. M. Burns, which was perhaps the first serious
attempt by English-Canadian academics to explore these difficult questions.

When the book was published in 1971, the October 1970 crisis had
come and gone, and English-speaking Canadians outside Quebec were
once more settling into the deep indifference and complacency which
has for so long marked their attitude towards Quebec. Now, in 1977,
we bear the costs of that complacency.

By 1977 the time seemed ripe for another hard look at the possibilities. The election of the Parti Québécois government in November
1976 meant that no longer was the question remote and academic. It
was urgent and pressing. English Canadians needed both to understand the situation which confronted them, and to search for new
initiatives which might permit Quebec and English Canada to work out
a new accommodation. But, if that were to fail—and the early reactions
offered little hope that it would not—they also needed to look further
into the future, at the possibility of a Canada without Quebec.

Hence this book in which many of the same authors are involved and
some new ones. As we reviewed the earlier volume, it became clear we

needed to concentrate much more directly on the hard issues; we could no longer afford the luxury of leisurely speculation. The result is a book which is virtually all new.

While we share many common perspectives, especially the desire for a peaceful and democratic resolution of the conflicts before us, we differ in many ways too. Some are optimists, some pessimists. Some would go further than others in modifying the federal structure to accommodate Quebec. All of us recognize the depth of sentiment represented by the Parti Québécois, but we differ in our assessment of many of its policies, economic, social, and cultural. Many of us adopt the liberal vision of politics; some, like the editor, have increasing doubts about it. In that, we probably reflect the quandaries of our fellow citizens, both French and English-speaking. We have tried to coordinate our efforts, but we have not developed a single party-line.

As teachers, we have in preparing this book felt uneasy at our departures from analytic detachment, and our willingness to rush into print before all the research is in. But time moves fast, and we, like all citizens, must make our voices heard before it is too late to do anything but write history.

As editor, I want to thank Dorothy Holman, who probably never believed that so many projects could be juggled at one time, or that publishers' deadlines could be met. That they were is in no small measure due to her efforts.

RICHARD SIMEON
June 1977

Queen's University

Contributors

JOHN ARCHER, an historian, is emeritus President of the University of Saskatchewan at Regina.

EDWIN R. BLACK teaches political studies at Queen's University, and has written widely on Canadian federalism.

R. M. BURNS has recently returned home to British Columbia after a long career in government, and, most recently, as director of the Institute of Intergovernmental Relations at Queen's University.

JOHN CLAYDON lectures in the Faculty of Law at Queen's University, specializing in international law.

JAMES DE WILDE teaches political studies at Queen's University, concentrating on Canadian and comparative political economy.

FREDERICK J. FLETCHER teaches political science at York University, Toronto, and has written on public opinion, the media, and Ontario politics.

WILLIAM P. IRVINE is a political scientist at Queen's University with interests in political behaviour.

W. R. LEDERMAN is a constitutional lawyer at the Queen's Law School.

PETER LESLIE teaches political studies at Queen's University, specializing in federalism and political economy.

JOHN MEISEL, of the Queen's University political studies department, writes frequently on parties, elections, and voting in Canada.

CHARLES PENTLAND teaches international relations at Queen's University and is an expert on the European Common Market.

GEORGE RAWLYK, head of the History Department at Queen's University, has written extensively on the political and social history of the Maritime provinces.

RICHARD SIMEON, director of the Institute of Intergovernmental Relations at Queen's University, is a political scientist.

HUGH THORBURN is president of the Canadian Political Science Association, and a professor at Queen's University.

JOHN TRENT teaches political science at the University of Ottawa, and is secretary-general of the International Political Science Association.

RONALD L. WATTS, principal of Queen's University, works in the area of comparative federalism.

JOHN WHYTE is a specialist on constitutional law at the Queen's University Law School.

Introduction

RICHARD SIMEON

What we intend to bring about, if people agree in a referendum and give us the bargaining power for it, is independence and association.

René Lévesque, March 1977

This is not an optimistic book. It offers no magic solutions to the Canadian crisis. There is little comfort in it either for defenders of the Canadian status quo or for those who believe that independence for Quebec can be achieved amicably with a mutually beneficial reassociation to follow. We argue that there is a vast reservoir of "will to survive" in the country as a whole, together with a willingness to contemplate new institutional arrangements and policies which might reconcile the political goals of Quebecers with those of other Canadians. The search for such accommodation is the central challenge for all federalists.

But we also recognize that this search may well fail: that however much good will there is, the fissures in the Canadian communities may be too deep to be bridged, and one of the communities may decide to seek its own independence as a sovereign state. Disintegration is no longer simply a possibility, as it was when the predecessor to this book, *One Country or Two?*, was published in 1971. It may not be a probability yet, but it is not far from it. If we do fail, what then?

We will be forced, and perhaps in the near future, to face some frightening and unpleasant possibilities. The civility and tolerance on which we pride ourselves will be severely tested. We will face a situation which, when faced by other countries, has frequently led to civil war.

Painful as they are, we must confront such questions. If we don't, they may well be forced on us anyway. Non-Quebecers have had a dangerous tendency to worry about Quebec only when some crisis loomed—such as de Gaulle's appeal for "Québec libre" in 1967, or the 1970 October Crisis—and after a brief flurry of concern, to bury their heads in the sand once more. So, when the next crisis comes we are once again unprepared. This ostrich-like stance is, perhaps, one reason for our current crisis. We must not let ourselves ignore Quebec yet again; indeed, it seems certain events will not permit us to. Although the tensions between English and French Canada have been building over many years, the cruel dilemma is that the failures of generations must be rectified within a very few years.

The Quebec election of 15 November 1976, in which the Parti Québécois defeated the Liberal government of Robert Bourassa, winning 71 seats and 42 per cent of the vote, was a staggering upset which took the country by surprise. Outside Quebec, the reaction was shock, tempered for the moment by the reassurance that the vote was not really a vote for separation, that independence still attracted only minority support, and that the vote was largely a vote against a discredited government. The reality was that a government, with all the levers of public persuasion and executive authority at its command, was now in power with an implacable commitment to attain independence followed by a new contract of association between Quebec and Canada. The effects of this power were soon apparent. First came Premier Lévesque's New York speech in which the drive for independence was reaffirmed. Second was the language legislation which asserted unequivocally that Quebec as a society would be unilingual in its essentials as a state, economy, and culture. Finally, we have witnessed a series of smaller acts, by which the inequities of federalism were demonstrated and the federal regime challenged. The PQ has moved much faster to lay the groundwork for independence than most observers had expected. The initial reaction in Quebec found federalists discredited, demoralized, and leaderless; and polls suggested growing support for the government.

For their part, non-Quebecers appeared in disarray. No federalist vision with widespread support appeared to offer an effective challenge to the exciting vision of René Lévesque. Regional conflicts and grievances in many parts of the country had eroded any clear sense of national unity and helped to weaken the federal regime. Reaction ranged from "let them go" to "we'll use force to keep them in." In opposing a "two-nation Canada," the government of Pierre Trudeau had staked everything on a bold and humane pluralist philosophy of bilingualism designed to demonstrate to French Canadians that they could be at home anywhere in the country and that the Ottawa government was theirs as much as it was that of the English. Now opposition to these policies was growing in English Canada while they appeared to have failed in Quebec. The question is whether, having undertaken this profound commitment, Trudeau is able to respond to the new situation. Opposition leaders also seemed to have difficulty in articulating a policy which would meet the crisis.

Even before any formal move towards independence, tensions have begun to escalate dangerously. The battle of rival balance sheets of federalism, designed to show how much Quebec gained (or lost) from the federal bargain, did little to illuminate the real issues. Stories of

English-speaking Quebecers packing up and leaving the province abounded. More seriously, so did actual or threatened withdrawal of capital and departure of head offices from Montreal, which heightened the possibility that the working out of the independence issue would be gravely compounded by an atmosphere of economic crisis. Many warned that the PQ should give up any hope of working out an economic association with Canada after separation. Some aspects of Quebec's new language policy seemed petty and vindictive. All these developments are simply a foretaste of the difficult atmosphere which is likely to develop.

On the other hand, there were hopeful signs. A crisis could also be an opportunity. Perhaps now the wrangling between Quebec and Ottawa, which had dominated Canadian politics for fifteen years, could finally be ended. The issues, at last, were clear. Moreover the Canadian "will to survive" could not be in doubt. Seldom, if ever, had there been such a massive mobilization of Canadians. The mass media provided blanket coverage, to some extent making up for years of neglect of developments in Quebec. By June 1977 more than seventy new groups, both local and national, with names like Unity Canada, had sprung up. A plethora of conferences, forums, and symposia were held, all exploring in various ways the possibilities of survival. Canadians were forced to rethink their commitment to the country and their sense of how it should be structured.

No consensus has yet emerged from the billions of words. Much of the debate has consisted of federalists simply talking to other federalists. Some of it has carried ugly overtones of ethnic hostility. But the debate has also begun to generate new ideas and new alternatives; it has revealed much flexibility—as if people had recognized that the old assumptions had failed and the field was open to almost any idea. Many debaters demonstrated a deep willingness to search for accommodations in which the real interests of both Quebec and other regions could flourish. Agreement is not likely to be reached soon. We are still in the period of generating and testing new possibilities. But the possibility of a consensus is there.

This book represents the attempt of a group of English-Canadian academics, based for the most part at Queen's University, to come to grips with some of the issues and to ask some hard questions about possible future paths of development. It is founded not on new research, but on our experience as students of Canadian politics and society. It represents a first cut at the problems, and as such it raises questions more often than it provides answers.

Several important values and assumptions underlie the enterprise.

First, we are all federalists. For all of us the promise of Canada, its uniqueness as a country, is wrapped up in its character as a bilingual and multicultural society. Quite apart from all practical difficulties, the breakup of the country would diminish our own sense of Canadianism.

Second, we recognize the depth and reality of Quebec's drive for autonomy, for cultural survival, and for control over the levers of economic and political power. We are committed to democratic procedures. There can be no question of coercing Quebec to remain in Confederation. Tragic as the loss of Quebec would be, we feel there could be worse outcomes, for example, mass violence. In a real sense, the *names* of political units and the shape of their political framework are less important than the ability of human communities to chart their own destiny and to coexist with each other.

Third, we believe that it is possible to work out an accommodation within the federal system, but that this search will not be easy. It could readily fail. The first task of all federalists, then, is to undertake the widest possible search for changes which are acceptable not only to Quebec citizens but also to those of other regions.

Fourth, we believe that it is essential to consider directly the alternative responses if Quebec does seek its independence. What are the processes by which such a decision might come about, what would be the political dynamics at work in the separation phase? What role might outsiders play, and so on. Most fundamental: could it be done peacefully?

Similarly, we must contemplate the future of the Canadian communities after independence. What would be the consequences for Quebec? For the rest of Canada? What are the chances for a "reassociation," for a common market and for close economic cooperation? What other issues—such as the rights of minorities—would have to be dealt with? What are the prospects of survival of the rest of Canada: would it continue as a nine-member federation? Would some other regions go their own way? Would all be absorbed into the United States?

In some sense, therefore, we propose to think the unthinkable: to look closely at a Canada without Quebec. In doing so we take many risks. It is difficult at best to see the future, especially when political events are likely to be so tense and confused. In looking beyond federalism we may even be legitimizing the very thing we seek to avoid. By talking about it, we make it more likely; we create a self-fulfilling prophecy. Our answer is that the dangers of *not* beginning to examine such questions are far greater. The costs of ignorance and unpreparedness if and when we are faced with negotiating separation would be immense. The field might be left to the extremists. We have shied away from such questions too much in the past. It may well be political suicide for politicians to be seen to contemplate such questions. But someone must—and not just in the dim recesses of federal security agencies. As for self-fulfilling prophecies, it seems clear to us that the writings of a group of English-speaking academics are unlikely to weigh heavily with Quebecers as they move towards a decision.

One of the most difficult questions here is how to argue at two levels. At the first, the argument is concerned with the advantages of federalism, the possibilities for accommodation, and the negative consequences of separation. Here the goal is to avert separation, not through threat, but persuasion. But at the second level, what does one say about the possibility of a harmonious relationship if independence occurs? Most of the writers in this book would argue that, difficult as it would be, it is *in principle* possible to work out the kind of association advocated by the Parti Québécois. Most would also agree that if Quebec does decide democratically to leave, Canada should not only accede to that decision, but also seek a close relationship. The reasons are both practical and moral; the economic disruption resulting from a total break would hurt Ontario and the Maritimes almost as much as it would Quebec, so there would be strong incentives for them to agree. It would be morally intolerable to accept a democratic decision and then to punish those who made it. Moreover, whether peaceful independence were achieved or not, Canada and Quebec would have to coexist on the northern half of the North American continent. Some form of *modus vivendi* would have to be achieved.

Having said all this, the analyses in this book indicate how difficult it would be both to achieve independence and to work out a stable relationship for the future. As Ronald Watts demonstrates, there are few hopeful precedents. The economic costs would be high. Separation itself is likely to involve deep hostilities and considerable turmoil, which could well overwhelm the voices of moderation and the rational calculation of costs and benefits. The potential for grave disruption is very real: and this reinforces our conviction that our primary obligation is to search for accommodation now.

The more we examine the problems of disengagement, the more convinced we are of the difficulties of putting humpty-dumpty together again—and the more afraid we are that all the king's horses and all the king's men might turn out to be either Canadian demagogues, or external interventionists.

This book is aimed primarily at an informed general audience, rather than at the academic community. It involves a set of English-Canadian views, but we make no claims to be representative. This deliberate stress on English-Canadian perspectives stems from our view that in the period since the Quebec election, English Canadians have been ideologically unprepared to deal with the drive for independence, both because of a lack of awareness of the social realities of Quebec and because of a basic uncertainty about their country. Fruitful dialogue with Quebec requires first a sense of one's own goals. We often ask "What does Quebec want?"; more realistic now is the question, "what do federalists want?" This book may help clarify this question. But that, of course, is only a prelude to the other vital task of dialogue with all shades of opinion in Quebec. Hence we hope the book will also reach a Quebec audience. Ignorance of events in Quebec has been one of the greatest barriers to accommodation; perhaps the reverse is also true: independentists, wrapped up in their great project, must also understand the risks and difficulties and must realize that few communities, however much they respect the drive for independence and acknowledge the importance of past injustices, can easily contemplate their own dismemberment.

In this book the terms "separatist," "separation," and "separatism" have been used sparingly. The PQ has seldom used these terms and they represent not so much an accurate reflection of PQ goals as a pejorative epithet imposed by their critics. "Separation" implies a total break, a fundamental fracturing, a cutting of all ties. The PQ has always talked in terms of "independence," "association," and "sovereignty." All such abstract words are inevitably subject to many meanings, to different interpretations, and to emotional loading. Our use of the words "independence" and "independentist" may be criticized as hiding the reality of the PQ drive and blurring its danger. It may also be true that independence for Quebec would involve the cutting of all links, although that would be a decision not of the PQ alone but also of the remainder of Canada. "Independence" is, here, the better and more accurate word.

If November 15 was a deep shock for most English Canadians, we must also recognize that for a great many French Canadians, and not only supporters of independence, it was a day of liberation, the beginning of a new era, in which Quebec had achieved maturity, affirmed its nationality, and begun the process of decolonization. Federalists, for many, were the voices of a dead past, independentists the voice of the future—progressive and optimistic. Federalists saw a breaking up of a more or less successful political regime; independentists saw the process not as nation-breaking but as nation-building. These differences in perspective are profound. They are not simply differences of preferred constitutional options, but are linked up with economic, social, and cultural drives. Most logically they relate to a sense of community. Even a federalist like Claude Castonguay has asserted in a recent speech: "We must understand that there is in Quebec a quite specific collectivity with an identity of its own, its own culture and its institutions, to which belong five million French-speaking citizens. This collectivity has by its cohesion, its numbers and its state of development, all the attributes of a distinct society. Quebecers want this society to remain dynamic, and they want it to develop." Nick Auf der Maur, writing in *Weekend* magazine, observed that "wherever one looks, be it in the arts, education, politics, the unions, the best and the brightest of the French element is apt to be péquiste." This is no atavistic, irrational, self-destructive movement; its leaders are sophisticated, pragmatic, and skilled.

Federalists ignore these characteristics of contemporary Quebec and of the Parti Québécois social movement at their peril. The arguments, rhetoric, and imagery—of Canada from sea-to-sea, of a brave experiment in multiculturalism, and so on—to which federalists appeal find no emotional response among many Québécois, just as their arguments and symbols find little resonance among federalists. This was well illustrated in the contrast between the rival leaders' speeches in New York and Washington early in 1977: René Lévesque appealed to the powerful symbols of cultural sovereignty and self-determination, Pierre Trudeau to the values of pluralism and internationalism. Each probably failed to reach across the great divide. Similarly the powerful drive behind the independence movement makes it unlikely that the goal of independence with association is merely a bargaining position in a conventional federal—provincial conflict in which Quebec would "settle" for something less.

However, we must be careful not to assume that all French-speaking Quebecers are supporters of independence. While the latter now dominate the debate, there is a wide variety of federalists, ranging from those whose support is perhaps based mainly on expediency and fear of the economic consequences of independence—exemplified in Robert Bourassa's phrase "profitable federalism"—to those with a more positive commitment to the kind of values espoused by Trudeau.

This book is not primarily an analysis of contemporary Quebec society. But some understanding of the social realities is an essential starting point in the search for solutions. James de Wilde seeks to locate the PQ within the context of the evolution of Quebec since the onset of the Quiet Revolution. He examines the complex mingling of traditional ethnic nationalism, the more "technocratic" nationalism of the new Quebec middle class, and a growing left-wing nationalism, based in part on a kind of communitarian socialism linked to earlier patterns of cooperative activity. The technocrats are presently in the ascendant, and their focus on Quebec-initiated and directed economic development under the guidance of a strong state provides the central dynamic of the PQ's drive for independence. This fuses with traditional nationalism which sees sovereign status as the symbolic recognition of cultural nationality. Socialist nationalism draws on both these strands, and, in addition, sees the political disengagement from federalism as a prerequisite to the emergence of a clearly class-based political movement.

We return to the Quebec milieu in Peter Leslie's chapter on the non-French communities there. His is the study of a "minority in the making"—of the move by Quebec governments to ensure dominant status of the majority language and to end what it sees as a threat to French language and culture—and of the diverse responses of anglophones, ranging from accommodation to the new realities to flight from Quebec. He shows that the traditional view of "les Anglais" as all rich Westmount "capitalists" is false—many are working class, and it is these who may be the main victims of change. Their potential reactions raise the possibility of great unrest. Leslie also examines the largely anglophone business world and shows how its reactions too have severe implications for Quebec, especially now that Toronto is already surpassing Montreal as the centre of Canadian business and finance.

We also return briefly to Quebec in John Trent's essay, which examines in more detail the specific proposals of René Lévesque with respect to federalism and independance. He contrasts this model with that of Trudeau, and with the views of other federalists. In some ways it is not easy to know precisely what the PQ seeks: at some times it appears to be little more than a symbolic independence retaining much of the present relationship; at other times, the break seems sharper.

It is equally vital to explore some of the central characteristics of English Canada. Independentists have often seemed to believe English Canada to be essentially homogeneous and centralist; after Quebec broke away, it was assumed, the remaining provinces would rally round a newly powerful central government. This may have been true at one or two periods, such as the immediate aftermath of the Second World War, but it is certainly not the case today. Not only do economic and social differences among the predominantly English-speaking regions remain very important, but these differences appear to have become more pronounced, partly under the leadership of strong provincial governments. Regional grievances in the West and the Maritimes have grown, and the federal government has been increasingly unable to act as a national government with strength in all regions. It has become, in the view of some, "delegitimized." It is a commonplace to argue that the west's grievances are economic and Quebec's are cultural—but this seems less and less true; Quebec's cultural drives are inextricably linked to economic goals, and in the peripheries economic grievances are becoming linked to greater identification of regional communities as the central focus of loyalty. Four essays seek to assess the views about Ottawa, Quebec, and Canadian federalism which are to be found in the various regions. What are the central grievances in each? What kinds of commitments are there to the Canadian union? What might be the levels of support for the different constitutional options before us? George Rawlyk stresses that the fundamental economic weakness of Atlantic Canada will condition all its responses. Frederick J. Fletcher finds in Ontario the strongest commitment to a united Canada, but also a surprising willingness to contemplate new arrangements. This also appears in his analysis of some recent national surveys. John Archer observes that recent events in Quebec have sparked a renewed focus on the country as a whole, despite the more widely publicized growth of movements for western separatism. Similarly R. M. Burns finds that although British Columbians are divided and schizophrenic, their national loyalties are perhaps stronger than usually realized. None of the regional commentators sees much likelihood of immediate absorption into the United States, or a sudden fragmentation of the country if Quebec separates, but the possibility remains—and, whether left in a rump Canada, or on their own, the dependency of all Canadian regions on the United States is likely to increase.

Canadians are entering a new and dangerous period in which our own past experience provides little guide to action or understanding. One important source of guidance is the experience of other countries which have undergone similar crises. Democratic societies which are also multicultural are uncommon. Societies which have divided peacefully are even more so. Ronald Watts surveys the experience of survival and disintegration in other federal systems, searching for the general conditions which have led to either integration or disintegration. He examines the record of other breakups and comes to pessimistic conclusions about the likelihood of doing it amicably or peacefully.

Another possible source of guidance is in legal precedent. In considering separation we are led directly to crucial questions about the legitimacy of decisions, the rights of self-determination and secession, and so on. John Claydon and John Whyte ask whether either Canadian constitutional law or broader international law would help in the current situation. They conclude that neither offers a conclusive guide, but that the preponderance of international law does not support the PQ claim. The British North America Act is silent about secession, but it seems clear that in formal terms it would require an appropriate amendment.

While economic considerations are not the only ones, the costs and benefits of Confederation are vital, and the subject of intense debate. Peter Leslie and Richard Simeon assess the "battle of the balance sheets," which seek to determine whether federalism is "profitable" for Quebec and other regions, and several other authors, such as Charles Pentland, touch on additional economic problems associated with independence and the PQ's plan for an economic association.

Four essays ask whether Canada can "re-confederate." Can we devise new forms of association or reform the federal system so as to accommodate the interests of Quebec—if not the PQ itself—and to redress the many other grievances and tensions within Canadian society? John Trent examines the positions of the federal government and opposition parties, and the perspectives of provincial political leaders, in order to chart the range of possibilities which might be acceptable, and to compare these with the position of the PQ. He is cautiously optimistic, but believes that, at least for some purposes, any alteration must include treating Quebec as a coequal partner with English Canada.

John Meisel touches on this theme in the concluding chapter. He stresses the need for a renewed commitment to bilingualism, together with radical alterations in the structure and operation of federal institutions so as to make Ottawa more truly representative of all Canadian regions. In making such changes, he suggests, we must contemplate substantial modification of the British parliamentary institutions we have known. Could it be, as the *péquiste* political scientist Daniel Latouche has suggested, in *This Magazine*, that we have the opportunity to create "a new kind of country which does not follow the old xixth century model of the nation state with its flag, national anthem, central political authorities, etc?" William Irvine makes a modest proposal for a recognition of Canada as a group of regions in which provincial governments are the most important and Ottawa serves mainly as a balance wheel.

In his exploration of the possibilities of decentralization, or special status, E. R. Black demonstrates the difficulties in defining the various alternatives and the pitfalls in reconciling the diverse interests in the country. Assuming there is some willingness to make change, Richard Simeon briefly discusses some of the ways such negotiations might be conducted.

If this search fails, the likelihood of a vote for independence in Quebec will grow immensely. We would then enter a period as difficult as any we have known. Richard Simeon looks at some of the possible political dynamics of the situation. Hugh Thorburn examines the rules of the game for the referendum and discusses the procedures and machinery necessary to negotiate independence if it is chosen. On the admittedly weak assumption that all this could be done peacefully, he then traces some of the many issues that would have to be resolved if two societies as deeply intertwined as Quebec and Canada were to be separated. Some of these issues would be once and for all matters, but others, like the St. Lawrence Seaway, would require continuous relationships into the future.

Central to the Parti Québécois' goal is the maintenance of an economic association with Canada. Whether that is in the interests of English Canada is unclear. And even if it were, we do not know whether it would be possible to work out such a relationship. Charles Pentland discusses the possible mechanisms. Whose interests would a common market serve? How might it operate? What would be the bargaining power of the units within it? A true common market, he says, would necessarily involve a great deal of reintegration of the two countries.

Another central issue in any future relationship is the role of the minorities—the non-French-speaking communities in Quebec, and the French-speaking outside Quebec. Any amicable settlement would probably depend on some mutual guarantees of their interests. W. R. Lederman examines how this might be achieved in his essay.

Finally, John Meisel asks whether we can work things out within Confederation and how English Canadians can come to terms with the present situation: can crisis breed opportunity—or will it breed defeat both for those who seek to make Quebec an independent and sovereign state and those who wish to preserve the Canadian union as a diverse North American society distinct from the United States? The stakes are high, and time is short.

I
Background

The Parti Québécois
in Power

JAMES DE WILDE

On 15 November 1976, the Parti Québécois was swept into power in Quebec with 71 out of 108 seats and 42 per cent of the popular vote. Both supporters of independence and federalists were taken by surprise. Whatever the particular reasons underlying the choices of individual voters, the central fact was that there was now in power a government committed irrevocably to the negotiation of a sovereign and independent status for Quebec. This chapter traces the development of the Parti Québécois, examining its social support and ideological goals, and locating it within the wider context of the development of a movement which has come to see the state as the central instrument, not only for the protection of the French language and culture but also for the economic development of Quebec. This gives the provincial government an interventionist—some might say socialist—stance more explicit than that of any other North American government. In addition, the party represents the fusion of the economic and cultural drives for sovereignty: cultural preservation has come to be seen as requiring control over economic life; economic development, in turn, is seen within the context of a French Quebec, rather than in terms of a wider pan-Canadian community. An understanding of these characteristics of the movement is essential if we are to avoid miscalculations and inappropriate responses.

THE GROWTH OF THE PQ

Nationalist movements in different forms have been a constant feature of Quebec life. Only recently, however, has that nationalism seriously tied its goals to political independence. The PQ emerged out of the social forces created by Quebec's Quiet Revolution. Its first leader, René Lévesque, and many of its most influential members were either

political or administrative advisers in the Liberal government of Jean
Lesage which initiated many of the policy changes that produced the
modern Quebec. Lévesque and others founded the Mouvement
Souveraineté-Association in 1967, after they were unable to persuade
the party to adopt a more autonomist stance. In 1968 the MSA joined
with two already existing movements, representing different
nationalist currents. The Ralliement National was a conservative
nationalist group, and the Rassemblement pour l'Indépendance
Nationale, led by Pierre Bourgault, represented a more radical strand.
The new Parti Québécois contested its first election in 1970, winning 23
per cent of the vote and seven seats. In 1973 it pushed its proportion of
the vote to 30 per cent, but fell victim to the effects of the electoral
system in a straight two-party fight, and won only six of 108 seats. Then
in 1976 came the dramatic breakthrough: the party won 42 per cent of
the vote and an overall majority. This remarkable victory was aided by
intense dissatisfaction with the Bourassa government combined with
the spoiler role of a renascent Union Nationale party led by Rodrigue
Biron, which siphoned off many traditional Liberal votes in predominantly English-speaking ridings. Even without the UN, however, the PQ
would have won a clear majority of seats.

Thus the PQ has steadily increased its electoral support in each
election. It is clearly no flash in the pan. It has steadily expanded its
geographic and social base, and has now built a broad electoral coalition. In part this was due to a largely unnoticed but highly successful
organization at the grass-roots, led by young militants for whom the PQ
was not just another party but an expression of profound personal and
cultural aspirations. Initially the PQ vote was concentrated in urban
areas and its electoral successes were virtually entirely within working-
class constituencies in East Montreal. By 1976 party support had extended deep into rural areas, into the ranks of the middle class, as well
as into the frontier industrial areas of Lac St. Jean and the north.
Indeed, the PQ won almost everywhere, except in the mainly English
areas of West Montreal, and in scattered ridings where Liberal members were able to hold on to personal followings. The Union Nationale
won 11 seats—all but one in rural areas.

What explains this breadth of support? The PQ evolution shows that
it was not a one-shot affair based on the transient appeal of a charismatic leader. Similarly, hostility to an incompetent Bourassa government
may explain much, but not everything. The PQ had succeeded in
mobilizing a wide variety of discontents. Workers were angered by the
anti-union policies of the Bourassa government, and by high unem-

ployment. Recent federal dairy policies angered farmers who felt they hurt the Quebec industry to the benefit of Ontario. In seeking their votes the PQ could easily demonstrate the inequities of the federal system. Similarly, the recent dispute over the language to be used by air traffic controllers appears to have persuaded many voters that language rights could not be protected in the federal system, even though this did not become an issue dividing the Liberals and the PQ.

It is true that the PQ somewhat downplayed its commitment to independence in the campaign, especially by its stress that no formal steps towards it would be taken until a referendum was held. But the campaign was directed as much against federalism and the federal government as against provincial Liberal policies, and certainly the Liberals themselves frequently reminded voters that a vote for the PQ was a vote for separation. Thus while it appears that only a minority of PQ voters directly supported independence, it also appears that few of them were frightened at the prospect. This view is reinforced by the increased popular support for the PQ since the election, despite its moving much more quickly towards its central goal than had been expected.

But to fully explain the basis of the Parti Québécois' success we must look not just at the results of a few election campaigns, but also at wider developments that have transformed Quebec society over the last two decades.

THE PQ AND THE EVOLUTION OF QUEBEC

Quebec has always been a distinct society—*une nation*—with a distinct culture, language, and network of social institutions. But traditionally this fact has not led to the assertion that the nation required its own sovereign state. How the ideology of nationalism led to the emergence of the PQ as a party seeking independence lies primarily in the dynamics of recent developments in Quebec society.

Since 1960 Quebec has undergone profound changes in its ideological, social, political and economic structures. These changes burst upon the Quebec scene following the death in 1959 of Premier Maurice Duplessis. Industrialization and urbanization, and its concomitant social changes, had been going on for many years before, but social and political institutions had failed to adapt. When change came it did so with startling rapidity. Quebec experienced a rapid modernization which overturned traditional patterns in almost every sphere of life. At the level of values the old hegemony of conservative catholicism disappeared and secularization spread rapidly, both at the individual level, where church attendance declined dramatically, and at the policy level, where, after considerable conflict, a secular educational system was established. New political ideologies replaced the earlier conservatism. Advanced industry required new technical and bureaucratic skills, and the educational system was forced to adapt. In some sense Quebec was becoming more like other western industrial societies, but this change, far from reducing ethnic tensions, increased them. For now English and French Canadians were contending for the same things, whether they were tax revenues or skilled jobs. In seeking entry to the higher positions in the capitalist economy, French Canadians found themselves confronted with the fact that it was predominantly owned and managed by people who spoke English.

Most fundamentally, there emerged a greater awareness of the existence of two sharply defined social classes: an industrial working class led by an increasingly class-conscious and politicized union leadership, and a middle class which, in contrast to the older stereotype of a clerical and professional Quebec middle class, was now much more bureaucratic and technically sophisticated. Both groups found, in different ways, that their search for a greater economic role was at least partly blocked by the foreign-owned structure of Quebec industry.

Hence both groups turned to the state, as the one instrument which Quebecers unequivocally controlled. The leaders of the Lesage government represented the beginnings of this development. Their slogan was "Maîtres chez nous." The state was to play two roles. First, it would be used to force open the doors of industry, to provide more jobs and more services in French, and to conduct itself, in its advertising and other areas, more in keeping with the Quebec milieu. This is one vital thrust behind the language policies of both the Bourassa and Lévesque governments.

Second, and even more important in understanding the PQ strategy, the state itself came to be seen as an agent whose expansion would provide a greater economic and political role for French Canadians. The expansion of the bureaucracy, of public—especially higher—education, of medical services, all vastly increased the avenues for those with technocratic and administrative skills. Similarly Hydro-Quebec, the Sidbec steel complex, and the pension and investment fund all represented tools for autonomous Quebec-oriented development.

These developments in turn spurred the growth of the two new classes. A high proportion of Quebec's middle class is now employed in the public sector and the best-organized and most effectively unionized sectors of the workforce are found in the public service.

Thus the state has come to play a dynamic role as the tool through which the Québécois will plan their own future, and will wrest at least some power both from the English-Canadian and American-owned economic structure, and from the federal government. This is not, of course, to say that the PQ wishes to nationalize all private industry; the crucial goal is to ensure that it operates in the interests of Quebec. Nor is it to assert that Quebec is unique in according such a role to the state. All modern governments have become more interventionist. The fusion of the economic and cultural drives in Quebec, however, has meant a far more explicit assertion of this role than anywhere else in North America.

These developments did not begin with the PQ. The Lévesque government differs from the Lesage government primarily in its greater commitment to planning and state enterprise, and in its development of a far more fundamental critique of the barriers placed in the way of autonomous Quebec development by the existence of the federal system. In fact, with the possible exception of the period from 1966 to 1970, there appears to be a steady development from 1960 to the present.

This stems both from the pressures generated by the new social and political climate in Quebec and from some changes in the operation of the wider Canadian federal system. The federal government was expanding too, playing a more aggressive role in such fields as regional development and cultural affairs, sometimes at odds with the priorities of the Quebec government. Quebec's expansion required a greater share of the tax resources, which Ottawa was unwilling to give up. Governmental responsibilities at all levels became increasingly overlapping and intertwined, making it difficult for any one level to develop coherent plans. Again these frustrations were felt by all provincial governments, but Quebec's drive for autonomy was more intense, and, whatever the simple balance sheets measuring federal expenditures and taxation in Quebec might show, there was a strong conviction that fundamentally federal economic development policies were directed more to the needs of prosperous Ontario than to those of poorer Quebec (or the Atlantic provinces).

The PQ argues that the logic of these developments in Quebec leads inexorably to political independence. Federalism, and Ottawa, were seen to place too many constraints on Quebec's development. Its control over areas such as communications and transportation could no longer be tolerated. Nor could the endless wrangling and competition between governments. Much better, the PQ contends, to transfer full responsibility to Quebec.

IDEOLOGY IN THE PARTI QUÉBÉCOIS

Traditionally, Quebec nationalism was concerned with protecting French Canada as a community defined by its faith and its language. Politically, it took the form mainly of seeking to isolate Quebec and shield it from dangerous "modern" influences. It was associated with a religiously based political ideology which was deeply suspicious of the corrupt secular state. It saw the church and the family as the main bastions of Quebec society charged with protecting its identity. The state was not unimportant. Federalism did actually provide minimal guarantees of cultural protection. The distinctive civil law assured that the legal system would reflect the dominant cultural values of Quebec. In fact, constitutionally, in 1867, Quebec really did have a form of special status. But in general, until the 1960s, the government used its role not to intervene directly, but rather to provide official sanction for the church and other private organizations. The Duplessis government stood for preservation of the culture, while simultaneously leaving the task of economic development to English-Canadian capital. It advanced Quebec's industrialization through transferring control of resources to outside interests, and assuring them of a compliant labour force.

Traditional nationalism of the purely cultural conservative sort has now almost vanished, even though, as recent language policies attest, the drive for cultural and linguistic preservation remains as strong as ever. The conservative Ralliement Nationale component of the original PQ is invisible. Similarly a figure such as Jean-Guy Cardinal who had been a major Union Nationale recruit to the PQ has had little impact on the party. Traditional means of cultural preservation were no longer effective in the new Quebec society; nor could the traditional nationalists build a coalition of the new social forces spawned by the Quiet Revolution, as the government led by Daniel Johnson and Jean Jacques Bertrand discovered. The battle for cultural preservation had now to be fought not only in the schools and churches, but also in the workplace, and inside the corporations which were the dominant institutions of contemporary society. Moreover, language policy was to be used not just to preserve a traditional way of life but also to extend French language participation into those areas of the economy which traditional nationalism had rejected as being the bastion of secular values. In addition, advertising, the mass media, and the like were now seen to be the crucial agents of socialization, and language policy must be directed at them. Thus, although the language policy embodied in the recent Quebec White Paper, and most aggressively promoted by Camille Laurin, minister of state for cultural development, builds on the traditional concern for cultural survival, it does so within a new social and economic context, and therefore new policy instruments are required. Moreover, language policy links up with the interests of the middle class, which can employ that policy as a means of opening up the economy and forcing it to adapt to the Quebec milieu. Just as the drive for greater economic planning grew steadily from Lesage to Lévesque, so too did the perceived need for ever more thorough-going attempts to make Quebec a society and culture in which French-language dominance could not be challenged.

The nationalism which developed after 1960, and which is now dominant in the Parti Québécois, differs in many ways from traditional forms of nationalism. It may be linked to the growth of the new middle class, and loosely labelled "technocratic." First, unlike traditional variants, the new nationalism accepted the logic of social and economic modernization: Quebec had to be a fully "North American" society. From this flowed the host of policies introduced during the Quiet Revolution (some of which, it should be said, had originated a few years before): educational reform, development of the welfare state, economic planning, and the rest. Second, where traditional nationalism had been inward-looking, seeking to preserve Quebec by building invisible walls, the new nationalism was activist and sought to expand its political frame of reference. Third, where the old nationalism sought implicitly to segregate French and English into separate spheres, now the Québécois were to penetrate all sectors, thus developing new forms of competition with the English. Fourth, where traditional nationalism had not usually called directly into question the federal structure itself—seeking just to be left alone, for the most part and only complaining when federal social policies seemed to infringe Quebec's jurisdiction—the new nationalism, as we have seen, challenged Ottawa directly, seeking to recover both powers and revenues. Finally, and most important, the traditional nationalist fear of the state was replaced by an utterly different conception: that the state—the Quebec state—was the instrument for survival and development. Indeed, one of the remarkable characteristics of leaders like Jacques Parizeau and Claude Morin is a seemingly unlimited confidence in the ability of clever men to create the society they want by the manipulation of state power.

Writers like Albert Breton argue that this new nationalism is nothing more than a device by which the new middle class opens up lucrative positions for itself, and that this development in fact imposes financial burdens on the working class. Persuasive as this theory is, it can at best be only a partial explanation. It makes it hard to understand the left-wing nationalism which has emerged more recently. It is crucial to realize that this fusion of technocratic ideology with the need for promotion of the French language has now become the dominant ideology in Quebec. Moreover, access to better-paid positions, and to positions of control in industry, is sought not only by Harvard MBAs but by workers at many levels. Finally, it should be noted that the goals of technocratic nationalism are supported, at least for the moment, by many intellectuals who on other grounds reject capitalism altogether.

There is, then, a third important strand of nationalism in the Parti Québécois, though it appears to be more prominent among party workers than in the cabinet itself. This is what we might call socialist nationalism. The economic *dirigisme* of the technocrats might be called by some socialist, but it is so only in a limited sense. The drive for a socialist nationalism arises in large part out of the industrial working class of Quebec, though its major exponents have been union leaders, together with many intellectuals, especially those based in the universities. It is a diverse set of social forces. All would agree that Quebec is a colony, subordinated not just to the English-language culture, but most fundamentally to American and English-Canadian capitalism. Independence for Quebec is a prerequisite for the development of a true socialism. In part the goals of socialist nationalism are the familiar ones of European socialism, namely, increased nationalization, and much greater participation by the working class, through the unions, in the activities of the government. But another element is perhaps unique to Quebec. It is based upon a long tradition of small-scale cooperative enterprise, similar in some ways to the cooperative movement in Saskatchewan. Its major expression in the past has been the caisse-populaire or mouvement Desjardins, which has provided a source for channelling the savings of Quebecers, and emerged as one of the dominant sources of capital in the province. Other expressions of this cooperative spirit in recent years have included worker takeovers (with government assistance) of failing firms, such as papermills at Cabano and Timiskaming, and Tricofil, a textile plant in St. Jerome. Throughout the Sixties "Operations dignites" or self-help movements sprang up all over the province. Building on this cooperative communitarian base, the second strand of socialist nationalism emphasizes worker self-management and control of industry, decentralization of power to the local level, and so on. The logic of such movements runs counter to the centralizing statist tendencies of technocratic nationalism. It is possible that conflicts between these two approaches will emerge.

While in recent years the Quebec labour movement has become well known for its radicalism and political activism, and left-wing ideologies have probably found a more sympathetic hearing in Quebec than anywhere else in Canada, it must be said that the socialist component of the PQ now plays a minor role within the party. The technocrats are firmly in the saddle. However, the PQ program does include many proposals which are linked to the socialist impulse, and the new government has in some minor ways moved to implement these ideas. Perhaps if it were not for the constraints imposed by Quebec's financial situation, and fear of the flight of capital, there would be a stronger commitment in this direction.

In any case, one major difference between the PQ and the preceding Liberal government is that the former does have for the moment the qualified support of the organized Labour movement. That may enable the party to reduce industrial strife and thus win the confidence of outside investors, despite the social democratic tone of its overall program. In the longer run, it may be that Quebec politics will divide more sharply on class or left-right lines. For the moment, the socialist nationalists are willing to cooperate with the technocrats, for the purpose of achieving what is for them the essential first step —independence. After that, one might expect that the issue of federalism and language would be essentially removed from Quebec politics, permitting the social and economic division to emerge more clearly.

Thus several different strands make up the PQ ideology. To some extent different elements are found in different sectors of the party: the leadership in the cabinet—especially ministers like Jacques Parizeau, Claude Morin, Bernard Landry, and Rodrigue Tremblay —is firmly oriented to the technocratic model. This is reflected in the policies pursued in the first months in power. At the constituency level, party militants appear more in tune with the socialist impulses. In the electorate as a whole it is likely that the general goal of cultural sovereignty has the most appeal. However, the divisions are not clear-cut, nor have the different strands in the ideology been fully worked

out. The cement which keeps all the elements together is the commitment to independence. Once that disappears the other tensions within
the party are likely to emerge. This may be one important reason why,
in its first months in power, the party has moved so much more
aggressively, both to promote independence and to implement sweeping language legislation, than many expected.

Growing out of the needs of contemporary Quebec, responding to
the interests of new groups, and building on a sweeping indictment of
Quebec's ability to attain its goals within a united Canada, the trend
toward independence may appear irresistible. It might seem that no
alternative exists. That, indeed, is what most PQ spokesmen believe;
for many it appears that it is all over but the shouting, and in spirit, if
not in form, independence has already been achieved. But before
accepting this analysis, we must look briefly at the other side of the
coin: who supports federalism?

According to the polls the majority do; even in its milder form of
sovereignty with association, only a minority of Quebec voters supports
the PQ option. At the mass level, it is possible that the major basis for
federal support is simply inertia, or the fear of taking a flyer into the
unknown, especially when its economic consequences may be disastrous.

At the leadership level, it must be remembered that on 14 November
1976 there was in power a federalist government with 96 out of 108
seats. After the election the Liberal party was leaderless, and federalist
forces had great difficulty reconstituting themselves. Federalism had
been discredited along with the Bourassa regime. Nevertheless, however dramatic the rout, federalist leadership has surely not vanished.

In social terms, the strongest support for federalism comes from the
non-French-speaking groups in Quebec, and from French-Canadian
businessmen who fear the economic consequences of separation and
are perhaps suspicious of the expanded state power it would bring. In
addition, big business, owned by English Canadians or Americans,
seems strongly opposed. The problem is that for the purposes of the
battle for support, in the context of Quebec today all these groups are
marginal or suspect. It will be hard for them to generate positive
arguments which are likely to win much support.

In addition, among many politicians support for federalism is conditional. Robert Bourassa's slogan "profitable federalism" carries with it
the clear implication that if it ceases to be profitable it can be scrapped.
The larger Canadian unit is not an important focus for loyalty or

support. Indeed, some provincial Liberals have argued they would be better equipped to take Quebec out of Confederation than would the PQ. Such tentative commitment—when faced with the self-confidence of the PQ—is a weak basis on which to pin one's hopes for the country's survival.

On the other hand, some independentist support may also be conditional. Certainly among many voters it is conditional on its economic feasibility, and for the PQ leadership itself, it is conditional on working out an association with English Canada (though some do say that if English Canada says "no" Quebec should go ahead anyway). Moreover, even among the most ardent independentists, especially those of a somewhat older generation, there is a lingering nostalgia for the wider partnership. Even René Lévesque talks of English and French Canada as brothers, and argues simply that they will get along better if they are separated. The idea of "association" is not simply a matter of expediency.

There is positive and principled commitment to federalism within Quebec. Its leader, of course, is Prime Minister Trudeau, who has spent much of his life battling the idea of parochial nationalism. As prime minister, he has a vision of Canada as a bilingual, multicultural society whose genius is its ability to reconcile French and English languages in a creative partnership. Such a commitment may still have considerable appeal within Quebec; and a central task of federalist leaders is to search out and mobilize support for it.

Four major conclusions follow from this analysis.

1. No single referendum will resolve everything. The social forces behind the quest for sovereignty are rooted in the social and economic developments of the past few decades. Most of the critical opinion leaders—in the bureaucracy, the mass media, and the schools—are committed to the cause. However, a referendum defeat, or even an ambiguous result, may well lead to deep splits within the PQ. That would not sway most of the critical opinion leaders in the bureaucracy, the media, and the schools. Even the defeat of the PQ government in the next provincial election would not end the movement, rooted as it is in the pattern of industrialization and economic development of Quebec. Whether a new government were led by an ex-Bourassa minister like Claude Forget, an "autonomiste" from outside the structure like Claude Castonguay, or a Trudeau lieutenant like Jean Chrétien, the federalist party would have to respond to the same social

forces that the PQ represents. It too would end up making "radical" demands on the federal government in order to consolidate its own political position.

2. The air traffic controllers' dispute and the massive reaction to it in Quebec show that the federal government is no longer a credible guarantor of francophone rights. That task has been appropriated by the Quebec government. Whatever party is in power, and whether or not it is independent, Quebec will continue to move toward unilingualism.

3. The crux of the problem is economic. Unless strong federal policies demonstrate a reason for Canada to exist as more than a fragmented trading association, Quebec's search for rational planning will encourage and will accelerate the centrifugal tendencies.

4. Faced with the problems of power, the present PQ cabinet must balance long-term goals against the requirements of practical policy-making. This will become more difficult as the glamour of the new regime wears off. Similarly Quebec citizens will confront daily economic problems in a new environment and a new set of political choices. The desire for stability, continuity, and security is powerful. If economic difficulties increase, that desire may be enough to ensure support of the status quo in the short run. Independence would be risky for Quebec. Its difficulties must give pause even to the most self-confident technocrat. The protracted negotiations would, in the best of circumstances, paralyse the bureaucratic apparatus, and set planning back for many years.

Perhaps the fundamental problem of federal policy is that it has failed to develop a raison d'être for federalism which could enlist the energies and support of the most influential groups in Quebec. The balance-sheet approach, listing the alleged fiscal gain to Quebec from federal taxing and spending activities, simply misses the point. Far more important are the benefits—and costs—of much broader economic policies designed to affect industrial strategy policies with respect to trade, investment flows, transportation, energy, and the like. The unwillingness of Ottawa to develop such policies either for Quebec or for the whole country is one reason why the technocratic elites have looked to the Quebec government as their instrument. From this perspective the problem, as Jacques Parizeau has often pointed out, is not that the federal government has been too strong, but that it has been too weak. It has been too weak politically, because of its failure adequately to represent all regions. And it has not chosen to exploit the policy instruments that it does possess.

The reluctance of federal governments of whatever party to mobilize their political resources for national development is partly responsible for the present impasse. If more ambitious federal policies can be adopted, it may be possible to develop common goals which would unite English and French Canadians. Similarly, it may be possible to capture for the wider Canadian political process many of the important ideas for social and economic policy, such as planning and worker self-management, debated in the PQ. If we cannot do such things, then the dynamics within Quebec society will lead to their logical conclusion.

Public Attitudes and Alternative Futures

FREDERICK J. FLETCHER

For much of our history, relations between Canada's two founding communities have been primarily a matter for negotiations between elites, within the federal government, at federal-provincial conferences, and in other forums. Increasingly, however, with the growing politicization of these relationships since 1960, and especially since the Quebec election of 15 November 1976, concern has spread to a wider public. The threat of separation has been made manifest by the election of a Parti Québécois government and anglophone Canadians have at last begun to take it seriously. The growth of concern in English-speaking Canada means that new public pressures are likely to emerge. As our political leaders grope towards new relationships between the two linguistic communities, they will inevitably be constrained by public opinion.

In order to examine future options, then, it is necessary to try to predict public reactions. Opinion surveys, especially when monitored over time, provide a useful basis for speculation about public responses to possible future events. Although opinions on such volatile issues as francophone-anglophone relations fluctuate with dramatic events and mass media content, they are nevertheless likely to reflect deep-seated attitudes. The patterns of response can provide clues to the environment of opinion within which political decision-makers and other key elites will have to work as they grapple with the present challenge to Confederation. Certainly, the leaders will be watching the polls.

I am indebted to the following for permission to use their survey data: Robert J. Drummond and Frederick J. Fletcher, "French-English Relations in Canada," Report no. 6 of the Canadian Attitude Trends Project, funded by the Privy Council Office; CTV and Complan Research Associates Limited, for "An Attitudinal Study About Quebec and Confederation"; The Canadian Institute of Public Opinion and *The Canadian* magazine for a special study, reported in *The Canadian*, 9 April 1977.

Among anglophone Canadians, there have been consistent and significant regional differences in attitudes towards Quebec and the French Canadians. These differences reflect distinct regional climates of opinion (or communities of sentiment) among English-speaking Canadians. A majority of Canadians do think of their country in terms of its regional divisions and identify with particular regions. An analysis of Gallup Poll data between 1960 and 1976 found clear differences in attitude between English-speaking respondents living east of the Ottawa River and those living west of it. Those living in Ontario and the western provinces have been consistently more pessimistic about relations between the two communities and less likely to support accommodative measures. This is especially true west of Ontario.

Here we will examine regional differences on a series of important questions regarding the future of Confederation and try to project them forward. These differences highlight the problem of creating national majority support for accommodative measures and provide the climate of opinion within which provincial leaders must operate.

Are English-speaking Canadians concerned enough about the threat of an independent Quebec to support serious attempts at accommodation?

On the whole anglophone Canadians do regard the implications of Quebec separation as serious, though only about half regard them as very serious. Since 1964, when the Gallup Poll first asked a national sample of Canadians to indicate how serious they thought it would be to the rest of Canada if Quebec were to leave Confederation, the level of concern has fluctuated in all regions. (See table 1.) Not surprisingly, concern has been the highest among anglophone Quebecers. (See table 2.) Prairie respondents have been the least concerned about the consequences of Quebec independence. By February 1977, well after the Quebec election, national concern had reached a new high, with 46 per cent viewing secession as very serious for the rest of Canada and 37 per cent viewing it as fairly serious. Although a clear majority of Prairie respondents viewed the prospect as either very serious (35 per cent) or fairly serious (29 per cent), concern was still lowest in that region. A plurality in all regions viewed secession as very serious but only in the Atlantic provinces and Ontario did a majority feel this was so. British Columbia was the most polarized, with relatively high proportions at each extreme. Quebec respondents were relatively sanguine: there appears to be growing feeling among francophone Quebecers that Quebec secession would not be all that disruptive, primarily because of the PQ's stress on economic association.

Overall, then, Canadians feel strongly that Quebec's independence would be undesirable: few seem to be willing to say "let them go." The latter sentiment may grow, however, as the PQ continues to challenge the federal structure. Western Canadians have the least commitment to preserving the union. Polls taken between 1963 and 1971 showed growing pessimism about French-English relations among westerners, many of whom appear to believe that nothing effective can be done to meet Quebec concerns.

A survey taken just three weeks after the election for CTV provides additional support for the view that anglophones want to preserve Confederation. Half the national sample wanted Quebec to remain a part of Canada "very much." An additional 24 per cent said they wanted it to stay "quite a bit," while only 23 per cent opted for the responses "not too much" or "not at all." Ontario residents were most likely to express a strong desire to keep Quebec in Confederation, with Alberta and B.C. residents following. Saskatchewan,Manitoba, and Maritimes residents were less committed to that goal. Surprisingly, given the drastic impact Quebec secession would have on them, 32 per cent of Maritime respondents expressed little desire to keep Quebec in. (See table 4.) Nevertheless, the overwhelming majority of respondents in all regions believe that Canada can " survive as a nation without Quebec," indicating a clear limit to the sense of danger engendered by the Quebec election and, perhaps, to the lengths anglophone Canadians would be willing to go to accommodate Quebec. Concern to preserve Confederation may produce various reactions: on one hand,willingness to make accommodation; on the other a disposition to force Quebec to remain.

How are Canadians likely to react to specific measures aimed at meeting Quebec demands and preventing separation?

Public debate in the months ahead is certain to revolve around such questions as these: Would further efforts to promote bilingualism reduce the threat of separation? Would they be acceptable to English-speaking Canadians? Would a special status for Quebec meet Quebec demands? Would a general decentralization be worthwhile? Some estimates of public reaction can be gleaned from the polls.

The Trudeau administration's attempts to promote the use of French outside Quebec have been an essential part of its strategy to make francophones feel at home in the rest of the country in order to broaden the identification of Québécois with Canada as a whole. Bilingualism had strong majority support in 1973, when efforts to promote it were accelerating. But by April 1976 more than half felt too much emphasis was being placed on bilingualism. Three quarters of English-speaking Canadians took that view. Clearly, disillusionment had set in.

A Gallup Poll taken in January 1977 for *The Canadian* magazine found that the Quebec election had produced little change. Only 28 per cent of anglophone respondents favoured extending bilingualism as a strategy for saving Confederation; the francophone figure was 56 per cent. Opposition to extending bilingualism ranged from 58 per cent opposed in the Atlantic provinces to 76 per cent against in British Columbia. (See table 5.) Readers sending in ballots to *The Canadian* (102,152) were even more likely to oppose more bilingualism. *The Canadian* writers concluded from accompanying letters that much of the opposition was based on the perceived cost of bilingual programs and a feeling that bilingualism neither worked well nor met Quebec demands. To many it had become a negative symbol. Bilingualism in the schools had much more support than bilingualism in the public service (or in the air).

In May 1976, for example, a majority of English-speaking respondents thought that education in both languages would improve understanding between the two linguistic communities. After the Quebec election a majority of anglophones in all regions but the Prairies expressed willingness to have French language and culture taught to their children throughout their school years. In Alberta, there was a small plurality in favour, while respondents in Saskatchewan and Manitoba were evenly split. (See table 6.) These findings suggest an increasing openness to French among anglophones which might provide the basis for meeting some of the demands of non-Quebec francophones, if not of the Quebec elite. However, the general opposition to bilingualism itself suggests that the options open to provincial governments for action outside of the educational system (for example, provision of services in French) may be limited by the threat of adverse public reaction.

In the present context, willingness to accept special status for Quebec is more important than responses to bilingualism. Although two-thirds of the French-speaking respondents in the 1977 Gallup Poll favoured a negotiated special status, a majority of anglophones rejected the idea. The concept was overwhelmingly rejected in British Columbia and the Atlantic provinces and disapproved of by a majority on the Prairies. Ontarians were almost evenly divided. (See table 7.) However, although opposed to special status for Quebec, Western respondents were willing to support a general decentralization of authority. In the CTV poll, the proposition that Confederation would be stronger if powers were transferred from the federal government to the provincial governments was supported by pluralities in Saskatchewan, Manitoba, Alberta, and British Columbia. However, it was rejected by majorities in the Maritimes and in Ontario.

These data do not provide much solace for those hoping for a new federalism to save Confederation. However, the even split on special status in Ontario suggests that a new settlement might be sold to the public by a committed leadership. Western desires for greater provincial autonomy might be tapped to provide support for a new federal bargain aimed at reducing secessionist sentiment in Quebec. Opposition in the Atlantic provinces might well be reduced by guarantees protecting their interests. The pattern of public opinion does not preclude a negotiated renovation of the federal structure to meet Quebec demands. Much will depend on the measures involved and on the support expressed for them by regional elites. It is also possible that Quebec government policies will erode the openness to Quebec concerns which appears to have emerged in the wake of the election. Nevertheless, there is convincing evidence that the vast majority of anglophone Canadians wish Quebec to stay in Confederation and are willing to make at least some concessions to that end. An Edmonton man in a letter to *The Canadian* seemed to speak for most anglophone Canadians: "I am sure most Canadians do not want Quebec to separate, but if the price of keeping them in is too great, then so be it."

How will English-speaking Canadians react if a majority of Quebecers vote for independence in a referendum?

Although anglophone Canadians are reluctant to accept a right of secession for Quebec, they are unwilling to contemplate seriously the use of force to prevent it. Apparently unwilling to accord legitimacy to separatism, Gallup Poll respondents rejected the view that Quebec should be allowed to secede "if a majority of its people want to" by 47 per cent to 40 per cent in 1971 and by 51 per cent to 39 per cent in 1976, just a few months before the Quebec election. (See table 8.) In the 1977 Gallup Poll, a small plurality favoured a negotiated settlement if a majority in Quebec should vote for independence. English-speaking respondents, however, continued to oppose the right of secession, by a margin of 47 per cent to 42 per cent.

Despite this reluctance to accept secession by majority vote as legitimate, few anglophones appear ready to support attempts to hold

Quebec in Confederation "by force of arms if necessary." The CTV poll, taken immediately after the election, found that only 15 per cent of its national sample (which excluded Quebec) would support the use of force to preserve the union. Support for the use of force ranged from 12 per cent in British Columbia to 19 per cent in the Maritimes, arguably the region most threatened by Quebec independence. A few weeks later, in the 1977 Gallup Poll, 19 per cent opted for the use of force, with no significant differences among the regions (or between language groups). Even anglophone Quebecers, the group with perhaps the most to lose, opposed the use of force. Whether this repudiation of force reflects a peaceable political culture, familiarity with the spectre of Northern Ireland, or simply a low level of patriotism is unclear. It does seem to mean that there is a base of support for a peaceful separation.

There are clear regional differences about the right to secede. In the 1971 survey, there was majority support for it in British Columbia and a strong plurality on the Prairies. Those not accepting the right to secede held slight pluralities in the other three regions. Francophones, especially those resident outside Quebec, were particularly reluctant to accept such a right. (See table 8.)

In the 1977 survey, which asked a slightly different question, the strongest opposition to a negotiated separation following a majority vote for independence in Quebec came from the Prairie provinces (50 per cent opposed) and Ontario. Pluralities supported a negotiated separation in Quebec, British Columbia and the Atlantic provinces. (See table 9.) Francophones were much more willing to accept separation by majority vote after the November 15 election than they had been before. The election campaign and its outcome must have altered attitudes considerably. Anglophone opinion appears not to have changed much overall, but the manifest threat of secession posed by the election of the Parti Québécois may account for the increased hostility to a right to secede found on the Prairies and in Ontario. However, anglophone opinion is evenly enough divided on the issue to provide the governments involved with room to manoeuvre.

Many Canadians did feel, however, that they should have some say in the future of the country. In the 1977 Gallup Poll, 47 per cent favoured a *national* referendum on Quebec independence; 42 per cent were opposed. Anglophones tended to be in favour and francophones against. On a regional basis, there was majority support for a national referendum in Ontario and British Columbia, while a plurality was in favour in the Prairie and Atlantic provinces. (See table 10.)

In the abstract, then, it appears that anglophone Canadians are neither willing to grant legitimacy to separation by majority vote nor to use force to prevent it. Of course, opinions might well change when faced with an actual majority vote for secession. Much would depend on the legitimacy accorded the referendum results by opinion leaders and on the capacity of political leaders to engage in a last effective act of elite accommodation by agreeing on a reasonable division of assets and establishing reasonable protection for mutual interests.

A major question surrounding the whole Parti Québécois strategy for achieving a painless separation has been the willingness of English-speaking Canadians to accept an economic union between an independent Quebec and the rest of Canada. The data from the 1977 survey suggests, as *The Canadian* put it, "that Levesque has a fair shot at getting what he wants in terms of an economic union if Quebec separates, but that it's far from a sure thing." Overall, 54 per cent of the national sample approved of economic union, while 30 per cent disapproved. Among anglophones, 45 per cent approved and 39 per cent were opposed. Economic union had overwhelming support in Quebec, a bare majority in Ontario and a plurality in British Columbia. Respondents in the Atlantic provinces were divided and a majority on the Prairies were opposed. (See table 11.) As many observers have predicted, the Prairie region would be the most difficult area to convince.

Taken at face value, these data suggest that there is much support for economic union, especially in the linchpin province of Ontario, and hence for a peaceful separation with a minimum of disruption. However, passive popular acquiescence may be insufficient. Among readers who felt strongly enough about the future of Canada to return *The Canadian* ballot, 54 per cent opposed economic union. Vocal minorities may well be crucial. More important, the prospects for a peaceful secession, like those for an amicable divorce, may evaporate when it comes time to divide up the assets, establish visiting rights, and, in the case of secession, set territorial boundaries. The combination of strong economic interests and high symbolism is sure to make rational bargaining difficult.

If Quebec were to separate from Canada, which of the various options for the rest of Canada would the public be likely to favour?

In December 1976, there was overwhelming support from all regions for the option closest to the present status quo, that the remaining provinces should continue as one country. Few respondents favoured the other options offered in the CTV survey: that each province become a separate country (4 per cent) or that the remaining provinces join the United States (5 per cent). There was, however, significant support for the latter proposition in the Maritimes (16 per cent). Thus, one can conclude that there would likely be an initial base of support for a federation of the remaining nine provinces. But this is clearly a case where economic and political difficulties could easily alter the distribution of opinions. Much would depend upon the success of the federal government in overcoming the practical problems of Quebec independence—such as communications with the Atlantic provinces—and in maintaining a reasonable degree of prosperity in the peripheral provinces. Also important would be the capacity of the federal government to mitigate the effects of the deep-seated suspicion of Ontario domination in the peripheries, especially in a federation in which, without Quebec, Ontario would be a veritable giant.

Table 1

Public Opinion Regarding Seriousness of Quebec Independence for the Future of Canada, by Region, 1964–1977

YEAR OF
SURVEY   PERCENTAGE VIEWING QUEBEC SEPARATION AS NOT VERY SERIOUS

ANGLOPHONES

	Atlantic	Quebec	Ontario	Prairies	B.C.	Total
1964 N = 414	20	13	38	40	39	36
1966 N = 398	24	27	32	42	26	32
1970 N = 428	23	16	37	45	32	35
1972 N = 426	39	21	34	42	39	36
1977* N = 1035	18	22	20	27	28	22

FRANCOPHONES

	Quebec	Rest of Canada	Total
1964 N = 198	9	23	11
1966 N = 224	19	21	20
1970 N = 195	18	15	17
1972 N = 203	26	20	25

* Not broken down by mother tongue.

QUESTIONS: 1964: "If it should happen, and Quebec did leave Confederation, how serious do you think this would be for the future of the rest of Canada—very serious, fairly serious, or not very serious?"

1966, 1970, 1972: "If Quebec should leave Confederation, how serious do you think this would be for the future of the rest of Canada?"

1977: "If Quebec should leave Confederation, how serious do you think this would be for the future of the rest of Canada—very serious, fairly serious, or not very serious?"

SOURCES: Canadian Institute of Public Opinion (Gallup Poll) surveys archived by the Institute of Behavioural Research, York University and, for the 1977 poll, *Toronto Star*, 23 March 1977, p. B–5.

Table 2
Public Opinion Regarding Seriousness of Quebec Independence for Future of
Canada, by Region 1964–1977

YEAR OF SURVEY	RATIO OF VERY SERIOUS TO NOT VERY SERIOUS RESPONSES						
	Atlantic (English only)	*Quebec English*	*French*	*Ontario (English only)*	*Prairies (English only)*	*B.C. (English only)*	*Total (all Language Groups)*
1964	2.46	4.34	5.13	.81	.83	.95	1.39
1966	1.43	2.25	1.80	1.09	.57	1.42	1.18
1970	2.35	4.25	2.71	1.00	.67	1.46	1.48
1972	.83	2.50	1.11	1.16	.67	1.00	1.08
Feb. 1977	3.50	1.82		2.55	1.30	1.71	2.09

QUESTION: Same as table 1.
SOURCES: Same as table 1.

Table 3
Public Opinion Regarding Seriousness of Quebec Independence for Future of
Canada, by Region, 1977

REGION	VERY SERIOUS	FAIRLY SERIOUS	NOT VERY SERIOUS	NO OPINION
Atlantic	63	14	18	5
Quebec	40	31	22	7
Ontario	51	28	20	2
Prairies	35	29	27	9
B.C.	48	23	28	2
Canada	46	27	22	5

QUESTION: Same as table 1.
SOURCE: Same as table 1.

Table 4
Desire for Quebec to Remain Part of Canada, by Region, December 1976

	VERY MUCH	QUITE A BIT	NOT TOO MUCH	NOT AT ALL	NO OPINION
Maritimes	37	29	24	8	2
Ontario	56	21	13	7	3
Prairies*	44	28	18	6	4
B.C.	49	25	17	8	1
Total	50	24	16	7	3

* For Saskatchewan/Manitoba, the percentages were: very much, 40; quite a bit, 27; not too much, 21; not at all, 7; D.K., 5. For Alberta, they were: very much, 49; quite a bit, 29; not too much, 15; not at all, 4; D.K. 3.

QUESTION: "How much do you personally want Quebec to remain a part of Canada?"

SOURCE: Complan Research Associates Ltd., "An Attitudinal Study About Quebec and Confederation," prepared for W5, Canadian Television Network Ltd., December 1976.

Table 5
Public Opinion on Extending Bilingualism as a Means to Prevent Separation, January 1977, by Region

	Atlantic	Quebec	Ontario	Prairies	B.C.	Canada
Approve	29	58	32	24	16	36
Disapprove	58	32	59	67	76	54
D.K.	13	11	9	9	9	10
	100	101	100	100	100	100
N	99	299	358	177	110	1043

QUESTION: "Should the governments of Canada and the provinces promote and finance more extensive bilingualism throughout the country to try to prevent separation?"

SOURCE: The Canadian Institute of Public Opinion, the organization which conducts the Gallup public opinion surveys in Canada, was commissioned to conduct this study by *The Canadian* magazine.

Table 6
Support for Compulsory Teaching of French Among Anglophone Respondents, by Region, 1965-1976

PERCENTAGE IN FAVOUR

YEAR OF SURVEY		*Atlantic*	*Quebec*	*Ontario*	*Prairies*	*B.C.*	*Total*
1965	N = 388	67	89	60	32	39	54
1974	N = 602	57	87	55	41	45	53
1976	N = 1023	53	—[a]	62	46[b]	58	57

a. Not included in survey
b. Saskatchewan/Manitoba, 44%; Alberta, 49%.

QUESTION: 1965 and 1974: "Do you or do you not think that French should be a compulsory subject like spelling, writing and arithmetic in all grades of public schools in English-speaking Canada?"

       1976: "In order to keep Quebec in Canada would you be willing to have your children study French and French culture all through school?"

SOURCES: 1965 and 1974: Same as table 1.
       1976: Same as table 4.

Table 7
Public Opinion on Special Status for Quebec as a Means to Prevent Separation, January 1977, by Region

	Atlantic	*Quebec*	*Ontario*	*Prairies*	*B.C.*	*Canada*
Approve	28	69	44	40	30	47
Disapprove	62	21	46	53	65	44
D.K.	10	10	10	7	6	9
	100	100	100	100	101	100
N	99	299	358	177	110	1043

QUESTION: "Should the government of Canada negotiate special political and economic agreements with Quebec to try to prevent separation?"
SOURCE: Same as table 5.

Table 8

Approval of Quebec's Right to Secede by Majority Vote, 1971 and 1976, by Region

1971 SURVEY (N = 714)					
	Quebec	Atlantic	Ontario	Prairies	B.C.	Total
English-speaking	45	39	42	49	51	45
French-speaking	27		24			26

OCTOBER 1976 SURVEY (N = 1042)		
	Approve	Disapprove
Quebec	32 (+2)*	53 (+3)
Rest of Canada	41 (−3)	51 (+7)
Total	39 (−1)	51 (+5)

* Change from 1971.

QUESTION: "Do you accept the principle that Quebec should have the right to separate from Canada, if the majority of its people want to, or do you think that Quebec should be held in Confederation, by force if necessary?" The 1976 survey deleted the phrase "by force if necessary."

SOURCE: Same as table 1.

Table 9

Public Opinion on a Negotiated Separation if a Majority in Quebec Votes for Independence, January 1977, by Region

	Atlantic	Quebec	Ontario	Prairies	B.C.	Canada
Approve	42	60	39	38	46	46
Disapprove	38	26	49	50	39	41
D.K.	19	14	12	12	15	14
	99	100	100	100	100	101
N	99	299	358	177	110	1043

QUESTION: "If a Quebec referendum favors independence, should Ottawa agree to negotiate separation?"

SOURCE: Same as table 5.

Table 10
Public Opinion on a National Vote on Quebec Independence, January 1977, by Region

	Atlantic	Quebec	Ontario	Prairies	B.C.	Canada
In Favour	46	37	51	49	56	47
Against	41	51	36	42	37	42
D.K.	13	12	13	10	6	11
	100	100	100	101	99	100
N	99	299	358	177	110	1043

QUESTION: "Should the government of Canada hold a national vote on Quebec independence?"
SOURCE: Same as table 5.

Table 11
Public Opinion on Economic Union with Quebec if Separation Occurs, January 1977, by Region.

	Atlantic	Quebec	Ontario	Prairies	B.C.	Canada
Approve	38	79	50	32	46	54
Disapprove	39	9	31	53	34	30
D.K.	22	11	19	16	20	17
	99	100	100	101	100	101
N	99	299	358	177	110	1043

QUESTION: "If separation occurs, should Canada enter into an economic union with Quebec?"
SOURCE: Same as table 5.

Survival or Disintegration

RONALD L. WATTS

The election of the Parti Québécois, with its commitment to independence for Quebec, has faced Canada with an unprecedented challenge to its unity. Since then there has been a growing realization that neither Quebecers nor the rest of Canada can continue complacently to delude themselves with the illusions which have dominated their thinking. One illusion is that Quebec would never opt for independence; another is that if Quebec decides to leave the divorce (not to mention some form of reassociation) will be easy. If the already emerging pattern of emotional confrontation and the apparent disarray and confusion about possible solutions are not enough, the experience of other federations under similar stresses provides abundant warning about the unreality of such illusions.

While every federation is to a large extent the product of a unique conjunction of conditions and institutions, there may be some valuable lessons to be drawn from the persistence or disintegration of other federal systems. It is not insignificant that four of the longest surviving constitutional systems in the world today are federal: The United States (1787), Switzerland (1848), Canada (1867), and Australia (1901). But it is equally significant that during the last two decades a number of other apparently stable federal constitutional systems have experienced the secession of some regions or total disintegration. While Canada may be numbered among the relatively few constitutional systems that have survived more than a century, its present crisis of confidence, arising not only from developments in Quebec but also from feelings of alienation in other regions, suggests the value of examining some of the factors which have contributed to the survival or disintegration of other federations.

Examples of severe stress and even outright failure in federal systems abound. Even the most long-lived and apparently stable have experienced breakdown. Examples are the United States, with its disastrous Civil War, Switzerland with a civil war in 1847, in which federal troops crushed a rebellion by separatist cantons, and Australia, where in 1933 one state voted by referendum for secession. The record of the federations established during the last thirty years, especially those formed out of former British colonial territories, is equally sobering. The partition of India and Pakistan was marked by a bloodbath in which about a million were killed and 12 million made refugees. Later Pakistan and Bangladesh fought a civil war leading to partition, and India has continued to be plagued by communal and linguistic tensions. Nigeria also underwent a bloody civil war over Biafra. The federations in the West Indies and Rhodesia and Nyasaland have broken up, while Singapore has separated from Malaysia.

STRESS IN FEDERATIONS

All these examples of disintegration or secession help us to understand some of the conditions which lead to stress within federations. While the specific circumstances have varied, in all cases political conflict polarized so that eventually compromise seemed impossible. Four sorts of conditions have contributed to this pattern: regional divergences of political demands; weakness of interregional communications; the evaporation of transitional inducements to union; and external influences.

Regional divergences of political outlook and demands are typical of all federations; that is usually why they adopted a federal solution in the first place. But a number of factors may sharpen such differences. Where several of these operate simultaneously to reinforce each other the cumulative effect may accentuate regional cleavages and political conflict to critical proportions.

Among the sharpest divisive forces have been language, race, religion, social structure, and cultural tradition. As in Canada so in Switzerland, India, Pakistan, Malaysia, Nigeria, and Rhodesia and Nyasaland, linguistic, religious, and racial minorities who have feared discrimination at the hands of numerical majorities have defended provincial autonomy as a way to preserve their own distinct identity. And when that provincial autonomy or cultural distinctiveness has been threatened, minority groups have turned to secession as the only defence against assimilation. Examples are numerous: the separatism of the conservative Roman Catholic Sonderbund in reaction to a dominant liberal Protestant majority in Switzerland; the secession of the Southern United States in reaction to an antislavery majority; the insistence of the Muslims on the Indian continent upon partition and the creation of Pakistan in 1947 to avoid domination by a Hindu majority; the growth in south India during the last two decades of the separated Dravida Munnetra Kazhagam; the pressure by Bengali-speaking East Pakistanis for greater autonomy and eventually for an independent Bangladesh; the resentment of the Singapore Chinese at their second-class status in a Malaysia ruled by Malays, removed by the separation of Singapore in 1965; the attempted secession of Eastern Nigeria to become Biafra; the insistence of black African nationalists in Malawi and Zambia that these modernized territories should break away from the federation dominated by white settlers of Southern Rhodesia.

The political impact of linguistic and cultural cleavages is often underestimated. Such differences are not only barriers to communication but go deeper because they are fundamental to the activities which are distinctively human. Language is a means of expression and communion which shapes the very way in which men order their thoughts and makes possible social organization. Not surprisingly, then, any community governed through a language other than its own has usually felt disenfranchised. This feeling has always been a potential focus for political separatism, as in Quebec. Moreover, like skin colour, language is a badge for those who wish to take issue with a different group, and so has provided a rallying point even for issues which were basically not those of language and race.

Other cultural factors can also be divisive. In several countries religious differences have been particularly explosive. An individual can learn to be bilingual, but the term "bi-confessional" is self-contradictory. Thus, Swiss political divisions have more often followed confessional than linguistic lines. In the newer federations of Asia and Africa religious differences such as those between Hindus and Muslims, or, in Nigeria, between the predominantly Muslim north and more Christian or Animist south, have gone much deeper than those in Switzerland or Canada.

Regional differences in language, race, religion, social institutions, and culture have had their strongest influence when they have reinforced rather than cut across each other, or where they have been associated with economic subordination. In Switzerland, for example, the division between Protestants and Catholics has cut across linguistic lines; in Canada the two divisions have reinforced each other. Thus in Switzerland cantonal alignments on political questions have tended to vary according to whether linguistic or religious considerations were at issue, and linguistic groups have not been solidified into unchanging political blocks.

In some federations regional differences in degree of modernization have greatly accentuated regional consciousness. Regions which have lagged behind others have been fearful of dominance by more modernized regions. In prepartition India and Northern Nigeria Muslim leaders in relatively undeveloped areas advocated extreme autonomy or separation as a means of protection from exploitation by the more advanced regional groups. The result in India was partition. In Nigeria, the north was conceded extensive regional autonomy to provide a breathing space in which to accelerate its own development. There are some parallels here to the situation of Quebec which, in the realm of education and technology, lagged behind the English-speaking provinces during the first half of the twentieth century, though it has now caught up.

Another important factor in the tensions within a federation are differences in prevailing political orientation, ideology, and political style. This has been important in Canada: until the mid-twentieth century Quebec, with its emphasis upon its own traditions, was distinctly more conservative than most of the rest of Canada. Since 1960, however, under the impact of the Quiet Revolution the situation has been largely reversed. The gulf now appears to be between an English-speaking Canada which is relatively conservative in political orientation and a Quebec which is more open to radical tendencies and movements.

In many other federations cultural tensions have been closely related to differences of political outlook and ideology. Malaysia, Nigeria, and Pakistan present the most obvious examples among the newer federations. Singapore's departure from Malaysia resulted not only from a struggle over the political roles to be played by the Malays and Chinese within the federation, but also from a clash between the conservative Alliance Party, and Lee Kuan Yew's more socialist People's Action Party which governed in Singapore. In Nigeria, southerners were frustrated by the political conservatism of the northerners. There was a similar split between East and West Pakistan. Going further back in history, the nineteenth-century separatist movements in Switzerland in 1847 and the United States in 1861 were both the reactions of conservatively oriented groups opposed to the liberalizing and reforming outlook of the majority.

Clashing economic interests have also contributed to regional consciousness. Even where federal union brings economic gains to a federation as a whole, specific economic influences may prevent certain provinces from sharing the benefits. An economic union may have not only "trade-creation" but "trade-diversion" effects. Inequalities may even be increased. Without adequate equalization policies, some provinces would be better off outside the federation. Complaints of economic hardship have contributed to separatist feelings within many federations just as they have in Canada. In an era of active public monetary and fiscal policies, it is inevitable that central government policies aimed at the economic development of the federation as a whole cannot equally accommodate differing specific interests and problems in particular provinces. Moreover, the very differences in provincial products which contribute towards the exchange of products across provincial boundaries may at the same time foster provincial consciousness because of related differences in problems of production, types of exports, sources of foreign capital, and appropriate policies for the promotion of economic development. In Pakistan, Malaysia, and Central Africa distinct regional economies were clearly discernible and contributed to internal political tensions, just as Western Canadians feel removed from Quebec not only by distance and language but by different economic concerns.

Sharp regional inequalities in wealth have invariably accentuated regional resentment and even secessionist movements, especially when equalization and assistance programs have been inadequate. Pakistan and Nigeria show that regional disparities in wealth can be one of the most politically explosive forces in a federation, when they coincide with linguistic and cultural cleavages. Yet by comparison with Australia, Canadian attempts to meet this problem have until recently appeared to be only half-measures. Australia has a long history of positive attempts to deal with this problem, with the result that by 1964-65 the per capita income of the wealthiest state exceeded that of the poorest by only 25 per cent. In Canada in the same year Ontario's per capita income exceeded Quebec's by 38 per cent and that of the Atlantic provinces by 86 per cent. In Australia, federal unconditional grants, the major form of intergovernmental transfer, in 1964-65 provided the poorest state with 63 per cent more than the wealthiest state on a per capita basis. Only in the last twenty-five years has Canada made any direct attack on the problem of regional disparities, and only in the last fifteen have relatively effective measures been accepted. Despite recent improvements, Canadian policies have done little more than prevent disparities from widening.

Apart from the direct influence of economic factors, many ostensibly linguistic, racial, or cultural separatist movements have had strong economic undercurrents. The linguistic regionalism and Dravidian separatism which have dominated independent India has been evident in the intense struggle for jobs among the different linguistic and caste groups. In Pakistan, Bengali demands for greater autonomy were closely related to discontent with central economic policies which appeared to give all the spoils to the landlords and businessmen of West Pakistan, and with the dominance of West Pakistanis in the civil services and armed forces. The anti-Ibo feeling in Northern and Western Nigeria was accentuated by the fear that the better-educated and aggressive Ibos would come to dominate the national economy, the civil services, and the officer corps of the army. Similarly Malays have resented the dominance of commerce by the energetic Chinese; the Chinese, in turn, have resented the constitutionally guaranteed dominance of the Malays in the federal civil service. Thus, as in Canada, local economic interests and the desire to legitimize a number of local spoils systems have promoted regional conflict. Political solutions aimed at accommodating regional linguistic and cultural demands have achieved little unless they also took into account the closely related economic factors.

Variations among provinces in ability to influence central politics have also been a factor in interprovincial tensions. The relative population, wealth, and remoteness from the centre of a province are important. The distrust of central Canada in the Western and Atlantic provinces and of Ontario by Quebec has been a fact of Canadian history and a major current source of political friction. The West Indies Federation, although relatively homogeneous in linguistic or cultural terms, was, nevertheless, torn asunder by tensions which grew out of the disproportionate size of Jamaica.

Similar pressures have been felt in other federations. Even in Switzerland the growth of Zurich as an industrial and commercial centre has created anxieties that it might threaten the balance among the cantons. In some cases this conflict has been severe enough to produce proposals for the splitting up of the largest units such as Uttar Pradesh or Northern Nigeria, or for the amalgamation of smaller units into larger ones, such as occurred in West Pakistan (1955–69). In Canada Ontario occupies a dominant position, and the anxieties of the French Canadians of Quebec have certainly been accentuated by proximity to the larger English-speaking province, as well as by the prevailing assumption in Quebec that the nine provinces of English-speaking Canada represent a monolithic political majority.

The character of interregional communications has had an important influence on intensity of conflict in many federations. The impact of geographical distance and topography has been felt in the remoteness of Western Australia, the mountain barriers in central Switzerland, the continental vastness of India, the separation of East and West Pakistan by a thousand miles of hostile territory, and the scattered nature of the West Indian islands. These parallel the remoteness from central Canada and the problems felt by some of the Atlantic provinces, the prairies, and especially British Columbia. In most federations technological advances in transportation and communications have strengthened interprovincial links. But even today in the wealthier federations such as the United States, Australia, and Canada, the sheer cost of transcontinental travel continues to limit the degree to which people in one region may know the problems of people in other regions.

Economic links are especially important. The proportion of a province's total trade which is with other provinces within the federation is likely to affect the willingness of its people to see their future in continued federation or "going it alone." To take one extreme example, only 1 per cent of Jamaica's total exports went to other islands within the West Indies Federation. There was little to discourage it from opting out. Similarly, in Canada provinces like British Columbia, which are less dependent upon interprovincial trade, have sometimes adopted the most independent stands.

In most federations the motives that led to the original union have continued to affect the operation of the federal system after its creation. But in some instances these pressures have evaporated, leaving little support for continued association.

Among transitional unifying inducements have been the drive for unity generated in opposition to alien imperial rule, the desire of some governments to see union as an escape from imminent insolvency, the agreement to wider union in order to surmount internal political friction, and the acceptance of union as a desperate immediate necessity when an external aggressor was threatening. A decade or a century later such motivations for union may lose their urgency, thus weakening the cement holding the federation together.

The experiences of some recent federations illustrate the rapidity with which original inducements may wane. In India, Pakistan, and Malaya, once independence was achieved, the unifying force of anti-imperial nationalism quickly began to evaporate. In India and Malaysia the trend was retarded, however, by the ability of a major political party, the Congress in one and the Alliance in the other, through skilful leadership to remain dominant for a considerable period after federation. In Canada, too, transitional inducements to unity operated in 1867 and later during the drive for self-government and in two world wars, but these are now weakened or even inoperative.

External threats have had an important impact upon the unity of most federations. It was one important motivation for federation in Canada, the United States, and Switzerland, but over a century or more the nature of these external threats has altered radically. Canadians are no longer alarmed by the threat of a Yankee army, victorious over the Confederates, being unleashed across the border. Instead the threat from the United States comes in the deceptive form of American influence upon the economy and the cultural life of Canada. Thus, although the fear of American domination may continue to unify Canadians, it no longer has the galvanizing impact which a direct military threat usually creates. Among the newer federations, both the West Indies and Nigeria, which were relatively free from any external military of diplomatic threat, suffered particularly from the lack of a positive impulse toward unity.

A particularly divisive form of external influence is the direct encouragement of a regional separatist movement by a foreign government. The threat to unity imposed by interventions from nations related to one of its own cultural groups led the Swiss to adopt neutrality as a fundamental policy in its foreign relations. Under the leadership of President de Gaulle, France overtly encouraged separatist movements not only in Quebec but also in the Jura region of Bern in Switzerland, and in Eastern Nigeria. Indeed, because of the French supply of arms to Biafra, de Gaulle's resignation was greeted in one Nigerian newspaper with the headline "Oujukwu's Man de Gaulle Resigns."

Foreign examples and precedents are another form of external influence. The Swiss in 1848 borrowed heavily but critically from the example of the United States. Canadians, with the lesson of the American Civil War before them, created a blend of British and American institutions. The Australians in turn took account of both American and Canadian experience, and most of the federations established subsequently learned from the experience of their predecessors. But while in the past such precedents favoured the establishment of larger political units or federations, the march to political independence and full membership in the United Nations of a large number of relatively small former colonial territories has provided within the last two decades a different sort of example. Whereas twenty years ago the watchword was the need for "viable" political units sufficiently large to maintain genuine independence, recent separatist movements in Quebec and elsewhere have been able to point to independent member countries of the United Nations which are much smaller than themselves. In Africa alone there are some twenty-five independent states each with a population less than that of Quebec. There may be some question about the real meaning of political or economic independence in many of these countries, but the existence of so many smaller African states has provided at least one argument for separatists against those who would argue that Quebec is too small to be politically independent.

THE ROLE OF FEDERAL POLITICAL INSTITUTIONS

Whether the stresses within a federation can be accommodated and resolved depends not only upon the strength and character of the conditions we have examined but also upon the institutional structure of the federal system. The way institutions channel the activities of the electorate, political parties, organized interest groups, bureaucracies, and informal elites contributes to the moderation or accentuation of political conflict. Indeed, Robert Dahl, in *Pluralist Democracy in the United States*, has described the primary function of the federal institutions as that of taming power, settling conflicts peacefully, and securing the consent of all. The way a federal system moderates conflict depends on many factors: the size, number, and internal homogeneity of the provincial units, the distribution of legislative and executive responsibilities and financial resources, the machinery of intergovernmental consultation and cooperation, the way regional groups are represented in the institutions of central government, the nature of constitutional safeguards for minority groups, and the flexibility of the political institutions in adapting to changing needs.

The size and number of provinces in a federation affect its politics. In contrast to the United States with fifty states and Switzerland with twenty-two cantons, federations composed of six or fewer provinces, such as Australia, Nigeria, Rhodesia and Nyasaland, and Pakistan, have produced fears that one or two provinces might dominate. Central governments have been weaker when confronted with a few large units. This was most severe in Pakistan where the biprovincial structure polarized most political issues into a struggle between the two provinces. Although Quebec may chafe at being only one of ten provinces, the creation of a biprovincial federation or confederacy seems unlikely, therefore, to provide a stable solution to the problems of Canada.

The distribution of functions and resources among governments has varied considerably from federation to federation. Where the distribution has failed to reflect accurately the aspirations for unity and provincial autonomy, there have been pressures for a shift in the balance of powers, or in more extreme cases even for abandoning the federal system, as in overcentralized Pakistan or the ineffectual West Indies. It has been hard to find the appropriate balance between, on the one hand, adequate central power in order to provide military and diplomatic security and economic development, and on the other, sufficient provincial autonomy to protect vital regional aspirations.

Moreover, a simple compromise between economic centralization and cultural provincialization has invariably proved to be no longer a realistic possibility. In most multicultural federations, as in Canada, regional linguistic or cultural groups have developed a deep-rooted anxiety that centralized fiscal and economic policies aiming at the rapid development of an integrated economy would undermine their cultural distinctiveness and opportunities for employment in culturally congenial conditions. In the face of such pressures, most contemporary federations have developed interlocking federal-provincial responsibility over a wide range of functions including many economic matters. In addition the sharing of financial resources has been a source of wrangling in all federations, since the distribution of such resources defines the limits of what provincial governments may do for their own regional groups.

Some federations such as Malaysia, India, Pakistan, and Rhodesia and Nyasaland have experimented with giving certain provinces more autonomy than others. A similar solution has been proposed by some for Canada in the form of a "special status" for Quebec. This has a certain logical attractiveness as a compromise meeting Quebec's desire for more autonomy while permitting English-speaking Canada to maintain a greater degree of reliance upon Ottawa. But such experiments elsewhere suggest that major differences in the degree of provincial autonomy have generally fostered, rather than reduced, tension. Such attempts have usually been followed either by a reduction in these differences in autonomy between provinces, as occurred with the reorganization of states in India in 1956 or the unification of West Pakistan in 1955, or by the eventual separation of the more autonomous states, as in the case of Malawi and Zambia in 1962 and 1963 and Singapore in 1965. The example of Singapore indicates that where one state is given greater autonomy than others, special care is needed to ensure that its citizens are not restricted in central politics to the point where they cease to feel themselves an integral part of the federation.

While regional distinctiveness is the basic reason for federal systems, some sense of positive consensus among the different regional groups is vital. The ability to generate such a sense of community depends largely on the central institutions. Particularly critical is how minority groups are represented in the central legislature, executive, civil service, political parties, and the life of the capital city. Where groups such as the East Pakistanis, the Singapore Chinese, the Jamaicans, or the black Africans of Nyasaland and Northern Rhodesia have been inadequately represented, the resulting alienation has directed itself into separatist movements.

In the United States and Switzerland the creation of a second federal chamber in which the states are equally represented has provided a check upon the sweeping power in the central legislature that representation by population would give the majority groups. But in Canada, Australia, India, Malaysia, Nigeria, and the West Indies, the adoption of a parliamentary cabinet system has in each case undermined the effectiveness of the second chamber as a guardian of provincial rights, even when, as in most of them, senators have been either directly elected or appointed by the provincial governments. In the United States with its congressional system and Switzerland with its collegial executive the framework of checks and balances within the central institutions has in most periods encouraged the search by politicians and political parties for compromises because of the variety of points at which minority groups could otherwise block action. The parliamentary federations, on the other hand, have given cabinets with majority legislative support an opportunity for more rapid and effective action, but at the price of complete sovereignty in a parliamentary majority with few institutional checks upon it. This has put the responsibility for reconciling political conflicts and for aggregating support from diverse regional and cultural groups more directly upon the internal organization and processes of the political parties themselves. Where the parties have become primarily regional in their bases, the parliamentary federations have been prone to instability, as in Pakistan before 1958 and Nigeria before 1966. In this respect one of the most ominous signs in the present Canadian scene is the apparent inability of each of the major political parties to attract support from some major regions of the country and thus to be truly representative of an interregional consensus.

In most multicultural federations it has proved necessary to recognize as official languages the languages of major minority groups and to provide constitutional or political guarantees of individual rights against discrimination. Where the language of a major regional group has been denied recognition as a federal language, extreme bitterness and tension has resulted. Pakistan, India, and Malaysia provide examples of the intensity of resentment that can be aroused.

Because the conditions in which a federal system operates inevitably undergo considerable change over time, the constitutional structure must be flexible and adaptable. Most federations face a dilemma here: some constitutional rigidity is necessary to ensure the confidence of minorities in the federal structure as a safeguard for their interests, but if federal institutions are too inflexible they may soon cease to reflect changes in social and economic conditions. Some federations such as Switzerland have managed to achieve flexibility through frequent formal constitutional amendments, while others like the United States and Australia have relied more heavily on judicial interpretation of the constitution, and on direct negotiation and agreement between central and state governments concerning political, administrative, and financial arrangements. Canada, still without an accepted formal amendment process, has had to rely especially on these latter processes, but it is now open to question whether these incremental means of adjustment alone will be adequate to meet the crisis of national unity.

THE PROCESS OF DISINTEGRATION

If the preceding survey has shown anything it is that no single condition or institutional arrangement has generated stress, or led to disintegration. In each case crises have been the product of a cumulative combination of factors.

The critical conditions appear to be of three kinds. The first is the development of a situation in which various regional demands and interests—cultural, social, and economic—instead of overlapping or cutting across each other, reinforce each other so as to polarize cleavages and conflict between regional groups.

The second is the failure of the federal institutions to perform the dual functions of accommodating minority fears through the provision of adequate provincial autonomy and of encouraging federal cohesion through representative and effective central policy-making. Where a federal system has proved inadequate to the task of enabling regional groups to maintain their own distinctiveness, secession and fragmentation have followed. But the devolution of controversial matters to the provinces in order to avoid conflicts within the central government has by itself never been enough. Equally important in the long run has been the ability of the central government to generate a positive federation-wide sense of community to counter-balance regionalism.

The third critical condition is usually an outgrowth of the other two. Where a cumulative political polarization has occurred and federal institutions have been unable to moderate these cleavages, and where negotiations have repeatedly failed to produce solutions, there has usually resulted a decline in support for political compromise or for the federal solution. Political conflict has then taken on the character of a contest with very high stakes in which each side becomes convinced that only one side can win and at the expense of the other. Consequently, intransigence and even resort to violence have replaced compromise and conciliation as political attitudes considered to be legitimate. Once such a situation of emotional confrontation and mounting frenzy has been reached it has usually taken only a relative insignificant incident to trigger off an act of secession or oppression resulting in civil war or disintegration.

The current crisis in Canadian unity has raised cries that it is time to consider a radical change in our constitutional arrangements. But we should be wary of embarking incautiously on such an enterprise for experience in several federations shows that the attempt to halt disintegration by instituting a total review of the constitution has in the end usually served only to encourage uncertainty and lack of confidence in the future of the federation. Furthermore such reviews have almost always aroused new expectations among different regional groups which have been difficult to satisfy. The Canadian efforts at constitutional review in 1968–71 demonstrate the point. Other examples are the formal constitutional reviews in the West Indies in 1961 and Rhodesia and Nyasaland during 1960–61 which led to intensified disputes. Within a year or two both federations had disintegrated.

Given the present lack of confidence in Canadian unity it may be that we have reached the point at which it might be even more dangerous to insist upon the status quo than to risk a major review. There is a stern warning from the examples elsewhere, however, that as the central and provincial governments proceed with the really hard bargaining involved in the review of our federal constitution, Canada might enter an even more critical period for her survival as a federation. This would be especially so if these conferences, having aroused expectations, again failed to produce effective results as they did at Victoria.

Most federal constitutions have explicitly or implicitly excluded a unilateral right of secession. First, it has been feared that the right to secede would weaken the whole system by placing a weapon of political coercion in the hands of provincial governments. Secondly, there has been anxiety that the possibility of secession would introduce an element of uncertainty and lack of confidence in the future, seriously handicapping efforts to build up federal unity and economic development. Thirdly, theorists have argued that if a provincial government acting alone is given the right to leave the federation, or if the central government acting alone is given the right to expel a member government, then in effect one tier of government would be subordinated to the other, thus violating the federal principle that member governments should be coordinate and not subordinate.

But constitutional restrictions have seldom prevented alienated regional groups from taking matters into their own hands. Once a province has declared its own secession the central government is faced with the dilemma whether it should enforce union upon the unwilling minority or simply accept the secession as a political fact. Most independent federations have chosen the former course, fearing that once the secession of one province is accepted there will be nothing to prevent other provinces from separating whenever they wish or at the very least using such a threat as a lever against the central government. Consequently, in both the United States and Switzerland the central government has resorted to military force to prevent secession. On much the same grounds Nigeria turned to military means to resist Biafra's secession. While in these examples the central government was successful in imposing continued unity, the effort of the Pakistan central government to do so failed. Among independent federations, only in Malaysia has a central government tolerated the separation of a state, but the separation of Singapore in 1965 was more a case of expulsion by the central government than of unilateral secession.

Furthermore, in practice it has proved difficult to work out a peaceful and rationally negotiated secession or disengagement of a unit from a federation. A federation which has been in existence for any length of time builds up many internal links and with them vested interests which have a large and emotional stake in their continuation. In addition, the confrontations and controversies which lead to the contemplation of secession inevitably generate a mounting frenzy of emotional responses with a momentum of their own, stirring up resentments and hatreds which make a coolly negotiated separation very difficult. Thus secession in the United States, Switzerland, Nigeria, and

Pakistan and partition in India produced civil war and bloodshed even where only a few years before their citizens foresaw no violence. The few cases of peaceful separation have usually occurred in colonial federations where an imperial government held the ring. Three other possibly encouraging examples of peaceful separation prove also on examination to have little relevance to the Canadian situation: the separation of Singapore from Malaysia was imposed by the central government; the separation of Norway and Sweden broke up a union which had in common only the monarchy and the diplomatic service; and the separation of Austria and Hungary in 1869 was made possible by the device of the Dual Monarchy.

One other case of political secession of particular interest to Canadians, although it occurred in a unitary system rather than a federation, is the separation of Ireland from the United Kingdom. It is of interest because it was eventually followed by economic association. The issue of Irish Home Rule came to the fore in British politics with the rise of Parnell's Home Rule party and the failure of both of the major British parties to retain the support of the Irish representatives as they had done earlier in the century. The defeat of Home Rule in the 1895 British election appeared for a time to be definitive but the real problems remained unsolved. In *England and Ireland since 1880* Patrick O'Farrell notes that the "Irish obsession, passion and agitation over matters relating to Union often encountered English incomprehension, lethargy and indifference," and such neglect enraged Ireland. The collapse of this situation into the bloody interlude between 1916 and 1921 was rooted in the politics of the British Conservative and Liberal parties, who used the issue as a stalking horse for party interests and consequently produced inadequate practical responses. The Anglo-Irish Treaty of 1921 established the Irish Free State as a separate self-governing Dominion. But while the treaty ended the war, the issue of the form of the connection with Britain continued to dominate Irish politics as a result of De Valera's campaign to cut the ties still linking the two countries. In 1933 the oath of allegiance was removed and in 1936 the office of governor general was abolished. From 1932 Ireland conducted an economic war with Britain which involved six years of mutually injurious tariffs until the war was ended by the London Agreement of 1938. Irish insistence upon neutrality during the Second World War drew British ire and was tolerated only because the ports of Northern Ireland were available for anti-submarine warfare. Finally, in 1949 the long campaign came to fruition with the formal declaration of the Irish Republic. But the problem of the partition of Ireland has remained unsolved because of the difficulty of drawing boundaries which do not leave a beleaguered minority on one side or the other. Consequently, since 1968 events in Ireland have again degenerated into a crisis which protracted violence has failed to resolve.

Generally speaking, once the complete independence of one unit in a federation has been conceded, other units have raised similar demands, which have often led to further disintegration. Moreover, the resentments aroused at the time of separation or dissolution have tended to persist and to discourage the subsequent creation of a looser form of association between the territories concerned. Whenever secession has occurred it has inevitably been accompanied by sharp political controversies which are not easily forgotten. In addition, the unscrambling of a federation requires the allocation of assets and liabilities among the successor states and rarely has it been possible to achieve this without adding further to the resentments felt by one or both sides. The continued hostility between India and Pakistan, despite Nehru's original belief that Pakistan would eventually have to return to the fold, is a good example. Nor in the West Indies or Central Africa has the creation of a new or alternative form of post-federal interterritorial political association proved feasible. It would seem, therefore, that René Lévesque's proposal for the establishment, following political independence, of a new economic association between Quebec and the rest of Canada is based on highly optimistic assumptions. The continued relations between Singapore and the Federation of Malaysia provide the only hopeful example.

CONSEQUENCES OF FEDERAL DISINTEGRATION

The actual secession of a unit from a federation has usually been followed by one of three possible consequences. One is simply the general acceptance of permanent separation, as occurred with partitioned India, the shattered West Indies Federation, and the separated territories of the former Federation of Rhodesia and Nyasaland. This solution avoids continued civil war, eliminates the central government as a centre of political controversy, and produces a number of more compact independent political units. But it involves a considerable price since it entails the loss of economic and diplomatic benefits associated with the larger political union. The economic difficulties experienced by the remnants of the federations in the West Indies and in Central Africa after their dissolution, and the contemporary international trend towards larger economic units suggests that political balkanization is a regressive step. In external relations, whether in terms of diplomatic influence or of security, smaller political units such as these have proved weak and vulnerable to pressure from larger and more powerful neighbours.

An alternative consequence of federal disintegration is the attempt to establish, as a substitute for the federation, an economic union or confederacy. This solution seeks to avoid the full effects of balkanization and has often appealed to supporters of regional autonomy, since it may obtain some of the benefits of economic association while retaining for the component units their political independence and a veto over all central political decisions. But such a solution is not as simple as at first sight appears. In practice such systems have found it almost impossible to isolate economic and political matters from each other. Economic unions, therefore, have proved politically unstable and have rarely lasted for long in the contemporary world. The European Economic Community represents an economic confederacy, but after an extremely effective beginning its progress has been slow and it has experienced some internal stresses. In any case, its main supporters regard it not as a final solution but merely as a stage on the road to fuller political federalism. Other contemporary examples, such as the East African Common Services Organization and the Central American Common Market, have not proved politically stable arrangements. It is perhaps worth noting that in the United States and Switzerland a federal system was adopted directly as a result of the deficiencies and difficulties experienced in the looser confederacy which had preceded it.

A third pattern of consequences following the declaration of secession by a state has been the resort to military force to maintain the union. The price of this alternative—civil war—may be high indeed in human lives, disruption, and the legacy of bitterness. Much depends, however, on the length and intensity of the civil war and upon the character of the federal reconstruction which follows. In Switzerland, where the war itself was brief and where the political settlement subsequently imposed was generous to the vanquished, the federal reconstruction was remarkably successful. In the United States, on the other hand, the length and ferocity of the civil war and the northern dominance which followed it left a much stronger and more enduring legacy of bitterness.

It is clear, then, that whichever of these three patterns has followed, the disintegration of a federation has generally exacted a high price in economic costs, diplomatic and defensive ineffectiveness, bitterness between the groups involved, and often in human lives. Furthermore, once complete independence for one unit has been conceded other units have raised similar demands which have often led to further disintegration.

AVOIDANCE OF DISINTEGRATION

It is clear that the Parti Québécois is fully committed to independence in some form for Quebec. Moreover, in the battle for the minds and votes of Quebecers, René Lévesque holds significant strategic advantages. In contrast to the Bourassa regime the fresh, energetic, and competent PQ government, supported by a largely enthusiastic provincial press, appears to have the sympathy of a large body of Quebecers. More important, holding the reins of government, the PQ is in a position to control the timing and wording of the proposed referendum. The PQ strategy for the interim period is clear: every action will be tailored to the goal of convincing Quebecers that they would be better off outside Confederation. Two strands of this strategy have already become evident.One is the heating up of confrontations in order to make independence seem preferable to continued friction within Confederation, both for Quebecers and other Canadians. The other is to withdraw from some of the voluntary intergovernmental arrangements upon which the effective operation of a federal system depends and to send mere observers rather than active participants to some federal-provincial meetings.

In the campaign for Quebec independence the PQ has a further major advantage: the disarray of their opponents at both the provincial and federal levels. It is hardly surprising that in such circumstances cries for a nonpartisan constitutional commission or a conference on national unity should receive such public prominence.

In the face of this unprecedented challenge to Canadian unity the tribulations experienced by other federations in similar circumstances suggest that we should emphasize four points. First, no matter what the provocations, we must do everything we can to avoid the emotional confrontation and cumulative polarization of positions which makes the search for rational accommodation and compromise impossible. Second, we must avoid the trap of thinking that the only alternatives are the steadfast maintenance of the status quo on the one hand and Quebec independence on the other, and instead seek genuine compromises which will provide both real and symbolic recognition of the aspirations not only of Quebec but of other disenchanted regional groups. Among the possibilities which require serious consideration may be significant adjustments in the responsibilities and resources assigned to provincial governments, a reform of the central institutions to ensure that central policy-making is more regionally representative (perhaps by the transformation of the Senate into a genuine Council of Provinces along the lines of the West German Bundesrat in which the state cabinets are represented), and the acceptance of predominantly unilingual provinces, French-speaking in Quebec and English-speaking elsewhere along the lines of cantonal linguistic territoriality found in Switzerland. Third, English-speaking Canadians will have to recognize the legitimacy of Quebec's linguistic, economic, and cultural aspirations, the present state of which is merely an outcome of the Quiet Revolution of the 1960s. A pro-Confederation majority in Quebec can only be preserved if Quebecers are convinced that Canada is just as much their country as anybody else's. Fourth, greater recognition of provincial aspirations across Canada will not by itself hold Confederation together unless we develop a wider sense of destiny for Canada. Canada has much to offer not only to its own peoples, but also to a world in desperate need of evidence that different cultures can live not only in harmony but in active unity under a common government.

II
Regional Opinion

British Columbia in Canada:
Perceptions of a Split Personality

R. M. BURNS

This essay has no basis in scientific sampling of public opinion. It is simply one observer's view of a confusing situation, based on discussions, interviews with a number of informed people, and a reading of the press. Others might come to quite different conclusions. It is a personal assessment, with all the prejudices that implies, of a changing scene in which the most vocal participants in the discussion seem often to be those who have given the matter the least thought.

The people of British Columbia and their governments, with some quite rare interludes of self-doubt, have always had an abiding faith in the province's destiny. But the framework of this future has not always been as clearly defined. Given the province's background it is not too surprising that the understanding and appreciation of its role in Canada should often have been less than clear. The common atmosphere of distrust in today's uncertain world of fragmenting loyalties has done nothing to improve the situation.

In the minds of many of its people, British Columbia is unique—a province unlike the others. And while no two provinces in this broad land are alike, it is probably true that British Columbia has no relationship with another province such as might be said to exist in a number of respects among the Atlantic provinces, and to some extent the Prairies. Even Ontario and Quebec, while different in so many ways, have a common bond of interest in their economic and political dominance. To the extent that this uniqueness does exist, the traditional remoteness of the province from the Canadian scene is easier to understand and appreciate.

But if a sense of uniqueness and isolation exist, they must have some basis in the factors which determine the character of a region, historical, geographic, economic, and cultural. All these have contributed to the basic political attitudes which have been characteristic of the province more or less constantly throughout its Canadian association.

It is sometimes alleged that British Columbia was a reluctant new-comer to Confederation in 1871. It would be more correct to say that the marriage was one of necessity, the Colonial Office lurking in the background with the shotgun. Canada needed the Pacific colony to tie the national expansion together and to forestall the extension of United States influence in the west. British Columbia needed the financial support of Canada and the offsetting influence it would provide to the growth of active political pressure from below the border. But, as is so often the case, once the immediate urgencies which had led to union had been eased, the battle for regional advantage began and it has continued with varying intensity ever since.

British Columbia began its life as an area of settlement separate and distinct from the other British possessions in North America. As a direct result of its background of exploration and development, it has always had a sort of cellular approach to its political life. One of its early pioneers, Dr. Helmcken, once said that "British Columbia is in, but not of, Canada." There was little, at least insofar as the centres of population on the Pacific coast were concerned, to link the growth of the region and its political development to the British possessions on the St. Lawrence and the Atlantic coast. The ties were directly to the Mother Country and indirectly to the settlements on the Pacific in the United States. Both these remained important influences in the early years.

Given the historical antecedents and the geographic base, it is not surprising that the differences have prevailed. Shut off from the rest of the country by an almost impenetrable barrier of not one but a series of mountain ranges, British Columbia's centres of population found little in the way of community with their fellow Canadians. Even in modern times, with the physical barriers bridged by road, rail, and air, the mountains remain as a mental support to the remoteness which must be experienced to be understood.

In economic terms the historical differences have also persisted. From the earliest times the province and its people have lived largely on the exploitation of its natural resources. Its philosophy of the "good life" has been tied to "boom or bust" and the richness of its assets has made the booms more common than the busts, even though they have sometimes been interrupted in a dishearteningly abrupt way. This has provided a way of life that few in the province would exchange. The "lotus land"conception of living that many hold, especially in the southwestern population centres, may indeed have a supportable base in reality. Admittedly the situation is not consistent throughout British

Columbia, for a variety of historical, geographical, and economic forces have operated in different ways, but, as a generalization, what has been said is a reasonably valid assessment of the prevailing point of view. Certainly, it reflects the dominant tone.

British Columbia's separatism, to the extent that it does exist, is the separatism of the cash register. Its disenchantment with its place in the Canadian federation has a strong foundation in economics. While the causes are varied and complex, essentially they originate in the basic characteristics of the province's economy. An economy based on the production and sale of natural resources is heavily dependent on world trade. This dependence on international trade, subject to the vagaries of a world economy, has made the people overly sensitive and often vocally belligerent about aspects of Canadian policy. This necessity of selling abroad and buying in the protected markets at home has coloured British Columbia attitudes for many years. Canada, it is earnestly believed, since the days of Macdonald's National Policy, has been absorbed primarily with the welfare of Canada's central heartland, even though this concern has had to be tempered from time to time with special consideration for the less favoured parts of the country. And the particular interests of Quebec are never forgotten. It serves no purpose here to argue the logic of the fact that the Dominion governments have generally had only a limited choice of action. The often conflicting demands of total national productivity and regional wants have placed some very real constraints on the choices of policy any government can exercise.

British Columbia's list of grievances is long and varied: freight rates, tariffs, transportation, immigration, the locus of public spending, and so on. In many cases they have had a basic validity but often their expression has been voiced emotionally and without any real attempt to consider the alternatives available. An observer may be excused for his confusion when at times these cries of hardship and discrimination become mixed with the complacent boasts of the "promised land."

Nevertheless, while it has often been an important contributor to its own isolation in terms of national policy, British Columbia has seldom been a prime beneficiary of federal policies, regardless of the political stripe of the government in power. Dominion governments have been only too willing to accept British Columbia's claims to the possession of paradise at face value. The result has been that with few brief exceptions, the relationships of the governments of the province with the governments of Canada have been marked by mutual irritations rather than by the cooperation that could add so much to the strength of each.

British Columbia's limited contribution to the national political life has been a further dimension of its insularity. Seldom in the history of Canada have British Columbia's politicians been in a position to exert any decisive influence on the direction of national policies. Aside entirely from the limitations on its impact due to the size of its representation in Parliament, no person from the province has made a mark of any great continuing significance on the national political scene. No British Columbian has ever been prime minister; no one from the province has led a major national political party.

It is tempting to seek complex reasons for this lack of influence. The common excuse might be that they lie in the domination of this country's power structure in the population centres of Ontario and Quebec, but that does not explain the greater roles played by those from other and smaller provinces. Alberta, Saskatchewan, Manitoba, and Nova Scotia at various times in our modern history have produced political figures of national consequence. The leaders of British Columbia have sometimes been men of substantial power and ability but they have generally limited their adventures to the provincial scene. It is perhaps that private attractions (as well as the political inducements) of life in the Pacific Province have been sufficient to outweigh the more prestigious attractions of service in the national capital.

If such is the case, the people of the province and their leaders have only themselves to blame for the political isolation of which they so often complain. Instead of becoming active and positive influences in the development of Canadian political life, they have been content to remain on the sidelines in too many situations, reacting in a critical way to national policies but only seldom producing positive alternatives.

British Columbia's cultural ties were originally directly to the Mother Country and not with the new Dominion. But once the union had been consolidated a gradual but inevitable substitution took place. Over time these new links were strengthened as the movement of population from the established provinces westward became the principal element in new settlement.

Canadian society has changed with the times, cultural ties have not remained the dominating factors they once were, and no strong new cultural influences have surfaced to set the province apart. Few people today in British Columbia would reject the province's part in the larger Canadian scene even though they may often be less than happy with its form and influence.

As long as all is well, this somewhat casual acceptance of the Canadian allegiance is not a matter of too great concern. Like the persistent belief in the good life which everyone is supposed to enjoy in this largely magnificent province, it is part of the accepted pattern. Unrest there usually is and complaints are a form of light conversation, but they are merely part of the accustomed background and taken more or less for granted. British Columbians have seldom worried much about national unity and except in times of crisis, have never been involved in contributing very much toward it. Problems such as those related to Quebec have been problems for the government of Canada and neither the governments nor the people of the province have felt any great responsibility.

But if the atmosphere of the past was one of mildly irritated complacency, events of the past few years have begun to disturb this detachment. The governments of the province, and perhaps the people as well, have had the realities of national political life brought harshly to their notice. The Quiet Revolution of Jean Lesage they could understand and even accept, for in its way it was only an extension of a pattern of political behaviour of which they had long experience. Not even the unrest in Quebec as it developed throughout the Sixties and Seventies could disturb the general equanimity. That there were problems was undoubtedly perceived but there was really no prevalent urge to develop an understanding of what was happening. Few people in the province had much interest in or sympathy for the federal language policies. In a province where fewer than two per cent of the people are French-speaking, this should not be wondered at. Of greater significance have been the increasingly large federal subsidies paid as equalization to Quebec, which many believe is a direct payment from their own pockets, to subsidize governments which are allegedly incompetent and now dedicated to the breakup of Canada. But, even with all this, there remains a detachment and a persistent willingness to leave the responsibility for solutions to others. It has often seemed, perhaps strangely, that while the people of British Columbia have not felt any great concern for the problems of the people of Quebec, neither have they shown any strong antagonism in response to the developments in that province. Illogically, their wrath, when aroused, has been more often directed at the government of Canada, which has had the difficult task of trying to hold this country together.

Recent events in Quebec have brought the urgency of the situation more into focus. While there have been the inevitable "jerk" reactions, some welcoming the departure of the French-speaking Canadians, and others supporting a similar course for British Columbia, such responses more likely represent the feelings of a vocal minority and not a very large one at that. There is to be sensed in the community a growing concern. No longer can the continuing life of Canada as a united country be assumed and there is slowly developing anxiety, not only for what the separation would mean for Canada but what it might also mean for British Columbia.

To speak of the people of such a large and diversified province as if there was a collective mind could, of course, be inaccurate and misleading. But there is little evidence to suggest any widespread differences of attitude. It is an unfortunate fact that most people in British Columbia have had very little chance to come to understand or appreciate the Quebec position. Even though this is a province of quite distinct regional loyalties within itself, there is only limited sympathy for the cultural and linguistic aspirations of the French-speaking Canadians. Rightly or wrongly, it is not uncommon to regard such aspirations as a cover for the less praiseworthy economic and political ambitions of a ruling class. To British Columbians this is something that they can understand for to them the federal problem has been, and is, one of economics, while the more esoteric and less definable characteristics of Quebec's search for authority do not enter easily into the assessment of the situation.

The easy world of detachment received an unexpected shock with the success of the Parti Québécois on 15 November 1976. The early reaction to the change in power was quite moderate. Quebec governments have not generally been held in high regard in British Columbia, and that of Bourassa proved to be no exception. People were therefore prepared to wait and see, hopefully believing that René Lévesque's deliberate policy of underplaying the separation theme in the election could be taken seriously. The wish, once more, was father to the thought and disillusionment has since set in. Few people here now believe that the Parti Québécois aims are likely to be open to reasonable adjustment in the terms of Confederation. The possibility of eventual Canadian national disintegration must now be accepted as a matter for deep and constant concern.

But if the people of British Columbia are concerned about the situation, what are they prepared to do about it? The sort of adjustments in the terms of the national relationship that would meet the current Parti Québécois demands are not likely to be the kind of adjustments that British Columbia would be prepared to accept. The risk of forcing the Quebec hand is very real, but so far at least, this fact does not seem to have been a serious factor in the western view of the situation. The responsibility remains that of Ottawa, and any solution that Prime Minister Trudeau may produce is probably going to be regarded with considerable suspicion and be one more element in the distrust that has traditionally been attached to federal policies in this province.

Fighting with the "Feds" has always been a popular and politically useful pastime in provincial politics, and British Columbia has been no exception. But fighting on particular issues is one thing. Advocating an open breach with Canada on constitutional ground is something else again. No British Columbia government is likely to chance the political risks that are attached to such a course, for the depth of the national attachment has yet to be accurately assessed.

Given a growing realization of the extent of the present uncertainty, it may, in the long run, operate to improve the political relationships between Ottawa and Victoria. Premier Bill Bennett has made it clear that while his government is not prepared to accept the status quo, neither is it prepared to take advantage of the preoccupation of the government of Canada with Quebec to force special concessions in constitutional change. There are already some practical indications of an effort on both sides to improve the traditional relationships, and, if continued, they can only be to the benefit of all concerned.

Though the breakup of Canada is probably beyond the bounds of credulity for the great majority of the people of the province, with the inevitable exception of those few whose regional biases or self-interest outweigh the traditional loyalties, the possibility has now become one that must be considered. And in the event of a national disintegration the province will have some difficult choices to make.

In any constitutional showdown with Quebec, the government of Canada could almost certainly count on the support of the present government of British Columbia, although some changes in the balance of federal and provincial power would probably be required. With the present growing doubt as to the intentions and the good will of the Parti Québécois, a mood of scepticism, strongly fed by the current language policy, is evident, and any sympathy that may once have existed for the Quebec position is rapidly disappearing. Certainly there would be very little support for any extension of official bilingualism or for extension to Quebec of powers not available to other provinces.

The reasons are not hard to find. British Columbians, despite an infinite capacity for complaining about their lot in Canada, are not really that unhappy with it. Perhaps they feel about it as Maurice Chevalier was said to feel about old age, it's not so bad when you consider the alternative. They are probably more concerned with the possible effects of the alternatives on their generally pleasant way of life than they are with the handicaps, real and fancied, that they claim to suffer under the existing scheme of things. The unknown future can be more disturbing than the known present.

If some new alignment eventually has to be found, any government in this province would, I believe, do everything in its power to continue the Canadian identity, with or without Quebec. Whether this is a viable option, or whether it would have to be modified in some way to take realistic recognition of the geographic separation of the Atlantic provinces, has not yet been worked out. But it seems likely to be the preferred course. There would be a good deal of hard bargaining on the terms of any continuing union but, in the circumstances and viewing the possible alternatives, it is hard to believe that the necessary compromises could not be worked out.

If the English-speaking Canadian federation, with or without the Atlantic provinces, proved impossible, there could be a movement toward some form of western union. But while union with Alberta might appeal to some, the logic of a larger scheme does not seem to rank very high in the list of possible alternatives. It is more probable that British Columbia would favour the concept of an independent nation on the Pacific. The former premier, W. A. C. Bennett, used to declaim that even if Canada were to disintegrate, British Columbia would remain as an independent member of the British Commonwealth. No one has seriously examined the economic and political prospects of such a situation. However, in the disillusionment with broader national affiliations that would follow any national collapse, such an option would appeal to a great many people in the province.

The realities of such an option cannot be analysed here. Certainly on the surface it is not hard to assume that a country as rich in resources as British Columbia could exist as an independent economic unit. This is undoubtedly a basis for the mercantilistic beliefs of the fringe separatist groups to whom union with the even richer province of Alberta would seem to be the ultimate objective. But the governance of a province as a unit in the larger federation is today a far more difficult job than that of the quasi-municipal responsibility which the Fathers of Confederation thought appropriate. And even that is a relatively simple task compared to what would be involved in leading a small "independent" power, dependent on the world at large for its existence. The ability of the people of the province to remain united under the inevitable stresses of independence is a question that cannot be ignored any more than it can be answered. British Columbia has not an enviable record of political stability and cohesion, despite the elder Bennett's twenty years of continuous power. Regional jealousies and independent ambitions have not been confined solely to the national scene.

In the possible circumstances of internal dissension under independence, the vulnerability to the influence of larger powers would be difficult to offset. Pressure from the United States, seldom direct but always there, would be emphasized under such changed circumstances. How long the province could resist, or for that matter how long its people would want to resist these influences, is an undetermined factor; one of which the British Columbia government is fully aware. Premier Bennett has openly expressed his anxiety at the vulnerability of the province in the event of Canadian disintegration.

Admittedly there is no immediate threat. Despite the part that the United States has played in British Columbia's history, and despite the close relationships that continue to exist in many aspects of life on the Pacific coast, there is singularly little interest on either side in political alliance. From the province's point of view it is hard to see how its problems in Canada could be solved by a new relationship with a much more centralized system. It is a matter that is obviously contingent on the future ability of the province to exist as an independent power. Pressure could work in two ways, internal and external. In the event of economic or political crisis in an independent British Columbia, its people might be more eager than they are today to seek a solution under the umbrella of their larger neighbour, having cast aside the shelter they already had. And while few people expect that the United States government would initiate any such movement, the temptations to respond and thus complete the integration of the Pacific coast north from Mexico might have a strong appeal.

The leader of the provincial Liberal party recently remarked that British Columbia had three main feelings about its place in Canada: "the 'aren't we lucky to be living in British Columbia' feeling, a feeling of economic disadvantage by association with Canada, and a feeling of political impotence in matters relating to the central government."

The feeling of luck is essentially a product of geographic location and nothing much is going to be changed by political realignment. The political and economic disadvantages might be eased, or at least altered, by independence or some new form of association. But, given the growing power of the western provinces, and the increasing recognition in Ottawa of the need to integrate national and regional interests, these aspects should be negotiable within the general context of the present political framework.

Basic political upheaval requires the existence and public awareness of some deep-rooted discontent and it must have leadership to translate these elements into effective political action. This is not now the case in British Columbia. People complain and governments argue about their real and fancied grievances, but nothing in sight at present is going to change the belief that despite the problems that arise from time to time, this is the best of all possible worlds. All in all, the great majority of the people of British Columbia, while never really satisfied that perfection has been reached, recognize that they have had a pretty good thing going for most of the years in Canada. The benefits of any of the perceivable alternatives have yet to be demonstrated. The province will not be content with things as they have been, but the situation appears to be negotiable. There is also a factor which we all too often forget, one not measurable in economic terms—the fact and effect of historical ties.

Federations seldom break up on purely economic issues. In the case of this province, the emotional pressures which can make or break a nation seem to be on the side of the continuing Canadian connection. Nationhood has been defined as the remembrance of great things done together, and the great events of British Columbia history are those of the history of Canada. The province has been, and is still, bound by what the Australians called the "crimson thread of kinship," first to Great Britain, and now to Canada. While we sometimes seem to have lost our hold on it in the years of our complacency, it may very well be the decisive factor in determining which way British Columbia will go, if the choice ever must be made.

The Prairie Perspective
in 1977

JOHN ARCHER

Significant differences divide the politics of the three Prairie provinces from those of other Canadian regions. To quote a distinguished western historian, W. L. Morton, these differences are "both of common observation and academic study." The explanation is historical in the main, the differences resulting from an initial bias which by cumulative process developed into a traditional attitude of mind. The initial blunder of the Dominion government in Red River was to regard the acquisition and development of the North West as compensation to Ontario for the latter's consent to the building of the Intercolonial Railway and to Maritime terms of union. The North West was to be a hinterland, indeed a colony of Ontario, not of Quebec. Louis Riel won a partial victory in 1870, for he gained provincial status for Manitoba which he thought would preserve the Métis language, religion, and existence as a group. Manitoba, however, did not gain control of its public lands, hence was not the equal of other provinces. This was the initial bias. It was sharply reinforced in 1905, when Alberta and Saskatchewan were created provinces with the federal government reserving control of natural resources for the purposes of the Dominion. By 1930, when the natural resources question was settled, the pattern of prairie politics was confirmed.

The Prairie provinces were settled under a National Policy that set out generally the terms, manner, and conditions of settlement insofar as planners in Ottawa could foresee future development. The National Policy was designed to nurture an industrialized heartland with a national transportation system serving industry's needs and national purposes in trade; a tariff policy to protect infant and essential industries; a fiscal policy to provide incentive to extractive industries, but also to monitor the strength of the Canadian currency. There were adjustments to tariffs, freight rates, and subsidies as regional disparities became marked and as protests affected political stability. The West has never viewed the National Policy as merely a policy of protection for industry located in central Canada. Rather the National Policy has been seen as a policy to create a national as opposed to a colonial economy. In this view the Crow's Nest Pass Agreement and its lineal descendant is as much a part of the National Policy as is the tariff. The defeat of the Reciprocity Agreement in 1911 came as a shock to westerners, convincing a majority of farmers that the tariff lobby would go to great lengths to maintain the advantages to the industrial heartland of the National Policy. The Prairie West, a minority region, could not dominate by numbers, nor had it the influence to effectively promote its own economic interests through legislation. It did not use the balance of power skilfully when opportunity offered and it became represented at the national level by fragmented voices. Today the West is barely represented in the party in power and is well aware that a federal election may have been decided before the polls have closed in Alberta. It is galling indeed to realize how little political clout the region wields.

Nevertheless, the Prairie provinces continue to feel a proprietary interest in the modern Canada they did so much to create. Canada was a bilingual nation in 1867. The successful settlement of the West gave it a sense of its multicultural heritage. In spite of the withholding of natural resources by the Dominion government and the constraints of the National Policy, the West is essentially federalist in outlook. The basis of Confederation was accepted and the exigencies of circumstances in the Twenties and Thirties proved the need for a strong federal authority. The process of developing shared programs appeared to be an earnest attempt on the part of Ottawa and the provincial jurisdiction to develop cooperative federalism, while negotiated fiscal arrangements appeared to offer a workable avenue for the resolution of problems stemming from regional disparities in income.

Federal-provincial relationships in the past decade have changed. Government spokesmen in the three prairie jurisdictions speak of a new and callous attitude on the part of the federal government. This attitude, it is stated, has much to do with the strains in federalism in Canada today. It has focussed the hurt and distrust, the feeling of alienation and resentment in the region, on the federal government, even though such issues as bilingualism, recognition of the French past, and the election of the Parti Québecois would normally have concentrated attention on the province of Quebec. The attitude of the federal government is regarded as a flaunting of power. Ottawa has drawn back from the concept of cooperative federalism and is peremptorily abandoning its responsibility for shared programs. There is a feeling that the federal government acts hastily, entering some arrangements without thorough preparation, barging into tax fields hitherto the preserve of the provinces, turning from income distribution to a punitive tax policy. There is a deep fear that the federal government is deliberately seeking ways of isolating provinces, so that a specified "enemy" may be attacked singly and reduced to a proper colonial condition. These views are not held with equal conviction in each prairie province, but each province can list time, place, and circumstance to document these views. Saskatchewan appears to be at odds with Ottawa in more areas, covering a wider spectrum of issues, than either of the sister provinces, Manitoba is the least shrill, Alberta lists the fewest issues, but feels these very deeply.

The election of a Parti Québécois government in Quebec was as startling to westerners as to others. In general, expressed opinion saw the Lévesque victory at the polls as a result of public dissatisfaction with the Bourassa administration rather than a positive vote for separatism. Some understanding was expressed of Lévesque's views on the need for a looser federal system. Many supported his opposition to the continuing centralizing thrust of the Trudeau government. Support and sympathy did not, and do not, extend to the separatist views held by members of the Parti Québécois, and prairie political leaders recognize the existence of a determined and closely-knit element within that party whose aims are independence from Canada at all costs. It is well recognized in Prairie Canada that economic arguments of themselves will not be a sufficient counter to the emotional appeal of separatist arguments.

One might expect some westerners to adopt a "let them go" attitude, since Quebec has little in the way of economic advantage to offer the West and is not seen as an important trading partner. Little is heard in this vein—perhaps because historically Quebec had been an ally of western farmers up to the Diefenbaker era. More likely, however, a politically sophisticated West realizes that a dominant protectionist Ontario in a union without Quebec would be quite unpalatable.

Economic facts and arguments do play on the issue, nevertheless, and will play an increasingly important role as Premier Lévesque's administration comes to grips with the realities of power and responsibility. The Prairie provinces emphasize economic grounds since any support for separation of this region from the rest of Canada is based on the economics of such a move. There are small groups advocating separation for the West. One such group, in Calgary, receives a certain measure of publicity, but there is no broadly based support. Unless conditions change drastically in the immediate future, there seems little possibility of any secessionist movement gaining strong official or unofficial support. Emotionally, prairie people strongly favour one Canada. There is no full understanding of the situation in Quebec where the economic facts draw Quebec in, but emotional forces call for separate status. The Prairie West feels that Quebec has benefited vastly from being in Canada and if that province is in a position to unilaterally declare independence it is only because it has been conceded much and this has lessened the appeal of economic arguments to the Quebecers. On the other hand, westerners would oppose using economic measures to force Quebec to remain in Confederation, feeling that such pressure would accomplish little and would add to separatist support.

The Prairie provinces are sensitive to federal pressure in the economic sphere and there is an almost paranoic hatred of federal policies in resource taxation in certain quarters. Alberta feels most deeply the "obstruction" of the federal government which has prevented fuller development of industries in that province and has appropriated its oil wealth to the whole country.

In general it is felt that any devolution of power should affect all provinces and not be special to any one. Manitoba, however, would not support further devolution of power to the provinces at the expense of the federal government. Premier Schreyer would agree that Ottawa needs a strong reserve of power to enable it to correct regional disparity of economic benefits. His government would support special treatment for cultural purposes. Saskatchewan, feeling the effects of oil and potash revenues, would seek a clear delineation of the present division of powers—federal vs. provincial—while supporting the need for a strong central or federal government. Alberta would support the Saskatchewan stance but seek a greater role in decisions on location of industry. There is no clearly defined single prairie view. Many would support transfer of responsibility for welfare, health, and education to the provinces if necessary funding was also transferred. Premier Blakeney would argue that education is a national concern in the broad sense hence the federal government should be more involved. The Prairie provinces might envy Quebec its success in gaining federal favour, but prairie politicians are in the same auction and they would not see Quebec's influence deliberately curtailed since a prairie province might later be singled out for similar treatment. Premier Blakeney expressed widely held views when he rejected the use of force to preserve Canada, saying the "force option is not open," but went on to say that separation by Quebec would exert significant pulls for the dismemberment of Canada. "There would be in Western Canada increasing sentiment for some separation, or alternatively, some re-negotiation of the relationship with Central Canada, now Ontario. I think that would be the first step." When queried on relationships with the federal power, he replied:

> The central government in Canada in the last couple of years has made some moves which have been adverse to provincial interests and adverse to the proper development of the country. I do not accept the general position that the federal government is too strong. It has been moving in a way which I would not have wished it to move, in some areas, but if Canada is to survive, we need a central government of some considerable strength.

The past few years have brought about significant changes in the attitude of prairie governments and people toward the French fact, the bases of Confederation, and the value of the Canadian experiment in bilingualism and multiculturalism. Changes in attitude have been re-flected in governmental action." As Premier Schreyer of Manitoba has said, "It is a challenge, but surely not an impossible challenge, to build and sustain a country with foundations based on bilingualism and multi-culturalism. . . . A country based on accommodation of diversity is more apt to show qualities of greater tolerance and understanding." Schreyer went on to say that the use of French as a language of instruction was authorized in Manitoba for prescribed subjects. This had been extended, while French as a class subject had come to the point where it was taught through primary, elementary, and high school grades. This Manitoba example reflected "the desire of so many of us to ensure that the rich bilingual and broad cultural basis of Canada's heritage is maintained and strengthened." Premier Schreyer has also stated in an interview:

> You either have an acceptance of the French fact and the meaningful presence of French language and culture or you encourage separatism. . . . Forget theory and get down to common sense on the part of both vocal English and French-speaking Canadians. There are limits to the extent to which bilingualism can be made to be pervasive. . . . Absolutely there should be more emphasis on teaching French in public school and up.

Premier Blakeney of Saskatchewan has pointed out that "the desire of French Canada to protect its own culture and way of life is fundamentally not very different from the desire of prairie wheat growers and Maritime fishermen to protect their unique communities." He added that some English-speaking Canadians view the bilingual nature of Canada not as a source of pride but as an annoying condition, while some French-speaking Canadians have lost faith in the rest of Canada. Nevertheless the majority of Canadians desired to make Confederation work. He emphasized that the cost of the bilingual nature of the country is worth paying—indeed it is no more than one quarter of one per cent of our gross national product—a trivial cost if we believe in Canada. He added, "Likewise, turning a box of cornflakes around in order to read the English is not too large a gesture to make for the unity of the country."

There has been a great change in all the prairie west in the attitude to the teaching and learning of French. French classes find ready takers. French radio and television is accepted, even appreciated. While it is true that bilingual signs affront some visitors to parks and public buildings, the recent admission that French will not best be learned by pressuring people has cooled opposition and left room for genuine appreciation of the cultural advantages of learning another language.

The official reaction of prairie provincial governments to the avowedly separatist aims of the recently elected Parti Québécois has been reserved and moderate. This same moderate posture has been adopted by the media and the business community. The *Edmonton Journal*, through its editor, Andrew W. Sneddon, took pains to point out that the "freeze in the dark" quip attributed to Alberta was in reality of Texas origin, first quoted in Calgary by a Texan. The *Journal's* editor strongly supports the teaching of French in all kindergartens and all grades up to and through university. He does not accept a customs union between Canada and an independent Quebec as a feasible proposal. Such an association could not last, since the tail would wag the dog, and there would be stalemate and recriminations.

The *Edmonton Journal* deplored the action of Calgary's mayor in publicly criticizing members of the Quebec government:

> For some reason that escapes us, the Calgary Mayor felt it necessary to use a radio show to launch into a tirade against members of the separatist Parti Quebecois government, characterizing them as "gangsters, saboteurs, murderers, jail people, fanatics, and criminals, members of the F.L.Q. and revolutionaries". . . .
>
> . . . it is a difficult enough job to try to convince people in Quebec and other parts of Canada that the "rednecks" haven't really taken over in Alberta.

The *Journal* took pains to dissociate itself from these remarks and to point out that whereas the separatist movement in Calgary was a fringe movement, some 78 per cent of Albertans had expressed the wish that Quebec would stay in Confederation.

The media and the business community in the Prairie provinces viewed the election of the Parti Québécois as a repudiation of the notion that anything could be tolerated in the name of keeping the separatists out of power. It showed a lack of trust in Prime Minister Trudeau's concept of national unity, a concept which appeared to favour centralization of financial, industrial, commercial, and political power in Ottawa. The *Calgary Herald* pointed out that westerners could no longer afford the luxury of detachment and while the assertions that Canada would be better off without Quebec were never based on reality, there was today "a late appreciation of the immense value of federalism in Canadian terms." There was concern lest in the rush of emotion too much be given away and the *Winnipeg Free Press* advised that the rest of Canada should make what accommodations must be made, but must keep in mind that an enfeebled Confederation with no central powers might not be worth saving.

The *Western Producer*, the organ of the Saskatchewan Wheat Pool and the most influential farm paper in the region, adopted a consistently moderate posture, providing opportunity through its "Open Forum" for readers to express opinion and editorially supporting the cultural value of bilingualism, and the value to Canada of the French fact. The *Saskatoon Star-Phoenix* found the schools at fault for failing to stress the bilingual nature of Canada. So it was difficult for a young Canadian of Ukrainian origin to appreciate the French fact. An article in the "Forum" of that paper came to the conclusion that Ottawa's best solution to the problem appeared to be in giving more power to the government in Quebec City alone—"special status, a concept that has destroyed many a political career in Canada, and is a scandalous concept to Westerners may well be Canada's last best hope." This position would not find general support. An editorial in the previous day's issue had suggested that perhaps the problem was that Quebec had long seen itself as one of two founding partners while other provinces saw Quebec and themselves as belonging to a ten-member partnership, which would exclude special status for one member. The writer nevertheless urged warm acceptance of the French fact. In the same issue, the Ottawa correspondent of the paper pointed out that in Quebec's view control of communications systems was essential if the province were to maintain its culture. This stance was vastly different to Saskatchewan's position on cable television, since

Saskatchewan did not challenge Ottawa's right to regulate programming. Its concern was primarily technical, having to do with how cable television systems fit into Saskatchewan Telephone's plans in other areas of communications. This difference in philosophy went to the heart of the difference between Quebec and any other province.

One of the most interesting aspects of the present discussion of Quebec separatism in the Prairie provinces is the almost total lack of reliance on economic arguments. There appears to be an appreciation of the emotional basis of Quebec's position. The main import of reasoning in the West sees room in Confederation for Premier Lévesque's views. Indeed, René Lévesque continues to command a high level of respect and liking, though prairie people appreciate that he is committed to separatism. There is no thought of coercion, and bullying Quebec is no part of anyone's program. As one writer to the "Open Forum" of the *Western Producer* put it: "If after our best efforts at compromise Quebecers still feel that separatism is their destiny we should yield gracefully, and with friendship and goodwill let them go their way." Indeed, there is a fear that the federal government, having in the past concentrated too exclusively on federal solutions, may again forget that Canada is not a unitary country and seek to deal with Quebec in isolation.

There is still some reaction to the language issue at the personal level but the heat has subsided. Most people would agree with Roland Bird, writing in *The Economist* of London, that "there is an essential decency about the concept of bilingualism, but there has been far too much gaucherie in the way it has been pursued. It does not directly touch the great majority of Canadians, but it angers too many of them at the emotional fringe." Certainly it has failed to convince the French-speaking element for whose benefit the policy was fashioned. It did promote resentment among the very people whose understanding was essential to success. Westerners saw the policies of both Ottawa and Quebec as short-term and arbitrary. An increasing number of people today are happy to accept the French fact, particularly as understanding grows of its implications for Quebec and the nation, but they have resented, and still resent, the attempts of the federal government to force the issue. Many, however, would agree that a certain amount of pressure was necessary to set the process in motion. It need not be said, but it is worth saying, that westerners are far from being rednecks and bigots.

In all the debate on separatism, and Quebec's declared intention to separate, there has been little criticism directed against that province or its people. The main brunt of criticism has fallen on Prime Minister Trudeau and his colleagues. Westerners feel that a highly centralized national policy has left little room for diversity, and has resulted in wide disparity of social and economic benefits. There was, and is, inequality of sacrifice and this policy of inequality has contributed to the unhappiness of French-speaking Canada, the Maritimes, and the West. Westerners are particularly alarmed at what they regard as sudden attempts to change the rules of Confederation, claiming that the rules regarding resources were well understood until the Prairie provinces uncovered some resources. The action of the federal government in arbitrarily setting a low price for oil from Alberta—oil that flowed into Montreal through a pipeline for which Quebec refuses to pay—together with the fixing of the export price of natural gas, has actually encouraged consumption at a time when it should have been restrained, and brought exploration to a standstill when it should have been encouraged. Premier Lougheed has fought hard for a constitutional guarantee of the provinces' right to mineral resources—rights which his government claims were laid down a century ago. The fact that a provincial government must fight for these, at this time, is indicative to westerners of the rapaciousness of federal politics. They wryly note that much of the money siphoned off in the West goes to pay for Mirabel airport, office complexes in Hull, and public works in Ottawa. Let any one of the western provinces strike off on a policy that appears to compete in a significant way with the industrialized heartland of Canada, and all the power and influence of that heartland is brought to bear on federal policy with the obvious result. The argument runs that if there were a new balance between the centre and the periphery; if there were a greater awareness of provincial and regional needs and sensitivities; if the federal power was not exercised in so peremptory and arbitrary a manner, then a new era would develop in which diversity of culture and heritage would be respected and some common basis of sacrifices and rewards would be provided.

No one has ventured yet to predict how Prairie Canada would react were Quebec to separate. The reticence of spokesmen for government, business, and industry is understandable, and commendable, for there is now some realization of the gravity of the situation. Until last November little credence was given to separatist threats in Quebec. The Prairie West had heard such threats before, and had recognized them as a weapon in the arsenal of "better deal" campaigns. The victory of a party campaigning on a separatist platform, confused though the issues were by the insertion of "clean government" planks, was significant enough. To have won so handily against traditional Liberal strength in Quebec at the provincial level was an electrifying achievement. The stance of Premier Lévesque's government has been made clear. The aim is peaceful separation from Canada. Some spokesmen for government and industry would explain the crisis away as a change in government rather than a change in status. Majority comment, however, accepts it for what it undoubtedly is—the determination of a body of Quebecers who no longer feel a sense of cultural fulfilment within the Canadian confederation. This is symptomatic of a division that goes deeper than economic disadvantage or unequal fiscal sharing. It has emotional bases that cannot be cemented over by tax points or subsidies.

Realization of the gravity of the situation has brought an appreciation of the difficulties of finding a cure before it is too late. Perhaps for the first time westerners have begun to think of Canada in idealistic rather than economic terms. They are finding it difficult to devise means of reassuring Quebecers that English-speaking Canada desires them to remain part of Canada. No longer is it simply a question of the economic advantages of Quebec remaining in Confederation. It is a realization that the Canadian nation stands for some ideals that cannot be wholly realized without Quebec. Many westerners seek the means to translate this feeling into tangible means of convincing Quebecers of their sincerity.

The media in the West has acted in a responsible manner in dealing with the probable effects of the Quebec election. The newspapers, in particular, have counselled moderation and restraint and have criticized some eastern colleagues for "premature" editorializing. While editorial writers have reviewed the factors that appeared to weigh in the election, the reporting has been objective. There was little or no speculation on what effect the Quebec result might have on prairie thinking and there was an obvious effort to explain that movements looking to prairie separation were weak in membership and local in character.

Perhaps one reason for the lack of speculation, official and unofficial, on the future of Prairie Canada were Quebec to separate, stems from the fact that there is no united front or declared policy on the part of prairie governments. There is no indication that government officials have discussed the matter, although each premier has made public statements supporting the ideal of a united Canada. It is no secret that young executives in Premier Lougheed's administration would favour Alberta going it alone, or perhaps making some accommodation with

British Columbia. Others would favour some investigation of a common prairie policy. However, Albertans do not view the Crow Rates with the same reverence as do Saskatchewan farmers. Alberta is now obviously a rich province, while Manitoba and Saskatchewan have less wealth and different views on how provincial revenues should be spent. Politically and culturally, Manitoba is much closer to Ontario than to Saskatchewan, and favours a gradual approach to development and a middle-of-the-road stance on the distribution of powers within the federal system. Saskatchewan is at odds with Ottawa in more areas than is either sister province, but Alberta's frustration with Ottawa's attitude to industrial growth in the province is deep.

There is one area that is receiving much quiet thought and comment. This has to do with the future of French-speaking groups in the Prairie provinces. While it is true that there is a growing appreciation of the cultural value of learning another language, the emphasis presently placed on instruction in French stems from the fact that Quebec is part of Canada, and the French fact part of our Canadian heritage. If Quebec were to leave Canada this emphasis would probably disappear. Certainly the accent on multiculturalism would continue and the French language and culture would become one of many ethnic threads proportionally less important than other more numerous strains.

What then is the prairie perspective today? There is less talk of a separate option for Prairie Canada. There is a greater realization that fragmenting Canada would almost surely mean the end of Canada. Not only are westerners not ready to take such a step, but they are ready to make sacrifices to ensure that it does not happen. Faced with a real threat to the wholeness of the country, westerners have reacted against fragmentation. They know that there is a price for maintaining a separate national identity. They feel that the goal justifies the cost because in their view the Canadian system of government is more efficient than most and our federation more balanced and more responsive to duality. Canada is not a melting pot. Confederation has served to maintain and nourish the French-Canadian culture, and the best security Quebec can have is to remain within Canada. But French-speaking Canada must be made to feel at home in Canada, not through any forced bilingual policy, but by making the federal system sufficiently flexible to accommodate the economic and cultural needs of the Quebec society.

Prairie Canada places much of the blame for the heightened tensions within the federal system on the actions of the federal government.

The anger over "forcing French down our throats" was directed at Ottawa rather than at Quebec. Prairie people shrewdly suspected that Quebecers would care very little if French was spoken in Regina, but would care much if the French language could not be used when desired. Prairie governments saw the outcome of the election in Quebec last November as the result of bad government, and, perhaps wrongly, view much of Quebec's discontent as stemming from exasperation arising from economic causes. In general, adjustments of powers within Canada and a recession of the centralizing tendencies of the federal government are seen as the means of bringing about a genuinely united Canada. As Premier Blakeney of Saskatchewan put it, groups in Canada

> are threatened by the powerful centralizing forces of the Canadian economy, and by the prejudices of other Canadians. We need more understanding on the part of all Canadians if we are to preserve a united Canada, but understanding alone is not enough. Governments, both federal and provincial, must actively resist the concentration of power and wealth in the centre, and Canadians in general must be prepared to pay the cost, in dollars and cents, of a unified country which sees itself, from coast to coast, as "One Canada."

There is heightened concern in the West about the actions that may be taken by the federal government. Few westerners see the federal authority as having the wisdom or vision to make the correct decisions for Canada. This lack of confidence may be a crucial factor in the expected negotiations concerning the future of federalism. Westerners know that the wording of a plebiscite may influence the answer given. The future of a country should not turn on this wording but rather should be decided cooperatively by the federal government and the provincial governments. Westerners are not prone to self-effacement. They may feel a sense of frustration over their lack of political influence, but they are well aware of their importance in the economic sector. They are willing to try to work out a new basis of Confederation before seeking any other course of action.

Quebec's Separation and the Atlantic Provinces

GEORGE RAWLYK

Without question, the region with the most to lose should Quebec leave Confederation is the Atlantic region. As the twentieth century advanced, and as economic, cultural, and political ties drew the Atlantic provinces into an ever closer relationship with central Canada, the often virulent anti-Confederation rhetoric of the nineteenth century was significantly neutralized by a growing dependence on the federal government. Because of their relatively weak resource and industrial base and because they have found themselves on the periphery far from the dynamic westward transcontinental thrust of Canada, New Brunswick, Nova Scotia, Prince Edward Island, and Newfoundland have become increasingly dependent upon massive federal financial assistance. If any Canadian region feels, with considerable justification, that it will be adversely affected by the undermining of the federal government's power to redistribute financial resources and equalize social services, it is the Atlantic region. And if any group of Canadians today is firmly and emotionally attached to Canada and feels especially threatened by the spectre of Quebec's separation, it is the residents of the Atlantic region. Although often unwilling or unable to articulate their sense of concern about the future, as well as their pride and faith in Canada, these people, nevertheless, have blended their local patriotism into a larger Canadianism. Premier Campbell of Prince Edward Island may have best described this development when he perceptively observed in January 1967, "If anyone entertains any doubts about the allegiance of Prince Edward Island to this nation, all he has to do is come here and talk to them. We may be Islanders first, but we're Canadians before we're anything else." Premier Campbell's insight could be applied to many Maritimers and Newfoundlanders in the 1960s and 1970s. They consider themselves to be Canadians "before we're anything else" largely because they are "Islanders" or "Newfies" or Nova Scotians or New Brunswickers *first*. Such a feeling may appear to be both paradoxical and illogical; nevertheless it seems to capture the essential reality of the Atlantic region's unique response to the forces of profound change which threaten to destroy Canada.

This pro-Canadian feeling owes little to the region's original response to Confederation and all that it represented. If a referendum had been held in the region in 1867, the anti-Confederation forces would have won an easy victory. Only in New Brunswick, the evidence suggests, would the supporters of John A. Macdonald's so-called "Botheration Scheme" have received more support than their opponents. And even in New Brunswick there was a strong minority opposed to Confederation. This opposition was to continue well into the twentieth century. New Brunswick's anti-Confederation point of view was eloquently expressed in April 1865 by W. H. Needham in a speech made in the provincial legislature. In this evocative statement Needham stressed the vital importance of protecting a New Brunswick sense of nationality threatened by Canadian imperialism:

> I know there are men whose souls soar away beyond us, who are satiated with all that little New Brunswick can give them, and they reach forward to the celebrated towers and palaces of the far-off Ottawa; for this they would let New Brunswick go to the winds and be lost for ever.
>
> When I forget my country so far as to sell it for Confederation, may my right hand forget its cunning, and if I do not prefer New Brunswick, as she is, to Canada with all her glory, then let my tongue cleave to the roof of my mouth.

In neighbouring Prince Edward Island, in 1866, the vast majority of the inhabitants would have shouted an enthusiastic Amen to Needham's patriotic outburst. Cornelius Howat, a member of the Island Assembly, cogently expressed what he knew was the majority opinion:

> And considering that we would be such a small portion of the confederacy, our voice would not be heard in it. We would be the next thing to nothing. Are we then going to surrender our rights and liberties? It is just a question of "self or no self."

Howat had shrewdly and deftly cut to the heart of the issue. The choice was indeed a simple one—or at least it seemed to be simple. Prince Edward Island could continue to be something or become "the next thing to nothing." It could have a separate identity of its own or it could be sucked into the mighty Canadian whirlpool and experience sudden oblivion. The editor of the *Summerside Progress* reiterated Howat's argument when he condemned those who wanted to "cheat, coax, drag, or drive us into a union where our individuality—our identity as a people—will be forever sunk and lost in the abysmal 'Dominion of Canada'!" Islanders were warned by their political leaders in the P.E.I. Assembly to resist being "devoured by the Canadians" and to beware of being "entirely swamped."

It is not surprising, therefore, that on 7 May 1866 Premier J. C. Pope would declare that "as ninety-nine out of every one hundred of the people are against Confederation, I think we, as their representatives, are bound to represent or express their views." And even the pro-Confederation paper, the *Charlottetown Islander*, had to confess on 11 December 1864 that "not one man in ten will listen to Confederation!" Edward Whelan, the leading pro-Confederation propagandist, admitted that there was "such a public phrensy against Confederation that no public man who looks to the future, dare advocate it." But pressure from the Colonial Office and economic difficulties eventually pushed a reluctant island into Confederation in 1873. Many islanders found it extremely difficult to adjust to their new dependent status in Confederation. And there was a pathetic ring of truth in the lines of the popular island folk song:

> With dishes fine their tables shine
>   They live in princely style
> These are the knaves who made us slaves
>   And sold Prince Edward Island.

Until 1949 Newfoundland refused to be "sold" to Canada. The essence of the island's response to Confederation is brilliantly captured in the well-known nineteenth-century folk song, "Come Near at Your Peril Canadian Wolf," in which "ye brave Newfoundlanders" are urged not to sell their birthright of liberty "for a few thousand dollars of Canadian gold."

In 1948 the special referendum to determine the future of the island found the electorate badly divided and very confused. The voters were caught between the advocates of "Newfoundland for Newfoundlanders" on the one hand and those promising "Baby Bonuses for Everybody" on the other. The referendum was actually the final step in a long-drawn-out political battle between those who favoured strong links with Britain or the United States and those who wished to see Newfoundland finally become the tenth Canadian province. Many in the latter group felt that Newfoundland's spirit of independence and its regional identity could be best developed and preserved within Canada. In the first referendum held on 3 June 1948 the result was:

Responsible Government	44.55%
Commission Government	14.32%
Confederation	41.13%

Then on July 22 the result was:

Confederation	52.34%
Responsible Government	47.66%

The margin of victory was disconcertingly narrow—but it was enough. And since July 1948 the Confederation movement has obviously gained much support in Newfoundland.

Nova Scotia's attitude towards Confederation was accurately expressed in the provincial and federal elections of 1867. In the former no fewer than thirty-six out of thirty-eight anti-Confederation advocates were elected and in the federal election eighteen out of nineteen. But despite the strength of the anti-Confederates by 1869 the back of the anti-Confederation movement had been broken in Nova Scotia. When Joseph Howe—"the Voice of Nova Scotia"—entered John A. Macdonald's cabinet in January 1869, the Repeal Movement, which he had led, received a fatal blow. Conceived in frustration, anger, and economic discontent the movement lost much of its momentum when signs of an economic upswing appeared and it became abundantly clear that the British government was adamantly opposed to Nova Scotia's leaving Canada.

The "Better Terms" agreement negotiated by Howe, and Macdonald's sympathetic perception of the problems peculiar to New Brunswick and Prince Edward Island, helped to draw the Atlantic provinces deeper into Confederation. Yet anti-Confederation and anti-Upper Canadian feeling remained near the surface of the collective Maritime mind and usually burst into bitter polemical rhetoric during periods of acute economic stress.

As the twentieth century unfolded the volume and intensity of Maritime regional protest vis-à-vis Upper Canada and Confederation gradually lessened. Even the Maritime Rights Movement of the 1920s, with its substantial elite and popular support in all three provinces, had little real impact on the national stance of the region. Unlike the Progressives of the Canadian West, the advocates of Maritime Rights exerted a minimal influence on Canadian federal politics. There is some evidence that in the 1920s, as in the following decade and during much of the post-World War II period, Maritime regional protest was effectively used by the region's economic, social, and political elite to deflect the often bitter and deep-rooted frustrations of the ordinary fisherman, farmers, and workers against Ottawa rather than against Halifax, Fredericton, or Charlottetown. Thus it may be argued that an ideological legacy from the nineteenth century has been used to try to preserve the status quo in the region.

It seems clear that the articulated regional protest of the twentieth century is not a serious manifestation of anti-Confederation feeling in the Atlantic provinces. Rather it should be viewed within the context of the region's peculiar political culture. The rhetoric of alienation not only serves to preserve the status quo but it is also an important means whereby a traditional and basically conservative people keeps in touch with a past which is regarded as far more important in many respects than the present and the future. Literary and political archetypes from the 1860s and the 1880s must help to provide Maritimers in particular with a sense of place and of time in a confused and disoriented world. Furthermore, regional discontent enables federal politicians from the region to apply pressure on Ottawa to provide certain political necessities for their constituents. For some critical observers this was a degrading habit; the cap was dusted off, the begging cup polished, and rich Mr. Ottawa approached for a little "conscience money." For Professor J. Murray Beck, writing in *The Government of Nova Scotia*, Maritime MPs have

> been more concerned with maintaining party solidarity than with safeguarding provincial interests. While the western Canadian Provinces have undoubtedly found it to their advantage to return third-party representation in strength, the Maritimes have rarely deviated from old-party lines to the extent of more than a single member, and the political leaders at Ottawa have had no difficulty in keeping them in line by what might be alleged to be little more than temporary sops.

By the late 1960s the Atlantic provinces had become, in many respects, virtually dependent upon Ottawa for their continued survival. It is not surprising, therefore, that the region reacted as it did during these years to the possibility of Quebec's secession. Those residents of the region who thought about the issue spoke with one voice in support of a strong and united Canada. Moreover, most of them showed very little sympathy for the aspirations of French Canadians. It was felt that the French Canadians should be quite satisfied with their lot in life since, as the *Charlottetown Guardian* put it, "the essential powers of the constitution cannot be defied or flouted." Quebecers were warned on 8 June 1968 to resist the blandishments of René Lévesque—"a mealy-mouthed apostle of the destruction of Canada," in the words of the *Halifax Chronicle-Herald*. A year later, Dr. Henry Hicks, president of Dalhousie University and a former Liberal premier of Nova Scotia, expressed what he knew many others Maritimers believed:

> I would *use force of arms* to restore order and maintain peace in Quebec.
> . . . The United States had to maintain the integrity of the union—if we don't believe in the integrity of this country enough that we wouldn't fight, then we don't deserve it.

What Dr. Hicks was doing, and survey data support this conclusion, was accurately reflecting a deeply embedded sentiment of national pride and sense of Canadian identity which most residents of the Atlantic provinces shared, though there is little evidence of a disposition to use "force of arms." It is not surprising therefore that a *Toronto Telegram* survey in May 1969 found that "many Maritimers almost choked with emotion when asked how important it was to them that Canada survive." And Robert Bourassa's two election victories in April 1970 and October 1973 provided both relief and joy to many distraught residents of the Atlantic provinces.

What the residents of the region desperately wanted to believe was that the Parti Québécois was a spent political force and that separation was now impossible. The four provincial premiers were delighted to turn their backs once and for all on possible contingency plans. Then came the unexpected results of the 15 November 1976 Quebec provincial election. When the four Atlantic provincial premiers were asked about the what plans they had if Quebec separated they could only say that they had none. And despite Premier Campbell's urgent request on 26 January 1977 for the setting-up of a Council of Maritime Premiers Commission to study the long-term impact of Quebec separation on Atlantic Canada, little has been done. As one civil servant put it, "we've been caught with our pants down." They still are. Why? Possibly the lack of decisive action can be traced to the basic fear of a self-fulfilling prophecy. Or it may be that the Atlantic premiers are really incapable of independent action. They have grown so dependent on central Canada that they must wait for Ottawa to provide them with an acceptable answer to the most important question they have ever faced. Or perhaps the answers are so obvious in their opinion that any commission would be an inglorious waste of money.

What might the Atlantic provinces do if Quebec decided to secede from Confederation? In seeking answers to this critically important question it may be best to look first at Newfoundland and then at the three Maritime provinces. Because of its economic dependence on Ottawa, many will argue, Newfoundland will have everything to gain and nothing to lose by staying in Canada. Moreover, the island province will need Ottawa's assistance in order to prevent an independent Quebec, under the PQ, from taking over Labrador. But if oil and gas are discovered in huge quantities near Labrador—and if these reservoirs can be easily tapped—then, as in Scotland, independent Newfoundland could be a possibility although still a highly unlikely one. An independent Newfoundland could, among other things, seek a common market arrangement with Quebec, Canada, and the United States. It should always be kept in mind that the Newfoundland economy could be easily integrated with the considerable American demand for Newfoundland electrical power, Newfoundland iron ore, and Newfoundland fish. And the discovery of oil or gas would, of course, provide an additional reason for the United States to consider seriously the advantages of some special economic relationship with Newfoundland.

For Prince Edward Island, New Brunswick, and Nova Scotia the separation of Quebec would create almost insuperable problems. What could the region do? First, it could be annexed to the United States. Since the 1860s there have always been some Maritimers who advocated this step. But the evidence is convincing that relatively few Maritimers wish to join the United States; moreover, there is no evidence that the United States wants what was once called "New England's Outpost." In fact, it is hard to imagine less American enthusiasm for a region widely regarded as a social, cultural, economic, and political backwater of despair. Annexation would upset the delicate balance of American politics, but of greater importance is the fact that it would saddle the U.S. Treasury with four debtor states.

A second possibility is the creation of an independent "Atlantica." Even though many Maritimers evidently believe that Quebec's separation will probably act as a catalyst for Maritime Union there is very little support for "Atlantica." The pragmatic and dependent Maritime "mentality," with its shrewd awareness of political and economic realities, cannot really envisage an independent nation-state. A Nova Scotia premier once described the scheme as being "not very practicable." He and other Maritimers have realized that "Atlantica" would result in a sudden and drastic drop in the region's standard of living. And, for that reason, as might be expected, nobody of any consequence in the Maritimes has during recent decades seriously advocated such a proposal.

A third and by far the most realistic and popular possible response to Quebec's secession is what has been called an "East Pakistan" arrangement. Such an arrangement would be possible with the existing three provinces or with a new super-province. As the *Cape Breton Post* observed, such a proposal might lead to "accelerated centralization." It is a policy which some Maritime premiers are not necessarily opposed to. For example, Premier Campbell of Prince Edward Island has argued that "Canadian requirements . . . necessitate a strong central government" and for him "Strength . . . means financial strength to provide a sufficiently large economic field within which a central government may exercise political and economic influence towards national ends."

In an "East Pakistan" arrangement the Maritime provinces would have to be concerned with the creation of a safe and direct communications corridor through New England and New York to Ontario or else through Quebec. Such a route would have to be open throughout the year, but especially during the winter months. It would be expensive to operate and would underscore the isolation and vulnerability of the Maritime provinces.

Existence in a position of dependence on some other region or some other power has been a basic ingredient in the historical evolution of the Atlantic region. Because of this and other factors most residents of the Atlantic provinces, if Quebec left Confederation, would opt for an "East Pakistan" kind of arrangement. They are tied emotionally, psychologically, economically, politically, and culturally to a Canada they have gradually learned to love. As Canadians they are something—removed from Canada, they are "the next thing to nothing." It is, as Cornelius Howat once said of Prince Edward Island's fragile identity, "just a question of 'self or no self'."

The View from
Upper Canada

FREDERICK J. FLETCHER

Ontario leaders see the province as the linchpin of Confederation. Ontario's centrality derives not only from its geographical position but also from its size and economic power, and its role as host to the national capital and to anglophone Canada's metropolis, Toronto. Of more immediate importance, Ontario plays a central part in the Parti Québécois scenario of a peaceful accession to sovereignty based on some form of economic association with the remainder of Canada. For these reasons Ontario's role in determining the future of Confederation is likely to be crucial.

ONTARIO IN CONFEDERATION

However it may rankle, few Canadians would deny that Ontario has been, in the words of former premier John Robarts, the Golden Hinge of Confederation. In a real way, Canada resulted from the dreams of expansion-minded Ontarians who saw economic and political benefits in a British North America stretching from sea to sea. Indeed, as the chief beneficiary of Confederation, Ontario has had every incentive to serve as a "golden hinge." A recent Ontario Budget Paper reports that Ontario had an interprovincial trade surplus of $4.2 billion in 1974 and gained $739 million from tariff protection for its manufactured goods. With 36 per cent of the population, 38 per cent of the labour force, and 40 per cent of the Gross National Product, Ontario has been the spider at the centre of the web of Confederation. Capital and labour (including immigrants) have been easy to attract.

Much of the analysis in this chapter is based on a survey of Ontario newspapers from 15 November 1976 to 1 May 1977. Descriptions of events and speeches not otherwise documented are from this survey. Much of the economic data is contained in the 1977 Ontario Budget and supplementary papers presented on 19 April 1977.

One consequence of Ontario's central role is that its citizens are more likely than residents of other provinces to identify with Canada as such. For example, they pay more attention to national politics—and less attention to provincial politics—than residents of any other province. They identify with the federal government and see it as more important than the provincial government. In short, they are more likely to regard the federal government as their government.

Yet there has been a long-standing and sometimes bitter rivalry between Ottawa and Queen's Park over which government was better suited to make policies—especially economic policy—for Ontario. Hence Ontario has often found itself allied with Quebec in challenging Ottawa's hegemony. Indeed, Ontario has had close relations with Quebec throughout its history. The two provinces have been both bitter rivals and useful allies. Economic relations have been close. In 1974, for example, their mutual trade created more than 100,000 jobs in each province.

Ontario has recently tended to be more sympathetic to Quebec's aspirations than have other provinces, despite a history of considerable intolerance. Recent polls have shown Ontarians to be more sympathetic to bilingualism than residents of other anglophone provinces, more anxious to keep Quebec in Confederation, and more willing to make concessions (including special status) to do so. At the elite level, John Robarts, premier of Ontario from 1961 to 1971, developed a close rapport with Quebec leaders and was a key figure in some of the accommodations of the 1960s. The Ontario and Quebec governments have had a close working relationship, one which has continued on many levels since the Parti Québécois took power. The province's leaders have a keen sense of responsibility for the maintenance of the system.

STRATEGIES FOR PRESERVING CONFEDERATION

It took several months for the government of Premier William Davis to develop a clear-cut approach to the Confederation crisis. Initially, Davis and his Progressive Conservative colleagues took a "business as usual" approach, stressing the need to keep calm and maintain ties with Quebec. The government discouraged Ontario municipalities from trying to attract investment from Quebec in the wake of the election. Davis met Premier Lévesque and they agreed to keep channels open and to "agree to disagree" on Confederation. Davis visited Quebec to speak directly to the people, appointed a Cabinet Committee on Confederation and an Advisory Committee on Confederation. The government also sponsored and funded the Destiny Canada Conference, which brought 500 people from all walks of life to York University in June 1977 to discuss the future of Confederation.

The premier explained his strategy in a speech in London on 6 February:

> This government's channels to the government and people of Quebec are open because—at a time when the channel between Ottawa and Quebec is clogged with by-elections and personality clashes—our channel will serve ideas, frankness, respect and dialogue. That more than anything else is Ontario's duty to Confederation today—a duty neither emotionalism nor pressure must deter us from.

As the PQ government began to unveil its policies, the Ontario line hardened. Premier Davis rejected the PQ assertion that discussion of alternative federal arrangements was futile, saying he would accept no limits on dialogue. He said some degree of decentralization in the federal system would be acceptable, as long as Ottawa could still manage the economy, and he endorsed extending further language rights to Franco-Ontarians (but as a matter of moral obligation rather than political bargaining). In early April he came out against proposed Quebec legislation restricting access to English schools, the first occasion on which he had opposed a specific PQ policy.

April 1977 was a turning point. Davis bluntly warned that "it would be absolutely foolhardy for the government of Quebec to believe that it could have both independence and economic association with the rest of Canada." Two days earlier, Provincial Treasurer Darcy McKeough had flatly contradicted Quebec's claim to have lost $4.3 billion to the federal government between 1961 and 1975 as a result of its membership in Confederation. McKeough's conclusion was that Quebec had gained at least $6 billion over the period. This was Ontario's first salvo in the battle of statistics initiated by Quebec.

As Ontario headed toward a June provincial election, the government's position became clearer. It had moved from a rather formless response, based on remaining calm and conciliatory, to an aggressive attack on PQ positions. This shift seems to have resulted from soundings of public and elite opinion as election strategy was formed. Party strategists seem to have concluded, presumably with one eye on Quebec and the other on the Ontario electorate, that a stronger approach was needed. The result was a crystallization of PC policy, which can be summarized as follows: a commitment to discuss a new federal bargain, including decentralization of powers to the provinces, as long as Ottawa retains the powers necessary to manage the economy; willingness to stand on its record of providing services for Franco-Ontarians (and to continue extending services as far as is practicable); readiness to refute Quebec claims regarding the balance sheet of Confederation; firm rejection of the view that Quebec independence is possible without significant disruption of economic relationships. Everything up to independence is negotiable, but if Quebec becomes sovereign, it is a new ball game and no assumptions about what the new rules will be can be made.

On a matter as important as the future of Confederation it is perhaps not surprising that the New Democratic Party has differed only in details from the government position. Immediately after the election Leader Stephen Lewis called for a "civilized" approach to the issue. Party spokesmen argued that the Trudeau strategy for Confederation, centred on bilingualism and a strong federal government with strong francophone representation, had been discredited. They called for decentralization and special status for Quebec. The major difference from the PC position has been the willingness of some NDP spokesmen to favour clear recognition of Quebec's right to self-determination, an issue the other two parties have avoided. Some PC spokesmen have accused the NDP of being "soft on separatism." The NDP rejects the charge, pointing out that it has taken the position that economic association after independence is unlikely to be acceptable. It is not conceding Quebec independence, but it is sympathetic to Quebec aspirations. Most notably, the party has abandoned its long-standing commitment to a more centralized Canada as the best route to democratic socialism.

The Ontario Liberal party, despite attempts to dissociate itself from its Big Brother in Ottawa, has supported the Trudeau Liberal views. From the beginning the party leader, Stuart Smith, a bilingual psychiatrist originally from Montreal, has attacked the "narrow ethnic nationalism" of the PQ and has made no effort to be conciliatory. This opposition to the PQ has been coupled with strong support for extension of services in French within Ontario. Other key Liberal positions are: support for bypassing the Quebec government in order to appeal directly to the people; unequivocal support for bilingualism as the best way to make francophones feel at home in Canada; the importance of setting an example by providing in Ontario a full range of French services and improving the teaching of French to anglophones; rejection of decentralization of the federal system or special status as a means of accommodating Quebec aspirations. Smith maintains that the present division of powers provides Quebec with full authority to realize its legitimate aspirations. In addition, while calling on the Ontario government to play an important role, the Liberals have argued that the prime minister must lead the effort to preserve Confederation. Smith has warned that any willingness to engage in rational discussion of post-independence options plays into the hands of the PQ by making the breakup of the country seem a routine matter.

Given their bases of support, the parties will be subject to different pressures as events develop. The Liberals will not be able to stray too far from the federal Liberal position, according to which Trudeau is the best hope for preserving Confederation. They will continue their traditional support for Franco-Ontarians. The NDP will face pressure from its radical wing to recognize Quebec self-determination and to press for an economic association between Quebec and a centralized anglophone Canada. It will also be expected to propose policies to reduce job loss in Ontario in the event of Quebec independence. The Conservatives will not be able to escape the Orange tinge of their traditional supporters, who may well push for a hard line on Quebec and on Franco-Ontarian rights. When it comes to negotiations, the Conservatives will ultimately follow Ottawa's lead while trying to maintain a distinct image. Tripartisan agreement in principle will likely continue on extension of services in French (with conflict over speed and extent) and on the need to accommodate Quebec (with disagreement over means).

PUBLIC OPINION

As suggested earlier, Ontario public opinion has been sympathetic to Quebec in recent years. Surveys taken since the Quebec election have failed to produce evidence of a strong anti-French backlash which would hamper efforts at accommodation or lead to support for repressive measures. Ontarians want to keep Quebec in Confederation, but not by force. A recent poll taken by the government found that Ontarians are willing to support a basic degree of bilingualism in the Ontario public service as well as the teaching of French in public schools. Most respondents agree that both Quebec and Ontario would suffer if Quebec achieved independence. The available poll data suggest that Ontarians want the government to make concessions to help maintain Confederation but that their willingness to sacrifice has limits.

The Quebec election galvanized many groups into action but so far most of their efforts have been directed towards self-education and patriotic affirmation. Lectures, seminars, study groups, and rallies have proliferated and there has been much talk of the need to preserve Confederation for the good of all. Support has been most common for efforts directed at mutual understanding—for example, youth and worker exchanges between Quebec and Ontario—and at reforming the division of powers, generally in the direction of decentralization and special status for Quebec. Some groups havs suggested a return to the dual majority system similar to that which existed before Confederation.

A group of intellectuals calling itself the Committee for a New Constitution, no doubt the first of many, called for a constitutional commission, made up equally of representatives of French and English-speaking Canada, which would draft a constitution and present it to a popularly elected constituent assembly and then to the electorate for decision. The group argued that Quebec should be accorded special status if it chose to remain in Canada or, if it chose independence, an association should be negotiated. The purpose was to convince Quebecers that there are options available between the status quo and independence.

In general, these public activities have offered few specifics but they do suggest the existence of considerable concern and goodwill which could be tapped by Ontario leaders in their efforts to preserve Confederation.

The newspapers have had little to add. Most editorialists have contented themselves with advising readers to remain calm and calling for leadership to save Confederation. The *Toronto Star*'s series of five editorials (27 November to 2 December) calling for radical reform of the federal system and a nonpartisan "save Canada" cabinet had little impact. Other editorials have set out scenarios for redistributing legislative authority or have opposed the notion of post-independence economic association, but have contributed few new ideas. The discussion has had an abstract and inconclusive quality. The newspapers have not been a major force in the debate and are unlikely to be so.

BUSINESS AND LABOUR

Although their formal organizations have taken few specific stands, some business and labour leaders have spoken out on the future of Confederation. Business leaders have been the more vocal and a survey of newspaper coverage of their statements turned up the following common themes: a decentralized federal system might be desirable if it met the demands of Quebec and the West, but Ottawa must retain control over essential economic powers, as well as foreign affairs and defence; bilingualism outside Quebec should be encouraged, especially in the schools, but the PQ language policies are unworkable for national or international corporations, which might be forced to leave Quebec; business leaders should demonstrate both sympathy for Quebec aspirations and commitment to Confederation. Not surprisingly, these positions are similar to those of the business-oriented Ontario government.

Echoing the pleas of political leaders, a number of Ontario business leaders have warned against providing ammunition for the PQ by reducing investment in Quebec or by pulling out. But there are indications that investments have been curtailed and that capital and offices are being moved out. The journalist Peter C. Newman, in a speech to the Canadian Club of Toronto on 25 April, said:

> the paladins of the Establishment—the men who make the investment decisions that count—have retreated into a kind of protracted sulk. They have withdrawn vital growth funds, cut Quebec right out of their capital investment plans, abandoned the province to its own dark devices. This in my view is an error of monumental proportions . . . if it continues to pursue its present course, [the Canadian Establishment] will become the main agent of its own destruction.

Few labour spokesmen have joined the debate. The thrust of their remarks has been towards decentralization of authority, special status for Quebec and even dual majority or binational central institutions, with equal representation for francophones and anglophones.

The support for decentralization among business and labour spokesmen in Ontario is a departure from past positions. Since World War II, both groups have tended to opt for greater centralization and economic management by Ottawa. Whether this new flexibility derives from their mutual alienation from the Trudeau government, new thinking about bigness and smallness, or the shock of the Quebec election, it does provide a basis for negotiating a new division of powers, perhaps including special status for Quebec. Neither group has locked itself into rigid positions.

THE SPECIAL POSITION OF FRANCO-ONTARIANS

The 500,000 Franco-Ontarians, though only 6 per cent of the

province's population, have inevitably become an important part of the Confederation debate. Their treatment in Ontario and their reactions to events in Quebec have come under close scrutiny in both Quebec and Ontario. Franco-Ontarian issues are followed with intense interest in Quebec, where their treatment is compared with that of Anglo-Quebecers. It is generally noted that the latter have long-standing rights and privileges, whereas Franco-Ontarians have been granted a few services as privileges, with careful attention to costs and the possibility of an anti-French backlash. *Le Droit*, Ottawa's French daily, commented on 5 March 1977 that it appeared that if Franco-Ontarians and Anglo-Quebecers were to become equal, it would be through the diminution of the rights of Anglo-Quebecers rather than the enhancement of Franco-Ontarian rights. The irony is that Franco-Ontarians are pressing to have their rights expanded at the very time those of Anglo-Quebecers are being contracted and reduced to privileges.

Although the situation of Franco-Ontarians has been improving gradually since the 1960s, the services available leave much to be desired. Ontario has a long history of restricting education in French. In the 1960s, however, the government changed long-standing regulations severely limiting education in French and in 1968 legislation was passed authorizing the building of French schools or classrooms where numbers warranted. Because implementation is left to local school boards, there have been numerous controversies over the adequacy of the facilities provided. A recent case is the Essex County dispute, which has taken on important symbolic significance since the Quebec election. For eight years, the 50,000 Franco-Ontarians in the area (one-sixth of the population) have been trying to get their own unilingual school to replace the present shared facility. The school board has rejected the request, claiming present facilities are adequate, despite francophone arguments that only a French school can provide a full range of services for French-speaking students.

Early in 1977, after much negative publicity in Quebec, the Ontario government, which had previously withdrawn funds for a planned French school as an austerity measure, proposed legislation to require the board to build the school, with the province to pay most of the cost. The motivation of the government is aptly demonstrated by the comment of Education Minister Thomas Wells that "the Essex County French-language school has become a provincial and national symbol of the treatment of francophones in Ontario." Although delayed by the 9 June provincial election, the bill was supported by all three parties and was passed in July (despite opposition from local MPPs).

In general, low priority has been given to education in French. It was reported that Ontario school boards had used only $17 million of $36.5 million in federal funds for that purpose, diverting the rest to other programs. Ontario ranks ninth among the provinces in percentage of anglophone secondary school students studying French.

Throughout the province, services in French are sparse. In the legal area, some documents are bilingual and there is a limited experimental program in Sudbury which allows certain courts to operate in French. The experiment is marginal because many francophones feel pleading in French may affect their chances of success and because appeals must be in English. (The Ontario Court of Appeal works only in English.) The attorney general of Ontario, Roy McMurtry, has said that there are too few bilingual crown attorneys and judges to make rapid expansion of French legal services practical, though the Sudbury experiment is to be extended to the Ottawa Valley in 1977. Jeff Simpson of the *Globe* (9 April 1977) described the government's approach as "timid, tardy and tight-fisted."

The government's record is probably worst in health care, where its major achievement appears to be the bilingual health insurance card. A government task force recently found no facilities for the sick, the mentally ill, or the handicapped offering services in French. Few Ontario physicians or psychiatrists can speak French. Basically, francophones are treated like other patients not fluent in English: needed translation is done by cleaners, other patients, or other untrained persons—or not at all.

The Ontario government has been on the defensive with respect to this record. Many commentators argue that Ontario must set a better example. Marc Lalonde, federal minister of health and welfare, has said that Ontario's failure in this area makes front-page news in Quebec and undermines the credibility of federalists. Premier Davis has responded by reiterating his government's commitment to the provision of French services and arguing that it is proceeding as fast as is practical. Understandably, he did not note that the Conservative base of support among Protestants of British origin makes it more vulnerable to anti-French sentiments than the other parties.

Franco-Ontarians have reacted to the PQ victory as both an opportunity and a threat. On the one hand, they see in the situation leverage to gain further extensions of services and, perhaps, some legal guarantees. On the other hand, they see the possibility of becoming pawns in negotiations between Ontario and Quebec and, if Quebec does achieve independence, of seeing their meagre gains of the 1960s washed away in an emotional anti-French backlash.

On an emotional level, most Franco-Ontarians felt pride in the affirmation of French-Canadian identity which the PQ victory represented, regardless of their views on independence. While some would certainly move to Quebec in the event of independence, most would stay, unless pushed out by an official or unofficial exchange of populations. Indeed, economic problems in an independent Quebec might bring a new influx. Relations between Quebec and Ontario would therefore continue even after independence to be influenced by the situation of the Franco-Ontarians.

ONTARIO AND A SOVEREIGN QUEBEC

There is no doubt that both provincial economies, given their close ties, would be seriously hurt by disintegration of the Canadian common market. But the data suggest Quebec would lose more: whereas in 1974 Quebec sold 30 per cent of its manufactured goods (most tariff protected) to other provinces and only 14 per cent outside of Canada, the figures for Ontario were 23 per cent and 20 per cent; whereas Quebec sells about 24 per cent of its manufactured goods in Ontario (65 per cent of its exports), Ontario sells only 15 per cent of its products in Quebec (just under half of its exports).

The PQ argument, as presented by Finance Minister Jacques Parizeau, is that Quebec sovereignty need not mean severing economic links, especially those with Ontario. "No part of Canada is interwoven with us like Ontario. Toronto and Montreal are economic suburbs of each other." Parizeau seems to assume that Ontario corporate business will insist on economic association to protect its Quebec markets, that it will be able to enforce this position on the Ontario government, and that together they will bring along the other provinces. How accurate are these assumptions?

Business analysts have tended to reject Parizeau's soothing words as a delusion. Simon Reisman, former deputy minister of finance in Ottawa, argued in a speech to the Canadian Club of Toronto that Quebec, with one-quarter of the population of Canada and one-fifth of the wealth, could not expect to negotiate as an equal on controversial economic issues:

> Why would the rest of Canada with quite different economic problems and goals accept this?
>
> And if the bargaining process and outcome reflected proportional population or economic power what in reality would be left of Quebec political independence?
>
> Most of Quebec's secondary industry— . . . textiles, garments, boots and shoes—depends heavily on the highly protected Canadian market.

Other Canadians are prepared to accept this cost only to the extent that they can believe it is part of the cement that binds a nation together.

A common market must be mutually beneficial and analysts like Reisman doubt that it would be in Ontario's interest to accept Quebec independence while maintaining the economic status quo. Certainly the attractiveness of the Quebec market would decline sharply if independence led to severe economic difficulties.

Ontario politicians stress that emotional reactions to the divorce might make economic association difficult. Spokesmen for all three parties have acknowledged that there might well be business pressures for economic association, but argued that public opinion would not permit it. Treasurer McKeough said the government would not "jump through hoops" to please corporate business and NDP leader Lewis said that business capitulates to intense public opinion.

In January 1977 half the Ontario residents interviewed in a Gallup Poll favoured economic association if Quebec should achieve independence; a third were opposed. However, the survey was taken before political and business leaders had begun to speak out on the issue and it is likely that public opinion remains fluid.

Are these protestations by business leaders and politicians simply tactical attempts to counter the PQ strategy? Or are they genuine reflections of strong sentiments and/or economic realities? Would the corporate elite favour economic association on terms acceptable to Quebec once independence was a *fait accompli*? Would they be able to bring public opinion and their friends at Queen's Park around? Perhaps the biggest stumbling block lies outside Ontario. It is extremely doubtful that Ontario could bring the West to accept continued tariff protection for Quebec.

Overall, it seems likely that relations between Ontario and Quebec, if the latter were to achieve independence, would be determined in large part by the nature of the divorce. At this stage it seems clear that acceptance and some form of accommodation would be preferred to repression. However, the inevitable emotional reaction to independence could easily be turned to anger. There is considerable potential for conflict in any independence scenario.

CANADA WITHOUT QUEBEC: THE PLACE OF ONTARIO

Given its central position on Confederation, Ontario would have a major role in reconstructing the system to cope with Quebec's absence. As the chief beneficiary of the present economic relationships, the province would have a strong incentive to work out new relationships with the other regions. In the reconstruction process, the historic rivalry between Ottawa and Queen's Park would intensify. In a federation without Quebec, Ontario would be mammoth, with about half of the population and more than half of the wealth and industrial strength. It seems likely that Ontario's long-standing demand for more say in economic policy-making would be pressed even more vigorously. In addition, Quebec's wooing of Ontario would likely continue, no doubt creating a potential for conflict.

Ontario's relations with its western hinterland would be crucial. The four western provinces would do very well as a unit without Ontario. They could go on selling their natural products at the same prices—or higher in the case of oil and gas—while buying cheaper manufactured goods from foreign suppliers. In 1974, for example, Ontario had a net subsidy (in tariff protected sales) of $231 million from the western provinces. The West has been in a substantial deficit position in interprovincial trade with both Quebec and Ontario. The temptation to be rid of both might be substantial.

It seems likely that the West would initially accept continuation of the present federal system without Quebec but that before too long it would want changes to deal with traditional economic irritants, such as tariffs, freight rates, concentration of commerce and manufacturing in Ontario, as well as more political influence, as the price for staying in. In order to preserve its traditional position, Ontario would almost certainly have to bargain some of its dominance away.

The Atlantic provinces are also in a substantial deficit position with respect to Ontario, but they have little leverage to press for concessions. The risk is that they would slide into an abject third-world style poverty now considered morally unacceptable. Unless offshore minerals were to bring a major change, the federal government would have to make substantial transfers from Ontario and the West to keep them going. The danger is that Ontario's attention would be turned westward in its attempts to keep its own economy functioning adequately and that it would have little sympathy left over for Atlantic Canada, which might end up turning to the United States.

The crucial importance of relations with the United States in any independence scenario was made evident by the visits of Premier Lévesque to New York and of Prime Minister Trudeau to Washington for the purpose of pleading their respective cases. Although few Ontarians now favour joining the United States, even in the event of Quebec independence, it seems clear that Quebec sovereignty would be a blow to those wishing to reduce Canada's dependence on her neighbour. Ontario's dependence on American money markets might well increase. Quebec would also be competing for U.S. money and markets—and possibly for more American branch plants, now concentrated in Ontario. The vulnerability of both to American pressures would increase. As Abraham Rotstein put it in the *Canadian Forum*, "The possibilities for American policy-makers in playing off English Canada and Quebec on every issue from pipelines to resources, to foreign investment policy, are too mind-boggling to contemplate." In the long run, if the centre (Ontario) cannot hold, all of Canada's regions might end up as northern Puerto Ricos.

Should an anglophone federation survive, pressures would surely mount to reform its institutions. Federations in which units differ sharply in size and wealth have generally been unstable and those in which one unit held a majority of the electorate were the most unstable of all. Could Ontario then be the centre of a stable federation, given its size and wealth? How could western feelings of exploitation and eastern feelings of powerlessness be countered? Would the federal capital have to be moved out of Ontario? Would national institutions—parliament, the courts, etc.—have to be reformed to reduce Ontario's domination? Would provincial boundaries have to be redrawn? Would Ontario have to be divided to make an anglophone federation work? These are only a few of the dilemmas that would face Ontario as it tried to create a lasting Confederation without Quebec.

ISSUES AND DILEMMAS

As Ontarians face the future, they must come to grips with a number of crucial issues. Having decided for the most part that they want to preserve Confederation, the most important current question is how? A commitment to accommodation is clearly there, but it has no obvious outlets. Neither the Conservatives nor the NDP find federal leadership satisfactory, but the absence of a viable federalist option in Quebec leaves them with no obvious channel for exerting influence there. In addition, the actual degree of independence needed to meet Quebec's minimum demands remains a mystery. In these circumstances it is difficult to frame alternatives to the status quo.

If Quebec does achieve sovereignty, Ontarians will face another set of dilemmas. Will the economic interests of Quebec and Ontario differ so sharply that economic association will not be possible? Will the inevitable conflicts lead to violence? Will the Ontario government, especially if it is a Conservative government, be able to resist pressures to retaliate against Franco-Ontarians? These issues will all have a bearing on the kinds of relationships worked out between Ontario and Quebec. Some *modus vivendi* will be required, simply because of the geographical relationship.

A major unknown factor is the reaction of Ontario's politically active citizens should their lives be disrupted by the Quebec issue over a long period of time. Will the strong commitment to stability in the Ontario political culture incline them to flexibility in negotiations with Quebec? Or will it result in vindictiveness towards those disrupting the tranquillity of their lives? Ontario leaders will have to grapple with strong currents of public opinion.

In the long run, the tremendous risks for all of Canada involved in Quebec independence may create a climate of moderation in both communities. Perhaps Quebec will see new possibilities for accommodation and pull back from its great adventure. If so Ontario will have a central role in formulating a new vision of Canada. If not, Ontario's linchpin role will oblige it to develop plans for a new federation of anglophone communities. In either case, Ontario will have its work cut out to retain its position as the golden hinge of Confederation.

Ethnic Hierarchies and
Minority Consciousness in Quebec

PETER LESLIE

April 1977. There is despondency, anger, and elation in Quebec: the government's nervously awaited white paper on language policy has just been published. Proclaiming as it does that "There will no longer be any question of a bilingual Quebec," it comes as a powerful reminder that the national unity issue is not all. For the people of Quebec —whatever language they speak—it is obvious that the provincial government already has ample powers to fashion the institutions of a national community and to accord what place it will to the other linguistic and ethnic groupings within its borders. For the people of Canada—in whatever province they live—it should now be clear that many of the values which make a Canadian state worth having may be nourished or destroyed by political action, much of it channelled through the provincial governments. National survival matters, and this is true whether we mean by this "the Canadian political nationality" or "la nation québécoise"; but it would be tragic if survival so preoccupied us as to blot out concern with the character of what survives.

Let us first be clear on one thing: Quebec nationalism is not merely economic self-interest in fancy dress. Even for those who are imbued with a different cultural tradition, it is not terribly difficult to sense the exhilaration experienced by those who have lately assumed leadership of the francophone majority in Quebec. They are intensely conscious, now that political power is theirs, of having a historic opportunity to build a country and to mould the character of its people; and the prospective rewards are gratifying to a degree which merely self-interested action cannot attain. For them, political sovereignty may be thought to bring an economic reward, but sovereignty is fundamentally a badge of collective self-respect and a guarantee that those who see themselves as agents of a nation will be able to manipulate the levers of state power untrammeled by a federal constitution.

The soaring ambition of Quebec's political elite is precisely what worries those who distrust visionary politics. The aggrandizement of the Quebec state throughout the Sixties and the awesome power now wielded by those who control it evokes apprehension among many, including virtually the whole of the non-francophone population. The election of a Parti Québécois government and the crystallization of its language policies have acted like a prism, refracting the minorities' apprehension into fear, into complacency tinged by suspected self-delusion, into resentment, assertiveness, and cautious optimism. Such variety of attitude derives partly from the fact that individuals who share a common experience nonetheless respond differently to events which they do not control; but perhaps more fundamentally the diversity of situation within the non-francophone population means that today's events affect its different segments in different ways. The 1.2 million non-French in Quebec (21 per cent of the population) are a heterogeneous grouping. Their various cultural traditions and the differences of economic circumstance among them bear heavily upon the way they interact with the francophone majority. Our first task, therefore, is to consider just who the non-French are.

THE NON-FRENCH POPULATION OF QUEBEC

Economic situation. "The English" in Quebec are frequently thought of as a privileged group or a dominant elite. This is not only because even casual observation reveals that the banks and the largest industries are run by English-speaking people; initial impressions of the favoured position of the non-French are reinforced by census data on occupation and income by ethnic origin. Public attention has been drawn to these data by John Porter's well-known treatise on class and power in Canada, *The Vertical Mosaic*, and by some widely-publicized parts of the *Report* of the Commission on Bilingualism and Biculturalism (vol. 3, 1969). In the latter it was shown that of fourteen national groupings in Quebec, male workers of French origin ranked twelfth in income from employment, ahead only of the Italians and the Indians. Attempts to explain these differences in wholly nonethnic terms do not succeed. Even when the possible influence of other factors such as age, education, or region were removed, André Raynauld found that in 1961 the income of the typical Anglo-Scot was $606 above the average, while that of the typical French Canadian was $267 below.[1] Thus "the net contribution of ethnicity to the income differential" was $873 or 15 per cent of the income-levels of those of British origin. As if this were not enough—for few were cautious enough to recognize, with Raynauld and the B and B commissioners, that "ethnicity" covers many inseparable elements including quality of schooling, work attitudes, and motivations and values—it even appeared that knowledge of French seemed to penalize those anglophones who took the trouble to learn it. If one looked at income from all sources, the *unilingual* person of British descent was marginally better off than his *bilingual* counterpart. (Unpublished work by François Vaillancourt reveals that the differential not only still existed in 1971, but had become wider.)

These data do easily create the impression that "French comes last," and contribute to the image of the anglophones as an economically dominant (i.e., controlling and self-perpetuating) group. Any careful assessment of the situation, however, must recognize two things. First, while Montreal's industrial and mercantile elite remains predominantly "Anglo," the character and relative position of the English elite have changed significantly since the 1961 census. Second, the affluent, even within the non-French minorities, are few in number relative to the economically insecure. In a nutshell, the rich and the owners of capital are still mostly English, but the typical anglophone is neither rich nor a capitalist. This fact is important, because the PQ government and its successors will undoubtedly continue, within Canada or without, to press for francophone primacy in Quebec. The non-French will have to make painful adjustments; and those adjustments will not be limited to the defence of acquired wealth and the sequestering of capital in more secure havens. The capacity of Quebec society—including its linguistic minorities—to adapt peacefully to a changing situation is at issue; and in this process, the behaviour of immigrant groups and the nonelite of British origin will be as critical as that of the wealthy English and, be it said, the francophone majority.

The 1971 census provides useful clues about the economic situation of various national groupings in Quebec. One can draw a profile of each group by first observing the distribution of ethnic groups among various occupations, and then looking at income-levels and stability of employment in each occupation-category. This has been done in table 1. It confirms the conventional images of ethnic stratification in Quebec in that the non-French groups (and especially the British) have a disproportionate number of the high-paying jobs and do not have their "due" share of jobs yielding below-average incomes. On the other hand, those who are of neither British nor French stock have slightly less stable employment prospects than the population of French origin. Most significantly for our purposes, however, the table indicates that among *all* ethnic groups the wealthy are still a small minority and that many workers are in unstable-employment occupations. Since many of those who are economically insecure have poor employment prospects elsewhere and would find it correspondingly difficult to move, this table should dispel the facile thought that the non-French who don't like it in a unilingual and/or separate Quebec will simply clear out. Many can't. Even many of those—such as teachers—who are in steady and well-paid jobs may be stranded in Quebec by age, family responsibilities, home ownership (when real estate values have slumped), and lack of jobs in other provinces.

National origin, migration patterns, and language use. Fears that the Quebec francophones may be an "endangered species" (to use the phrase of Camille Laurin, the PQ minister responsible for language policy) reflect the phenomenal drop in their fertility rates during the Sixties and the concern that they will be swamped by immigrants oriented to English North America rather than to French Quebec. Hence the insistence that all those moving to the province, including English-speaking people from the rest of Canada, should go to French schools and accept minority status in a basically unilingual society. In these circumstances it is the Quebec anglophones who regard themselves as the endangered species. But are measures which drastically restrict individual freedom of choice, such as those announced by the PQ, necessary to protect the French language and culture? To answer this we must look at demographic trends and patterns of assimilation.

Quebec nationalists rightly assert that the future of the French language in the province will be determined within the Montreal area: in an industrial society the language of the metropolis dominates the hinterland and reduces any other language to the status of a dialect. In table 2, which reports ethnic origin and language use, anglophones are likely to notice that even in Montreal only a quarter of the population speaks English in the home. By contrast the Québécois, especially those of nationalist persuasion, emphasize that only a 16 per cent "cushion" separates them from becoming a minority. This cushion seems under-stuffed when, as in the Seventies, the birthrate is a mere 14 per 1,000, compared with the 16 necessary to barely reproduce the population and the 30 or so which had prevailed until the Sixties.

Even more significant than fertility rates (the impact of which is felt about evenly throughout the province) are immigration to Quebec, internal migration, and the assimilation of new arrivals to either the English or the French culture. All these factors bear especially heavily on language use in the Montreal area, since that is the main destination of immigrants and is also the focus of regional migration by francophones deserting the countryside. High net immigration tends to reduce the proportion of francophones in the total population, especially in Montreal. Although debate often dwells on gross immigration statistics and neglects those who leave, this gives a false and alarmist view of the situation. For example, from 1946 to 1966 more than 620,000 immigrants settled in Quebec, but net migration was only an estimated 291,000; obviously many immigrants, and no doubt some long-standing residents of Quebec, left the province during this period. Heavy immigration ended in the mid-Sixties together with prosperity, and in the past decade there has been a net outflow of 38,000, most of it apparently anglophone. Indeed, Anglo-Canadians both enter and leave Quebec in substantial numbers each year. Fragmentary data for 1970 and 1971 (years of strong net outflow) suggest that at least three per cent of the anglophone population left the province each year, being partially replaced by newcomers (four immigrants for every five emigrants in 1971).

Even in the absence of any new stimulus to emigration, the implication of these figures is that blocking off the influx of anglophones (as the proposed measures regarding language of instruction would tend to do) would progressively reduce the size of the English-speaking community in Quebec. They would also alter its character, since its most highly mobile members are probably also the wealthiest and most highly skilled.

If economic prosperity normally draws immigrants from Canada and abroad, economic stagnation outside the metropolitan area drives people from the rural areas to the towns. Such internal migration swells the francophone population of the area surrounding Montreal, and to a lesser extent of the Island of Montreal itself. It is evident, though, that the relative size of each migrant group *by region* is difficult to predict; it is also critical in determining linguistic ratios in and around Montreal.

This is why projections made for the Commission on the Position of the French Language (the "Gendron Commission," 1972), which ought to have been broadly reassuring, were not. Demographers hired by the commission estimated the probable size of linguistic groups in the province, in the Montreal region, and on the Island of Montreal. They made several projections based on different assumptions regarding fertility, immigration, and regional migration. Even on the assumptions least favourable to the francophones, the population of

French mother tongue in Montreal was expected to decline (in percentage terms) only marginally; and on more favourable assumptions, it would increase significantly. (See table 3.) Although, especially after the recent period of economic stagnation in Quebec, the low level of migration hypothesis (i.e., the more reassuring one) seems more plausible, these highly authoritative projections have not served to allay fears that the French language will be overpowered by a wave of immigrants assimilating to English. When the Gendron Commission recommended no immediate change in language legislation relating to education, which at that time guaranteed to the parent freedom of choice regarding language of instruction for his child ("Bill 63," 1969; replaced by "Bill 22," 1974), its proposals met with vehement condemnation. By February 1974 its chairman, Jean-Denis Gendron, had changed his mind and was proposing amendments to the law that would impose more coercive measures, rather than relying on incentives for the *francisation* of business. The Gendron Report had originally suggested that the extension of French in the work world would in turn encourage immigrants to send their children to French-language schools. Gendron, having observed the public reaction to his report, now saw in Bill 63 the source of a "collective fear" among the Québécois, who were searching for linguistic and cultural security. "I still think," he said, "that we were right in logic. But we had not taken account of the psychological aspect .... It's only when the francophone majority of Quebec starts to behave like a majority—whereas it now acts like a minority—that these fears will be alleviated."[2]

At the moment the fears which are the hallmark of a minority consciousness are fed by assimilation patterns among immigrant groups. The most obvious indicator of these patterns is school enrolments by language, especially in the Catholic schools in Montreal. In some of these schools English is the language of instruction. Of pupils whose mother tongue is neither English nor French, the proportion receiving instruction in French has dropped steadily during the post-war period from about 35 per cent to, in 1971-72, 10.8 per cent. This figure has led to emotional assertions that in the absence of restrictive language policies only 10 per cent of immigrants would opt for the French language. More dispassionate analysis softens this somewhat. The demographer R. Maheu estimated an "attraction index" towards French, which showed that in the Montreal area 23 per cent were gravitating towards that language-group, and in the rest of the province, 57 per cent. The discrepancy between school-choice and prospective assimilation patterns is accounted for by a number of considerations. The gist of these is that immigrants resist assimilation to either group but want their children to be fully bilingual for economic reasons. Even some of those clearly tending towards French, as evidenced by language use at home, have been sending their children to English schools.

The overall picture which emerges is one in which there are strong but not overwhelming tendencies for immigrants to assimilate to the anglophone community. In public debate, however, nuance is generally smothered by strident assertion, and not infrequently, by selective presentation of evidence. The controversy over language policy in Quebec has been an emotion-laden one marked by excesses on all sides, and only rarely has advocacy divested itself of overstatement. The Gendron Commission managed to do so, but more overtly political statements such as the PQ's language paper have not. This paper crystallizes the nationalist thesis on the position of the French language in Quebec. While it reflects genuinely-held attitudes and legitimate apprehensions, in expressing them it has sometimes resorted to the sloppy use of data, so much so that some observers have suspected deliberate falsification.[3] The feelings of collective insecurity which lie behind such shallow analyses of the situation have also apparently blinded many francophones to the very real and substantial changes which the English business community has undergone during the past decade, and to this theme we now turn.

THE CHALLENGE TO THE MONTREAL BUSINESS ELITE

Nervousness about the prospects for the French language and culture in Quebec stem from a conviction that in a plurilingual society the language of a ruling class will eventually predominate. The language of economic elites is presumed to have a corrosive impact on other languages, even one spoken by a majority, and to invade it with foreign vocabulary, foreign turns of phrase, and foreign habits of thought (which can scarcely be dissociated from language). Eventually, it is argued, nonelite languages are relegated to the sphere of "folklore" and survive, if at all, only in corrupted form. This is why, quite apart from the economic aspirations of a middle class, the language of high technology, senior management, and the boardroom is considered to have special significance.

That language, in Quebec, is still mainly English. Nonetheless, the overall position of the anglophone elites is undergoing substantial change, partly because of the augmented role of the state in the Quebec economy and partly because of the language policies of the Quebec government. There have been noticeable shifts in the income-levels of various national groupings over the past ten or fifteen years, and the use of French in the upper echelons of business has increased sharply. All in all, it is quite clear that the anglophone business community of Montreal is operating in a vastly changed social context, is acutely conscious of this fact, and has been adapting to these changes in a way which no observer of the Fifties or even the Sixties could have imagined possible. Moreover, developments within Quebec have been complemented and reinforced by the rapid growth of the Toronto region. Toronto is now by far the more important financial centre, and southern Ontario is more and more the industrial heartland of the country. This means that in the Canadian context the business leaders of Montreal are, as a group, simply less important than they were. Perhaps they are even coming to think of themselves as regional rather than national figures, and are correspondingly readier to adapt themselves to conditions prevalent in the region, i.e. to recognize that their operations are conducted in a basically French environment. Their attitudes towards the use and prevalence of French do suggest this. But, just as the Montreal anglophones have come to realize that bilingualism applies to them, they find that the majority are now, through the Quebec government, moving to establish French unilingualism.

Anglo-Quebecers and the Quiet Revolution. The Quiet Revolution of the earlier Sixties was a time of cultural renaissance and political maturation in French Quebec. English Canadians reacted positively to these changes, foreseeing a more tractable partner in Confederation and a population better adapted to the industrial age. Much of the sociological writing of the time—especially what came from the pen of French-Canadian authors—concerned itself with the social and psychological difficulties occasioned by modernization. Others emphasized the changing class structure of French-Canadian society; but at first no one seems to have foreseen a fundamental challenge to the economic and social role of the English Quebecers. Why so? If we try to answer this question, perhaps we will see the present situation more clearly.

As every observer knows, at the political level francophones have held the leading positions in Quebec for more than a century. Thus the Quiet Revolution would not displace an anglophone political elite. Moreover, French Canadians have always enjoyed the power to fashion their own institutions in those matters having the greatest impact on national culture: education, health care and social security, and the law pertaining to the status of the individual ("property and civil rights"). Except in the last of these areas the Church played the main part while the state supported the Church's initiatives by providing an appropriate legislative framework for action and by assisting financially. All this could (and would) change, thereby bruising the traditional elites of French Canada but scarcely disrupting ethnic hierarchies. Indeed, only in the economic sphere did English Canadians occupy a dominant position; and it would occasion no alarm—quite the reverse—if French Canadians started to enter the competition in greater numbers and with better business and technical training.

So far there is nothing to suggest that the Quiet Revolution would threaten or much change the position of the English business leaders in Montreal. Missing, however, from this account is an awareness of the changing attitudes and aspirations, or the overall self-assessment of the language groups. Here, on both sides, was to occur a change of breathtaking magnitude.

If a sociological majority is a grouping who feel (collectively) in charge of the situation, who define human rights in individual terms, and for whom social conflict is largely a matter of individual competition for preferment, then the English Quebecers have until recently felt like a majority. Conversely, as has often been remarked, French Canadians *in Quebec as in other provinces* until about 1960 lacked this self-confidence and sought to survive by creating institutions which would insulate them from the rest of North America. This was particularly true in the sphere of education, but it expressed itself also in a preference for the liberal professions over a business career. The early Sixties witnessed the complete overturn of these attitudes among the nationalist elite of Quebec, at least as far as the design of national (communal) institutions was concerned. This elite temporarily gained the upper hand in the Lesage government of 1960-66 and used the state to redesign the educational system of the province, transfer administrative responsibility for social security and health care from the Church to the state, improve the legal status of women, extend the realm of collective bargaining into the public sector, and initiate the planning of economic development through a number of state agencies and public corporations.

These changes bespoke a change in values amongst the Québécois and a modification of the class structure of French Quebec. But what seems not to have been recognized at first is that remaking the class structure of French-Canadian society could not be accomplished without measures which would impinge seriously on the position of anglophone business leaders. From about the middle Sixties, however, many Québécois came to think that it was not enough to sweep away the traditional reluctance to pursue a business career and, through far-reaching educational reforms, to equip French Canadians to take their share of the top jobs in an industrial society. They began to believe that collective measures, i.e., state action, would be necessary to create new opportunities by more vigorous expansion of the public sector and by policies that would pry open more doors in the private sector.

In short, there developed among the most zealous of the reformers a desire to achieve primacy over the non-French groups and to displace the English-speaking minority, the traditional holders of economic power. This process is well under way, though as yet far from complete.

The state and the Québécois managerial class. Anglophones, as far as ownership of major enterprises is concerned, still have the field virtually to themselves; they also predominate on the boards of directors and in senior management. Some major enterprises are in French-Canadian hands, especially in the financial sector. But in general, as Pierre Fournier has pointed out, if one is searching for signs of the development of an *haute bourgeoisie* among the Québécois, it is more rewarding to look at the public and para-public sectors than to search within the ranks of private enterprise.[4] Fournier argues that existing studies have underestimated the current size and the prospective expansion of a francophone business class, and that they have done so because they disregarded the cooperative movement, public corporations, and mixed enterprises. He suggests, persuasively, that it is much less significant that major firms include one or two French Canadians on their boards than that there are now large enterprises in which ownership is indigenous to Quebec (often by virtue of state participation) and the language of management is French.

The establishment of a francophone entrepreneurial class has been an objective shared by all Quebec governments since the middle or latter Sixties. If the *péquistes* are more widely known to have such a policy than was the case with, say, the Bourassa Liberals, that is because they link it with the expansion of public enterprise and the cooperative movement (which is important in finance and in the food industries). The fact remains that it has been and will undoubtedly continue to be the policy of successive Quebec governments to promote the development of a Québécois economic elite. Already much has been accomplished through the establishment of crown corporations, the prime examples being Hydro Québec and Sidbec-Dosco. These not only employ francophone engineers and managers in their own operations, but also exercise their substantial purchasing power to promote the development of Québécois-controlled firms which supply business services, components or machinery, and office space. The *Caisse de dépôts* (the investment agency of the Quebec Pension Plan), the General Investment Corporation, and the Quebec Industrial Development Corporation have all aided nonstate enterprise by equity investment and by loans. Conditions are typically attached to such assistance, including the hiring of francophone managers and directors, the purchase of primary materials and production equipment in Quebec, and the use of Quebec business services (accountancy, insurance, engineering). Although it is difficult to judge the impact of these measures, there is no doubt that opportunities are being opened up where previously they were negligible. English control of the private sector is as yet little affected, but the overall place of English capital in the Quebec economy is undergoing a significant change, and this in turn continues to work upon the attitudes and behaviour of anglophone members of the industrial and mercantile elite of Montreal.

The changes stimulated by the expansion of the public sector have been accelerated by the public clamour for unilingualism and by government policies in relation to language. The Bourassa language legislation, Bill 22 (1974), contained provisions requiring the *francisation* of firms if they were to become eligible for government contracts or outright state assistance. The supervisory agency (*la Régie de la langue française*) which was authorized to grant the certificates of *francisation* was instructed to take into account the conditions in which the firm operated but basically to aim for extension of the use of French at all levels and to assure an adequate "francophone presence" at management levels. The *Régie* had, then, wide discretionary powers with which it could implement, at its choice, a soft or a tough language policy in relation to the language of work. The PQ government ordered it to cease its activities in this sphere in December 1976; there were newspaper reports that the policy about to be announced would employ too loose a definition of what constituted a "franchophone presence."

It is hard to know how effective Bill 22, and the policies formulated within its very roomy confines, were or would have become. Those who have not wanted much government action in language matters have claimed that businesses were already engaged in the process of *francisation* even before Bill 22 was passed. On the other hand, the *Mouvement Québec français* and a large number of organizations supporting its demands for unilingualism had been vociferously active since about 1968 and any prudent businessman who intended to stay in the province would want to take advantage of all the lead time he could get. So there should be little surprise if the main effect of political action, insofar as the language of work is concerned, has been an "effect by anticipation."

Ethnicity, bilingualism, and economic status. Even if it is impossible to sort out the effects of political action (or its anticipation) from the general impact of changes in the milieu, we do have data which indicate extensive and increasing bilingualism among anglophone Montrealers, and some striking evidence that they are not unhappy about learning French. Table 4 reports the linguistic skills of the white male labour force in Quebec in 1971, for selected occupations. Although, evidently, bilingualism is more widespread among francophones than among anglophones, I would guess that it is only very recently that bilingual anglophones have come to outnumber the unilingual ones in each of the occupation-categories except production workers (where the percentages are equal) and professionals. This supposition is reinforced by the results of a 1976 language-use survey commissioned by the *Montreal Star*.[5] Respondents were asked: "Has there been any change in the language used by most people in your company in their ordinary work activities?" One in five, both in the sample as a whole and in the anglophone group, reported more French; only three per cent reported more English. The same survey, though it revealed substantial linguistic segregation in the work force (in the sense that anglophones worked mainly with anglophones, etc.,) also demonstrated the great importance of bilingualism in the work world. Bilingualism was least important to the francophones (50 per cent), rather more important for anglophones (55 per cent), and greatest for the "Other" grouping (66 per cent). In a sense this is misleading, however, because it must not be thought to indicate that in any one occupation, anglophones need bilingualism more than francophones. The opposite is almost certainly true. If anglophones find it more important to be bilingual, that is probably because they are more heavily represented in the higher-paid occupations and these (with the notable exception of "professionals") tend to require greater language skills. The importance of bilingualism in various occupations ranges from 83 per cent (managerial) to 24 per cent (construction; also professional). Another indicator that English-speaking workers increasingly need to know French is that bilingual anglophones, except professional and production workers, have higher incomes from employment than unilinguals. (See table 5.)[6] In the top-paying category, the managerial occupations, the advantages of bilingualism are substantial.

The Anglophones' commitment to bilingualism. What do the anglophones think about these changes? Evidence drawn from the *Montreal Star*'s 1976 survey reveals very positive attitudes. For example, although 20 per cent of the anglophones say more French is now used in their own firm, less than one per cent indicated that they were unhappy about this. Nine per cent judged the language changes positive for themselves personally, and only 2.3 per cent felt the effects were negative.

The general willingness to adapt to a social and economic environment where French is increasingly used is also indicated by enrolments of children of anglophone parents in French immersion classes: in 1976–77, almost a quarter of those entering grade one in the Protestant schools of Montreal were enrolled in the immersion course, while in 1975–76 the special immersion classes for grade seven (set up to accommodate those who had not taken this option through elementary school) accommodated 40 per cent of all students at that level.[7] It should be noted that immersion classes have a particularly large clientele in the wealthier parts of Montreal; in the largest elementary school in Westmount the immersion stream now outnumbers, in grade one, the "regular" stream by about eight to one.

In short, the Montreal anglophones are now strongly committed to bilingualism. Perhaps a little more surprising in view of francophones' apparently enthusiastic reception of the Laurin language paper is *their* strong support for bilingualism—at least in March 1976. When in the *Montreal Star*'s survey, respondents were asked whether they thought "Everyone in Quebec should be bilingual," the replies among all groups were very positive (English, 89 per cent; French, 78 per cent; and Other, 83 per cent). Replies to other questions suggest that the majority of anglophones accept the primacy of French—though they qualify this with a strong commitment to freedom of choice in language use.

This was the set of attitudes which prevailed when the Parti Québécois came to power. These attitudes were formed in a context in which English-speaking Montrealers still predominated in the top echelons of the largest firms in Quebec, but found themselves operating in a much-changed political and social milieu. Business leaders were facing strong pressures for the expansion of French and the hiring of francophones at all levels in their operations. The anglophone community as a whole has come to recognize that the environment is predominantly French and that business cannot isolate itself from that environment. It has called for a great deal of personal readjustment, and it appears thar this process is well under way with, on the whole, positive attitudes rather than grudging acceptance of the new situation.

In short, the anglophones are committed to learning French and to using it when the situation requires; and many are willing to work partly or even entirely in French. But they also insist on being able to use English in dealing among themselves both at work and in local institutions such as municipal councils and school boards, when these are located in predominantly English areas. Schooling, particularly, has a symbolic importance; time and again one hears: "I'm sending my child to Immersion; but I want the right to choose." (Even the immersion class after grade three is only forty per cent in French.) It is also the case that corporations insist on using English in head office operations and when they deal with a mainly English clientele.

The Montreal anglophones have changed a great deal in the last few years, both in behaviour and attitude; but these changes are not great enough for large parts of the francophone political elite, who are now committed to institutional unilingualism. These persons regard unilingualism as essential to their future as a French-culture community. Demographic trends ought to be broadly reassuring. But these trends are not *conclusively* reassuring, and that is what is needed in the present context. Given the collective insecurity of much of the francophone political elite, the mood which has prevailed in political debate has been glum and at times highly agitated. The *péquiste* reaction to this situation, as it is now shaping up, is one which appears to the anglophones as aggressive and unnecessary; and they, unquestionably, are in turn feeling the gnawings of collective insecurity.

THE VULNERABILITY OF THE QUEBEC ECONOMY

The business community of Quebec appears to have three major worries about the evolving political situation. One is that an adventurous leap into a shadowy constitutional future (or merely worrying about it) will create a climate of uncertainty which will disrupt the economy, particularly as many persons do not take it for granted that political independence could be achieved without introducing separate currencies and a variety of trade barriers including tariffs. Another concern lies with the social-democratic platform of the Parti

Québécois. The party membership wants to further expand the role of the state in the economy and to introduce universal and compulsory unionization of the labour force. Indications are that the PQ government will not be very adventurous in such matters at first; but these policies remain in its program. And the third concern lies with the language policies which may impose serious costs on business and increase the difficulty of recruiting managerial and technical cadres.

In any one of these areas the promulgation of a tough or radical policy could be expected to cause serious disruption; in combination, the effect would be devastating. Right now, though there is extreme unease at the top echelons of finance and industry, sang-froid prevails, even if there are occasional puffs of steam to show that, within, the blood boils. In general, there seems to be a determination not to expose the business community to charges that it is blackmailing the government. One danger, though, is that if one or two large firms packed off to Ontario, the financial community might be subjected to public vilification which would enable, or force, the government to take strong action against business as a whole. In other words, the situation is highly volatile; and one must ask, what if the Montreal business elites panic? If there is a massive economic pullout, what might its consequences be?

Here we enter the realm of speculation, guided by some knowledge of the structure of the Quebec economy. Well before nationalist economic policies were formulated—before unsettled political conditions could be thought to have had any impact on investment decisions—a process of economic change was under way in which Toronto was steadily gaining the upper hand over Montreal. These two cities have long been in competition with each other to assume the functions of a metropolis for the whole of Canada—that is, to become the city which provides the widest range of financial and other services to business, the country's main communications centre, and the hub of its most technologically innovative manufacturing industry. Such activities make an area the focal point for extensive regional migration. Once initiated, an influx of population tends to set up a self-reinforcing cycle in which industries establish in the area to service people and other industries; manufactures gravitate to the region to be close to their most lucrative markets, to obtain or to take advantage of subcontracting opportunities, and so forth. Although processes of urban growth (and the factors which bring on the decay of a metropolis and the region which surround it) seem not to be very well understood, it does appear that a rapidly-growing population centre, once it has reached a certain size, spawns a ring of satellite cities around it. The interaction among these cities augments the vitality of the whole region.

Whereas Toronto has become the core of an urban network, Montreal has been noticeably unsuccessful in stimulating the growth of satellite towns of a size comparable to Hamilton, Oshawa, and so forth. Montreal itself has been losing ground as a metropolis, having been clearly surpassed by Toronto as a financial centre. In manufacturing, the economies of Quebec and Ontario have become more specialized during the past half-century, with Quebec serving an increasing share of the Canadian market in products from labour-intensive (relatively low-wage, technologically stagnant) industries, epitomized by clothing and to some extent by textiles. These two industries were estimated in 1970 to provide 37 per cent of all jobs in manufacturing in the Montreal region. They are, like almost all Canadian manufactures, heavily dependent upon protective trade policies to give them a captive market.

For some years it has been alleged that head office operations are being transferred from Montreal to Toronto. The allegation is only partly borne out by the data on major corporations listed in the *Financial Post*'s annual *Survey of Industrials*. These listings suggest that Quebec has experienced little net change over the past ten years. On the other hand they also show that the number of head offices of major firms has increased both in Ontario and in the rest of the country, and thus the relative importance of Montreal as a location for head offices seems to have declined. Moreover, the significance of the data is limited because they do not measure the relative size of regional and head offices; there have recently been some celebrated (or notorious) cases of selected operations being transferred to Toronto although the head office remains in Montreal.

The overall picture, then, is one of the relative economic stagnation of Montreal and the region surrounding it (i.e. all Quebec except those regions based on primary industry). The outflow of population in the past decade, together with the high rate of unemployment in Quebec, suggests that the province has been unable to support a population growing at only the rate of natural increase. (Births still do exceed deaths.) The problem should be alleviated in a few years as the drop in fertility rates during the Sixties is reflected in a diminution in the number of persons entering the labour force each year.

To what should one attribute Quebec's weak economic performance in the past decade? One hypothesis is that there is not a close enough relationship between political and economic elites, due to differences in language and culture. Many academic and government economists in Quebec emphasize the active role of the state in economic development. They argue that even in advanced capitalist countries such as the United States there are close ties between government and the heads of the largest corporations. The most innovative sectors of industry are said to be stimulated by government contracts, subsidies to research and development activities, and export assistance. This happens, it is argued, to a much lesser extent in Quebec, where the relationship between government and business is tenuous. Not only is decision-making power not in the hands of francophones, it frequently lies outside Quebec or outside Canada altogether; thus the largest firms in Quebec, though they have some operations there, are externally-oriented in terms of sources of supply, of hiring technical services, of subcontracting, and of the further processing of raw material or semi-manufactures. Such an analysis underlies the belief that an active policy to establish Quebec-controlled firms and to assert a "francophone presence" in top management will have great potential benefits in terms of augmented spin-off effects from any given economic operation.

This theory suggests that Quebec's fundamental economic problem is to make a smooth transition to indigenous (i.e. Québécois) control of the Quebec economy. Economists, including those of independentist persuasion, appear to acknowledge that the Toronto region will continue to drain industry and head office operations away from Greater Montreal. Some firms—those tied to Quebec by ownership, sources of supply, or markets—will be relatively immune to the attractions of southern Ontario, but established trends will continue and probably become more pronounced. Head offices will become regional ones, now staffed by francophones; but the decrease in employment occasioned by the efflux of head offices will be at least partially offset by the expansion of the regional offices of firms now centred in Toronto or elsewhere. Some firms, especially those in the resources sector, will have no option but to make the best of the new situation because "you can't move a mine." Others, in the manufacturing sector, will adapt; if they don't, their plant will be taken over by francophone entrepreneurs, and their operations be better integrated into the Quebec economy as a whole.

I do not discount the possibility of eventual transition to a

Québécois-run economy, but it is clear that the whole scenario is based on a gradual process of orderly change: on a no-panic attitude in the anglophone business community.

The likelihood of a massive, jolting rush to quit Quebec as a result of government policies is the greater since such policies would reinforce existing tendencies which are already pulling business away from the province. A contributing factor in these trends is that small firms of professionals may re-establish elsewhere—indeed, some have done so—thus reducing the availability of business and personal services. So far as I know, no independent study exists which has attempted to estimate the direct and indirect employment effects of head office operations in the Montreal area; but according to the Montreal Board of Trade, the headquarters of thirteen major firms—representing one third of the province's total head office activity—provide 13,260 jobs and contribute $430 million to the provincial economy. These are the direct effects. In addition, head offices are what keep engineering, accountancy, and legal firms in business, and when such operations close down the high salaries attached to them disappear and substantial purchasing power is withdrawn. Thus there is substance to the board's claims that indirectly the head office operations covered in the study contribute a further $1 billion and 40,000 jobs.

In manufacturing, failure to maintain existing plant and to replace machinery as it becomes outdated or worn results in a gradual decline in profitability; eventually the firm may relocate elsewhere, leaving behind exhausted installations. In the meantime, the absence of investment depresses the economy and contributes to unemployment in industries such as residential construction—a very important industry in terms of direct employment and its extensive spin-off effects.

In short, a depression of appalling dimensions may descend upon Quebec. Such an economic crisis always has profound political ramifications. In the present context where depression may appear to have been deliberately brought on by "les autres" as an act of spite or fiscal blackmail, it could induce a sharp rise in social tensions and accompanying acts of violence.

THREATS TO THE DOMESTIC PEACE

Suppose nonstate investment plummets, head offices move out, and a number of manufacturing establishments close down. Many of the wealthier Montreal anglophones will, naturally, follow their jobs out of Quebec. (In some cases their losses in real estate will be underwritten by their employers, though the necessity of doing this may be a factor in preventing some companies from moving.) Many of the non-French, however, will not have the opportunity to move, since their prospects for employment elsewhere will be dim and the costs of leaving Quebec prohibitive. Many of them will be the older, the lower-income, and the more economically insecure part of the population. Their rights or privileges as a community—as members of a minority—had hitherto been protected by the economic power of English capital. This has lost its force: what do they do now?

The political role of the non-French. One option which already seems closed off by past political stand-offishness is for the non-French to mobilize electorally in order to secure legislative protection for their rights as a minority. Until the latter Sixties the two major parties shared the English vote. With the anglophones, as with the rest of the population, a rural-urban electoral cleavage was evident; and both parties had some electoral incentive to keep their non-French voters. As a community, however, the English Quebecers did not much rely on their votes to maintain an influence with the provincial government; the anglophone ministers who were in every cabinet represented an economic rather than a strictly political constituency. However, when the Parti Québécois was formed and the Union Nationale became a walking cadaver, the non-French vote aligned massively behind the Bourassa Liberals. The Parti Québécois tried to prevent this. It made an effort to dissociate the constitutional issue from that of majority-minority relations in Quebec, and, with the "bogeyman" of independence revealed as harmless, to woo anglophone support. The appeal was apparently genuine but the anglophones were cold to it. As a result, the PQ quickly perceived that it had nothing to lose by endorsing language policies which were being promoted by the more exclusivist wing of the Quebec nationalist movement.

The Liberals, on the other hand, easily conceived the notion that nothing they did, as long as they told the people of Quebec that federalism was profitable, could alienate the non-French vote. They passed Bill 22. Its lack of clear policy content—for it was merely a container into which almost any language policy could be poured —antagonized all sides. The nationalists thought that under cover of a few generalizations about promoting French, the Liberals would engage in administrative foot-dragging or obfuscation and thus stultify any serious or effective policies to protect the French language and culture. The non-French, of course, saw it as Machiavellian in quite the opposite sense: for them, the failure to retain full freedom of choice in the language of instruction was an attack on their very existence as a community. In the 1976 election many of them switched to the Union Nationale, which had opportunistically promised to support them (it has since recanted and basically supports the *péquiste* language policy).

The end result is that the anglophones are left without a political instrument. In any case, as a minority they cannot afford to create political controversy over legislative guarantees for their rights; inexorably, every time minority interests are isolated and are set against those of the majority, the minority loses. Thus the first rule of political strategy for an ethnic or cultural minority is to find some allies and to promote their interests as those of a class or region rather than of an ethnic group. In this way they may be able to contribute to forming a majority electoral coalition. The most dangerous course of action is to form an ethnic party; parties which appeal exclusively to a minority interest, where legislatures are not based on proportional representation, are wiped out or become politically impotent. Rather better is to form a bloc within another party, thereby putting all one's political eggs into one electoral basket. This incurs the danger of harsh treatment when the party favoured by such support is out of office; it is a risky strategy, not least because it may promote political controversy on ethnic issues. This may partly explain the history of the language controversy since 1969. The third strategy for the non-French is to divide support between the major parties, thus recreating one feature of the party system during the pre-PQ period. The problem with this strategy, which encourages compromise within the major parties and tends to dampen down political controversy on ethnic or linguistic issues, is that a minority must be of a certain size to carry any electoral weight within two or more parties simultaneously. The non-French in Quebec are probably too small for this.

In any case, the PQ may have succeeded in splitting the non-French political constituency. One of the major grievances about Bill 22, as voiced by some of the ethnic groups (that anodyne "Other" of statistical compilations), was that it created a distinction between them and the anglophones, since children entering the English schools had to pass a language test. This imposed heavy psychological strains on the children and in some cases divided families which had one or more children in the English school but were forced to send younger ones to French schools. These objectionable features of Bill 22 will be abolished under the new legislation. The PQ policies tend to place English on an equal footing with other minority languages, and while this is highly offensive to the anglophones it is gratifying to other groups. In consequence, the PQ may effectively distinguish the interests of anglophones and "Others," and if it does so the non-French will find it all the more difficult to exercise any political influence in Quebec.

Two dangers. Quebec anglophones, then, have every reason to feel politically powerless. In this situation the desire to assert oneself, to stage demonstrations calculated to offend the majority, is very high. Deliberate terrorism or the planned operation of a guerilla-type movement (which I think one can discount) are not necessary preconditions for social disruption; events of a trivial character can, in an already tense situation, spark the escalation of violence when a déclassé population feels itself the victim of illiberalism and a discriminatory nationalism. Thus the first danger presented by economic distress and the flight of wealth is disorder emanating initially from the non-French who feel themselves trapped in a hostile social environment. The seizure of political independence by Quebec, or its negotiation, would contribute to attitudes and behaviour of this sort;but it seems just as plausible, if such evils are visited upon Quebec society, that they will precede independence and precipitate it rather than the other way around.

The threat of social disorder could also arise from another quarter. An accentuation of the economic decline of Quebec, though without the sudden collapse envisaged in the preceding scenario, could well increase tensions between ethnic/linguistic groups as competition for jobs became more acute and perceived discrimination in the job market more prevalent. Here the main antagonists would probably be the Québécois and immigrant groups, in which case those individuals who are evidently assimilating to the anglophone minority would be the most obvious target of nationalist action. Events such as the schools dispute in the Montreal suburb of St.-Léonard have demonstrated the existence of substantial hostility between the Québécois and the immigrant population.

It has sometimes been thought that such hostility is an instance of displaced aggression. Class antagonisms in Quebec have become sharper in the past decade, and ideological polarization appears stronger there than elsewhere in Canada. Perhaps ethnic/linguistic differences contribute to this, since the majority of managers and owners are anglophone: capital in Quebec has an alien face. But overt acceptance of such a conflictual view of economic relations is far from universal among the working class. Paul Cappon among others has argued that many Québécois who resent English wealth are too dependent on it to acknowledge (even to themselves) the real object of their hostility; and immigrants become scapegoats. They qualify for the unenviable role of surrogate Anglos, Cappon argues, because they tend to assimilate to that community, and are weak enough to attack.[8] Some observers will think this theory fanciful, but it illustrates a general point: ethnic tensions and class antagonisms in Quebec may well be sharpened by the difficulty one experiences in trying to distinguish them from each other.

If this is so, an economic crisis would accentuate existing social conflicts. With strong competition for scarce employment opportunities, the political demands for the sort of language policies which would victimize the non-French, and the union pressures on employers for discriminatory hiring practices, would inevitably increase. Political oratory already contains frequent allusions to "les vrais Québécois"—a phrase sometimes used not only to distinguish francophones from the rest, but to distinguish political nationalists from all those indifferent or hostile to independence. Such expressions suggest an intolerance which is the least attractive feature of Quebec nationalism.

In a period of economic distress the danger of a sharp rise in social exclusivism is great indeed. Intolerance may then become unblushing and discrimination overt, particularly if the withdrawal of capital is perceived merely as punishing Quebec for taking away privileges that the British had won through conquest and subsequently maintained through superior economic power. This is not pure fantasy—one has only to think of the furor caused by "la coup de la Brinks," when a convoy of seven armoured cars bearing securities made its way to Ontario, publicly, just before the 1970 election.

One of the dangers of economic hardship, then, is the emergence of an ugly mood in the majority accompanied by acts of public and/or private reprisal against the non-French. The victims would not be the English capitalist class (which presumably would already have decamped) but the larger and by no means privileged sector of the anglophone and immigrant population.

The distinction I have drawn between disorder originating within minority groups on the one hand, and the majority on the other, is merely analytical. In practice the escalation of tension and violence is a dialectical process in which none of the groups involved remains passive. Thus, though I have written of two threats to domestic peace there is in reality only one; but it possesses dynamic qualities of the most frightening kind.

A DEGREE OF OPTIMISM

The Montreal anglophones may not call it optimism. The mercantile-industrial elite which has been the pinnacle of this community is in eclipse. It is caught between the self-assertion of the Québécois and the pre-eminence of Toronto. The one nudges them from economic power if they stay, and the other attracts them to more lucrative employment elsewhere. This does not mean that Quebec will assimilate or ultimately expel its cultural minorities, although it may do so. It would be a less interesting and I think a less vital society if this were to happen; and it is hard to believe that in these circumstances Montreal could be anything but a big provincial town. However, this danger, provided the more dreadful happenings envisaged in the preceding section are avoided, seems slight. The main point is that even without xenophobic nationalism in Quebec, the English-speaking Montrealers will lose their control of the Quebec economy—to the extent that they have not already lost it to the Americans—probably within a generation. This outcome will not hinge on the political longevity of the PQ government or on its success in achieving statehood for Quebec: the Bourassa Liberals too were committed to creating a francophone entrepreneurial class; any prospective government will presumably retain this commitment; and membership in the Canadian federation (even as now constituted) is no bar to its realization.

So, for a person committed to a multicultural society in Quebec and in a Canada which includes Quebec, what are the grounds for optimism? One reason for being cheerful is that an unhealthy situation which has been with us for some time will not persist. Where differences in social class or economic condition in a society correspond even roughly to ethnic or cultural differences, there is ample room for alleged discrimination; indeed, discrimination (conscious or otherwise) often does exist. The social discontents associated with discrimination produce racial tensions and encourage the growth of an inward-looking national or ethnic-group consciousness. Such movements are characteristically illiberal and intolerant; the sort of French-Canadian nationalism which was prevalent before the Quiet Revolution epitomized this genre. Current Quebec nationalism is far from free of such tendencies, and the danger does exist that they will, perhaps in a flash, come to dominate the movement. One ought not to disregard this possibility. Nor, on the other hand, should its existence prevent us from realizing that racial or cultural exclusivism reflects the insecurity of a people. A closed outlook is the likely consequence of economic inferiority and uncertain capacity to shape major social institutions. That these marks of a minority status are rapidly being erased is profoundly gratifying.

A second feature of the present situation which offers some encouragement is that a substantial part of the Montreal anglophone community is showing some readiness to adapt to the predominance of the French language in Quebec. Admittedly, not all of it. I suspect that there is a big difference in this regard between those who have lived a long time in Quebec and intend to stay there, and those who have moved to Quebec in the course of a business career and expect eventually to be transferred out. There is no apparent way of identifying the proportions of anglophones in these two categories; but it may be significant that the "West Island" of Montreal, where the turnover of population is high, has been the area to show the most hostile response to the Lévesque government. One cannot, then, honestly depict an anglophone population suddenly converted to the idea of integration into a French Quebec, and certainly not into a unilingual French Quebec. Responses to recent developments have been diverse, and any attempt to describe the behaviour and position of the non-French minorities must take account of such diversity.

With this reservation, and in spite of some expressions of bloody-mindedness (as in the "Eleventh Province" movement), it can truly be said that anglophones' readiness to adapt to an increasingly French milieu—provided it is generous to its minorities—is impressive. Further rapid evolution is likely to occur.

Curiously, Toronto's surpassing of Montreal may have facilitated the adjustments which Montreal anglophones have made. It has been entirely salutary that those who could not accept that Montreal is a French-speaking city still had an easy "out"; this, no doubt, was especially true for the professional classes who can at relatively little cost make individual decisions about where to live and work. The exodus continues at a sharply accelerated pace. Those of the younger generation who stay, stay by choice; and they could scarcely do so if they were not prepared to come to terms with the prospect that francophones will step into most of the leading positions in all spheres of social life, including the economic.

The integration of the anglophones into a society which they acknowledge must henceforth be predominantly French does not mean that they will be absorbed by it, or that the end of the "two solitudes" is at hand. The mutual isolation which this phrase denotes can only slightly (unless a society assimilates its minorities) be broken down. We should get away from the idea that social distance between linguistic communities is a dangerous thing. What counts is not intimate mutual understanding—how much of this do we have even in unilingual societies?—or regular social contact, but mutual awareness and respect, distinctive institutions for specific purposes (especially education), some ability to communicate, and the absence of hierarchy among language groups.

Finally, on the side of optimism, we have the possibility of refashioning a Canadian federal state which includes Quebec and which works a little more harmoniously than the Canada of 1977. We tend to think that it is difficult to make Canada work because one of the big provinces has a distinctive culture. Perhaps the real "Quebec problem" is that within the province the numerical majority do not really feel in control, and resent the prominent—or dominant—economic role of "les Anglais." The complaints against the federal system may not be regional—representing a distinctive economic interest or cultural concern—so much as a reflection of internal problems. The independentists see the federal state as a prop for the anglophone minority, and they want out of Canaada for this reason.

Quite possibly, if it survives, the Canadian state will run more smoothly if in each province the numerical majority enjoys clear primacy. This need not entail cultural homogeneity. In all parts of the country there must be tolerance towards minority groups and support for their cultural distinctiveness. Such tolerance is a condition of making Canada a going concern. Conversely, Canada's existence as a multicultural state supports linguistic and cultural diversity within the provinces and contributes to their being more open, more liberal societies.

Table 1

Quebec Male Labour Force by Ethnicity, Showing Employment in Selected Occupation-Categories, 1971

ALL ETHNIC ORIGINS	NUMBER	PER CENT
All occupations	1,447,365	100.0
High-Income Occupations*	128,025	8.8
Below-Average Income Occupations**	924,045	63.8
Unstable-Employment Occupations***	554,780	38.3
BRITISH ISLES ETHNIC ORIGIN		
All occupations	169,135	100.0
High-Income Occupations*	28,650	16.9
Below-Average Income Occupations**	89,750	53.1
Unstable-Employment Occupations***	42,560	25.2
FRENCH		
All occupations	1,097,015	100.0
High-Income Occupations*	77,115	7.0
Below-Average Income Occupations**	728,715	66.4
Unstable-Employment Occupations***	437,460	39.9
OTHER		
All occupations	181,215	100.0
High-Income Occupations*	22,260	12.3
Below-Average Income Occupations**	105,580	58.3
Unstable-Employment Occupations***	74,760	41.3

* Occupations yielding, on average, an income of $10,000 or more. In 1970, 19% of the employed male population earned this much.

** Average employment income for male workers in 1970 was $7,663. Occupations yielding, on average, less than this were classified as Below-Average Income Occupations.

*** Occupations in which less than 66% of male workers were employed for 49 weeks or more in 1970, except "health diagnosing and treating occupations," where if one worked less than 49 weeks this assumed to be voluntary.

Columns do not sum as categories are not mutually exclusive.

SOURCE: Canada. Census, 1971.

Table 2
Ethnic Origin and Language Use, Quebec Province and Montreal (Census Metropolitan) Area, 1971)

(percentages in brackets)			
PROVINCE OF QUEBEC	FRENCH	BRITISH ISLES/ ENGLISH	OTHER
Ethnic Origin	4,759,360 (79.0)	640,040 (10.6)	628,365 (10.4)
Mother Tongue*	4,866,405 (80.7)	788,835 (13.1)	372,525 (6.2)
Home Language**	4,870,100 (80.8)	887,875 (14.7)	269,785 (4.5)
MONTREAL AREA			
Ethnic Origin	1,762,695 (64.3)	438,500 (16.0)	542,040 (19.8)
Mother Tongue*	1,817,285 (66.2)	596,305 (21.7)	329,645 (12.0)
Home Language**	1,818,865 (66.3)	683,390 (24.9)	240,985 (8.8)

* Language first understood, which the respondent still understands.
** Language most frequently spoken in the home.
Tables sum horizontally.
SOURCE: Canada. *Census*, 1971, bulletin 1. 4–8, tables 23 and 24.

Table 3
Population Projections for the Island of Montreal, by Mother Tongue, 1961–1991

		FRENCH	ENGLISH	OTHER	TOTAL
		%	%	%	%
High level	1961	62.7	24.0	13.3	100
of migration	1971	63.6	23.0	13.4	100
hypothesis	1981	62.4	22.5	15.1	100
	1991	61.2	22.4	16.4	100
Low level	1961	62.7	24.0	13.3	100
of migration	1971	63.6	23.0	13.4	100
hypothesis	1981	66.8	21.1	12.1	100
	1991	70.2	19.2	10.6	100

SOURCE: Calculated from *The Position of the French Language in Quebec* (Quebec: Report of the Commission of Inquiry on the Position of the French Language and on Language Rights in Quebec ["Gendron Report"], 3 (1972), 174–75.

Table 4
Linguistic Skills by Occupation, White Males, Quebec 1971 (Percentages)

OCCUPATION	UNILINGUAL ANGLOPHONES	BILINGUAL ANGLOPHONES	UNILINGUAL FRANCOPHONES	BILINGUAL FRANCOPHONES	N
Managers	13.2	17.5	13.9	55.3	(803)
Professionals	19.1	10.9	16.7	53.1	(412)
Teachers, Health Employees	5.7	8.0	29.1	57.0	(696)
Clerks	9.7	10.7	29.2	50.3	(1314)
Salespeople	7.3	11.9	32.8	47.9	(1240)
Production Workers	5.2	5.2	53.0	36.3	(2716)

SOURCE: Unpublished data supplied by François Vaillancourt, to whom I wish to record my thanks. Vaillancourt obtained the data from the 1:100 Public Use Sample Tape, produced from the 1971 Census. Calculations performed at the Université de Montréal using SPSS.

Table 5
Mean Income From Employment, White Males, Quebec, 1971 According to Linguistic Skills (Selected Occupations)

OCCUPATION	UNILINGUAL ANGLOPHONES	BILINGUAL ANGLOPHONES	UNILINGUAL FRANCOPHONES	BILINGUAL FRANCOPHONES
All workers	8,372	8,412	5,012	7,007
Managers	14,727	16,112	7,666	11,167
Professionals	11,330	9,336	6,385	8,726
Teachers, Health Employees	8,766	8,544	6,463	9,165
Clerks	5,783	5,741	4,730	5,869
Salespeople	8,440	8,910	5,729	7,368
Production Workers	7,458	6,812	5,275	6,329

SOURCE: As for table 4.

NOTES

1. André Raynauld, "The Quebec Economy: A General Assessment," in Dale C. Thomson, ed., *Quebec Society and Politics: Views from the Inside* (Toronto, 1973), p. 147. Raynauld here is reviewing the work he did, together with Gérald Marion and Richard Béland, for the federal Commission on Bilingualism and Biculturalism. Other data quoted here on income by ethnicity are drawn from the commission's *Report*, III, pt. A (1969), 23, 63, and 77.

2. *La Presse*, 26 fév. 1974, p. 1. The demographic data in this section of the chapter are drawn from *The Position of the French Language in Quebec* (Quebec: Report of the Commission of Inquiry on the Position of the French Language and on Language Rights in Quebec ["Gendron Report"], 1972, vol. 3, *The Ethnic Groups*. References in the text to this report are to pp. 57, 93–102, 161–66, 182–90, and 485.

3. I refer specifically to the following passage in the White Paper: "English predominates clearly in the general communications at work: 82 per cent of all communications are carried out in English in Quebec as a whole, 84 per cent in Montreal, and 70 per cent in the province outside Montreal." As William Johnson has pointed out (*Globe and Mail*, 6 April 1977), this passage is based on a section of the Gendron Report which refers only to language-use among the anglophone work force; but the White Paper treated the percentages as if they applied to the whole employed population. Other parts of the White Paper are also highly selective in their use of quotations, e.g., demonstrating the intolerance to be found among some English Canadians without giving any sense of the variety of attitude expressed to, and reported by, the Commission on Bilingualism and Biculturalism.

4. Pierre Fournier, "Vers une grande bourgeoisie canadienne-française? Le développement de la bourgeoisie nationale au Québec: 1962 à 1975," unpublished manuscript, 2 juin 1976. I am grateful to Pierre Fournier for sending me this manuscript.

5. *Montreal Star*, 27 March 1976, p. A-8. This excellent survey is the source of several sections of this chapter referring to language use and attitudes towards language matters. For this survey, 739 telephone interviews were conducted with working Montrealers 15 years of age and older. Interviews were conducted between 20 Jan. and 6 Feb. 1976, by Data Laboratories Limited. Findings were reported in the *Star* in a seven-part series by Dominique Clift, 27 March to 3 April 1976.

6. Although, as mentioned earlier in this chapter, unilingual anglophones have higher incomes than bilinguals, this is true only if one considers income from all sources (e.g. including investments). Where anglophones' employment income alone is concerned, the census data shows that bilinguals have the edge.

7. Data on enrolments in the French immersion program supplied by the Protestant School Board of Greater Montreal, whose assistance is gratefully acknowledged.

8. Paul Cappon, *Conflit entre les Néo-Canadiens et les francophones de Montréal*, publié pour le Centre international de recherche sur le bilinguisme (Quebec, 1974).

III
Working It Out

Common Ground and Disputed Territory

JOHN TRENT

Underlying the great debates about federalism, French-English relations, and the role of Quebec in Canada are widely divergent images,
assumptions, and values concerning such central concepts as state and
nation. Given such different philosophical approaches, is it possible to
find any common ground on which some form of compromise might
be built? Is there room for accommodation, or must one or other image
prevail? Two of the central figures in the debate, each representing a
well-articulated analysis of the past and conception of the future, are
René Lévesque and Pierre Trudeau. Understanding their views, and
the usually less well-developed images of other actors in the drama,
provides an essential key to exploring the possibilities of reconciliation.

Let us first look at the arguments of the "plaintiff," M. René
Lévesque, in the case of Quebec vs Canada. Lévesque first produced
his theory on sovereignty-association in September 1967, in a series of
articles in *Le Devoir*. They were published as *An Option for Quebec* in
1968. The essential ideas may be summarized as follows.

1. The Québécois are a people defined by the facts that they speak
French, they live in Quebec, and they have a collective personality
formed by three and a half centuries of common history. They are
marked by their will to survive, their ability to recognize each other
("with no one else listening"), stemming from a common language and
personality and their attachment to Quebec as the only place they can
really be at home. They are a "nation trying to build a homeland in
Quebec," to live as themselves, in their own language, and according to
their own ways. The difference cannot be surrendered.

2. Quebec society has been subjected to rapidly changing conditions,
internal and external, which have broken down "old protective barriers" and created a "terrible collective vulnerability." This is com-

pounded by a long list of inadequacies (in education, the economy, sicientific technology, government, and ownership), a sense of inferiority, and a minority position on an Anglo-Saxon continent.

3. The only way for the Québécois to overcome these handicaps is to created a progressive, French-speaking homeland for themselves, where they will be equals, not inferiors.

4. To secure once and for all the "safety of the collective personality," the nation must obtain power for unfettered action in the fatherland of Quebec where it is a majority. The nation cannot tolerate policies conceived and directed from outside.

5. The years of the Quiet Revolution have helped the Québécois to catch up. They have found that they are as capable as anyone, that the more they take charge, the more they accept their responsibilities, the more they can achieve. Now they must make a crucial choice in order to keep up the momentum.

6. The impetus will be lost by the Québécois if they don't undertake a number of necessary tasks. This they cannot do because of the basic difficulty of living in a country made up of two nations. Because there are "two majorities, two complete societies, quite distinct from one another," Lévesque believes it to be "evident that the hundred-year-old framework of Canada can hardly have any effect other than to create increasing difficulties," Both sides must. recognize that the present regime has had its day and must be profoundly modified or a new one built. Because the Québécois have put up with the main disadvantages and are menaced by the current paralysis they are in the greatest hurry to get rid of Canada.

7. Quebec cannot accomplish its essential tasks because of the "sclerosis of Canadian institutions." The confusion created by overlapping laws and regulations has paralysed change and progress. One government thwarts the actions of the other, leading to conflict and impotence. There is an "incredible split-level squandering of energy."

8. The state gives form to everything. It is absolutely necessary that it be able to direct, coordinate, and humanize. English Canada, too, needs for its own security a strong state that can be used for "simplifying, rationalizing and centralizing" certain institutions. Order must be reestablished in the chaos of governmental structures for rational economic planning as well as administrative efficiency and responsibility.

9. Quebec's demands for jurisdiction over its economy, social security and welfare, culture, international relations, citizenship, immigration, and employment, for a massive transfer of fiscal resources, and for restructured federal institutions, add up to a "basic minimum" that is completely unacceptable to the rest of the country.

10. Constitutional reform is not possible because Quebec's demands surpass both the best intentions of English Canadians in terms of compromise and the capacity of the regime itself to make concessions without becoming crippled.

11. Federalism is an outdated regime, suited to the last century. Maintaining it will only lead to increased confrontation between "two collective personalities" that are in a parallel search for their own national security. Continued wrangling will so weaken them they will "drown themselves in the ample bosom of America."

12. Thus another solution must be found to get rid of obsolete federalism. The answer lies in the "two great trends of our age": "the freedom of peoples" and the "formation by common consent of economic and political groupings."

13. Quebec must seize all the essentials of independence, mastery of "every last area of basic collective decision-making." It must become sovereign.

14. But we must recognize the facts of interdependence in the world. Quebec and the rest of Canada could create a "new Canadian Union," based on a voluntary association of equal partners. There would need to be mixed permanent committees of officials for fiscal coordination, a common administrative authority for the association, a court of arbitration, agencies to deal with other areas of coordination and planning, and regular meetings of joint Councils of Ministers and sessions of delegations from the two parliaments, all on a basis of equality.

15. Sovereignty will be achieved once the people choose leaders capable of taking the first judicious steps—as they have now done—and through "the democratic participation of a majority of citizens who will have made their decision calmly."

If one compares these fundamental ideas with those expressed by Parti Québécois leaders since the November election or with the party platform the degree of consistency is nothing short of extraordinary.

To give just one example, the 1975 edition of the PQ program states:

> Four centuries of common history have made the Québécois a nation.
> The Québécois possess an undeniable will to live together and preserve
> their own culture. Our existence as a distinct nation can only be assured
> to the degree which we completely master the instruments of our politi-
> cal life.... But, others exercise political power dangerously in our stead ...
> we are a minority in Canada. ... The only government controlled by the
> Québécois is that in Quebec. Quebec is blocked in almost all domains by
> duplicated structures. ... The French language is menaced. ...
> Federalism is not profitable.

The basic ideas of Pierre Elliott Trudeau have not been as concisely
expressed as those of Lévesque, but most of their elements are to be
found in his book *Federalism and the French Canadians* (1968):

1. The nation can be defined juridically or sociologically. In the
former sense it is simply the entire population of a sovereign state. In
the latter it is a cultural or ethnic community. The will to be one is
fundamental to the nation. This is more important than language or
culture, history or geography, or even force and power. Canada was
formed by a consensus to create the Canadian nation. The vocation of
Canada is to be a pluralist nation made up fundamentally of two major
cultural communities both of which have equal power in the sense that
both can destroy Canada and neither can assimilate the other.

2. The tendency to confound ethnic nation and sovereign state is
illogical and retrograde. Most of the recently independent states are
polyethnic. Nations have no biological reality and cannot be considered
an extended family. Even supposedly homogeneous populations have
been formed over generations by immigrations and the intermixing of
peoples. And if the right to independence of ethnic minorities were
carried to its extreme, each one would find within itself other
minorities claiming the same right. Appeals to ethnic nationalism are
emotionally based and arouse similar passions in surrounding peoples.
This is true of the nationalism of British Canadians who have attempted to define Canada as an English-speaking nation, thus creating
French-Canadian nationalism in self-defence. It will also be true of
attempts to define Quebec as a French nation.

3. The task of the state is to seek the common good of all its citizens
without distinction by sex, colour, religion, or ethnicity. It is to install
and maintain a legal order in which the citizens may reach full attainment. The most difficult problem is to justify authority without de-

stroying the independence of the human person, that is, to create institutions which guarantee liberty without destroying order. This is best achieved in systems where there is an equilibrium of forces, a just measure of rival claims, a system of counterweights which can correct excess and abuse and maintain liberty. Ideology and dogmatism are the enemies of liberty. The Canadian people enjoy a degree of liberty and prosperity which, while not perfect, has few equals in the world.

4. Ethnically defined states lead to intolerance because they are founded on an exclusive idea. If the idea of the nation is given priority, it inevitably pushes people to define the common good in terms of one ethnic group rather than the whole population. History shows that emotional nationalism often leads to despotism, chauvinism, racism, and jingoism, especially when a "strong" government is called upon to satisfy the deceptions of a "liberated" people that finds it is as poor as before.

5. The values of the French-Canadian nation can best be advanced through the Canadian federation. Economically, it shares resources and markets with another people while being forced to learn to compete in a relatively protected situation. If French Canadians can't compete on a two-to-one basis in Canada, how will they compete internationally at more than a hundred to one? French Canada is economically integrated with a continent. In this interdependent world small communities have great difficulty financing and manning all the functions of a modern state. Culturally, French Canada avoids becoming isolated in a ghetto while at the same time having in Canada and the federal government an amplifier which can multiply the impact of the French culture in North America. Politically, it maintains a system of balances which prevents Quebec from sinking into a narrow parochialism.

6. Nationalism wastes a people's limited energy in sterile debates without seeking workable solutions. French-Canadian nationalism has always tended to formulate unrealizable social goals. Nationalism produces stagnation and is by essence right-wing, as it emphasizes what sets men apart and not what they have in common. The best path for French Canadians is to seek excellence and self-discipline, in their education, industry, and government and to put all their energy into reforming their cities, agriculture, and public administration.

7. Federalism offers a compromise between the extremes of isolation and unity. It is an ideal system because it can be adjusted flexibly to

meet various requirements. Thus it has a pan-Canadian scope in matters such as international affairs, defence, and economic development, while the provinces have jurisdiction over matters central to regional and ethnic values. Federalism promotes social progress because it permits new ideas and parties to be tried out in individual provinces. The provinces also provide a barrier against the effects of giantism in modern society. As a form of organization based on law, rationality and compromise federalism is more civilized and humane than a system based upon emotional appeals to ethnicity and exclusiveness.

8. All the practical changes Quebec nationalists have ever sought can be achieved within the framework of the present Canadian constituion. In fact, the system is moving rapidly toward decentralization without changing a comma in the constitution. Quebec is free to undertake the economic and social reforms it desires and even to modify its own internal constituion. Changes in constitutions should be considered with caution; they should not be accorded an absolute value in themselves.

9. Before rejecting Canada, French Canadians must learn to participate fully in it and to remake it as a pluralist, polyethnic society. This means English Canadians, too, will have to change their image of Canada by redefining it as a bilingual country where the two linguistic communities are equal partners. If any reform of the constitution is necessary it is to overcome the ethnic conflicts which have marred Canada's history. At the federal level both languages must have an absolute equality. French education rights in the other provinces should be equal to those the English have enjoyed in Quebec. In provinces where there is a sufficient French or English minority government services should be freely available in both languages. Canada can serve as an example to other polyethnic states.

10. Provincial autonomy must be protected. It is the main training ground for self-government and the chief domain for the growth of national values. Quebec is the only territory in North America where French Canadians are sufficiently concentrated to give themselves social and political institutions in their own image.

11. Paradoxically, independence or self-government does not guarantee either good government or self-determination. Independence will not in itself make French an important commercial and industrial language in North America, or give Quebec greater bargaining power with business or other countries. The likely victims are the working classes who live close to the economic margin. But the nationalists

never calculate these costs or explain their potential dangers to the workers.

12. A common market would simply bring Quebec back to approximately its current levels of powers and independence. It would have to renounce its autonomy over the movement of capital, technology, manpower, and production, as well as with regard to policies dealing with money, external commerce, tariffs, and customs.

It would be an understatement to say that most of Trudeau's thinking has become federal government policy. His ideas and priorities are incarnated in government documents such as "Federalism for the Future" which laid out Ottawa's approach to constitutional revision at the Federal-Provincial Constitutional Conference of February 1968. In addition, they have become part of federal policy on official language rights and bilingualism. More recently the prime minister referred to the same values and images of Canada in his address to a joint session of the United States Congress.

This speech signalled a major change in Trudeau's thinking—a greater recognition of the responsibility of the Canadian government to the individuals and peoples of which Canada is composed and of the need for constitutional changes. This was anticipated in an earlier speech in December 1976: "Our task is to build a more enriching federalism to guarantee even more firmly the liberty, self-realization, and well-being of the people and communities of Canada. The politics of federalism are the politics of accommodation."

The theories of Trudeau and Lévesque reflect fundamentally different concepts of the nation. Lévesque has adopted the organic theory, founded on the biological ethnic group, developed by German nationalists and romanticists in the nineteenth century. Any nation worthy of its name should have its own state founded on one people and one language. Trudeau follows the British and French ideas of the "elective" nation, based on choice and will, as expounded especially by French thinkers in the late 1800s. It is "desired solidarity" rather than a union to which a people is obliged to submit.

Trudeau fears the potential aberrations of an ethnically based nationalism but has habitually underestimated the contribution of nationalism to promoting and defending a people's communal values. Just the opposite may be said of Lévesque on both counts. Nevertheless, the similarity of the political goals of the two men is striking. Both seek equality for the French-Canadian nation, the assertion of the French fact in North America, and the most effective form of government. Their priorities are, however, reversed. Trudeau believes that happy competitive individuals living in liberty will produce a progressive nation. Lévesque thinks that only the collective independence of the nation will allow it to progress and the people to benefit from their democratic rights. To a large extent the real political battles the two men have been fighting for the past decade can be explained by these differences. Lévesque has been struggling to preserve democratic processes and human and minority rights within his nationalist movement, while Trudeau has been fighting against English-Canadian obduracy in order to achieve francophone rights in a democratic Canada.

It is over the paths to the political goals, however, that the two leaders show seemingly insurmountable differences. For Lévesque there is only one reasonable, logical, possible solution to the "French problem": political independence.

Trudeau, on the other hand, believes that the Canadian system can be reformed. It is better to seek progress within the federal system, because it has proved more supportive of liberty than has ethnic nationalism and because franchophones enjoy a much larger sphere for economic and cultural growth than they would outside the system. At the same time, without becoming an ethnic ghetto, Quebec can ensure the protection of French-Canadian culture within Confederation.

The similarity in aims of the two philosophies provides some possibility that the differences over means could be bridged. Both accept the reality and legitimacy of the cultural collectivity, even though according it a somewhat different priority. Both insist on the autonomy of Quebec. Both believe democratic government must prevail. Whether or not agreement on the means to these ends can be found largely depends on two factors. One is whether we can deepen our concept of federalism so as to create innovative institutions that may accommodate the notion of French equality within Canada. The other is whether current political conditions will permit the flexibility needed to change attitudes and develop negotiable solutions before it is too late.

These broad analyses of Canadian federalism have shaped the role that the federal government has played in discussion of constitutional change since 1968, and have determined the positions that the Parti Québécois government adopted as it began to participate in federal-provincial conferences after November 15. Between 1968 and 1971 the eleven governments had sought agreement on a method for amending the constitution and on possible change in its substance. Tentative agreement was reached on the so-called Victoria Charter of June 1971, but it was then rejected by Quebec. The issue of constitutional reform faded into the background until 1975, when Prime Minister Trudeau suggested a more modest attempt to secure agreement at least on a means of domiciling the constitution in Canada, rather than in Britain, and on a formula for constituional amendment. The provinces, displaying an unprecedented degree of unity, responded that any discussion of these matters must be accompanied by real changes in the distribution of powers. These were to include entrenchment of language rights, greater provincial control of immigration, culture and communications, restrictions on the federal spending and declaratory powers, greater provincial authority over natural resources, changes in federal institutions and other matters. The federal government showed little sympathy for such broad alterations. The matter was due to be threshed out at a new conference to be held in December 1976, but the Quebec election suddenly cast the whole matter in a new light.

Even the changes proposed by the provinces did not come close to meeting the demands of the PQ government for the powers it regards as necessary to Quebec's sovereignty. In a statement to the federal-provincial conference of ministers of finance, shortly after the election, the new minister of intergovernmental affairs, Claude Morin, stated that Quebec would continue to cooperate while it was a member of the federation, but that its central goal was political sovereignty with economic association. The current federal regime must be replaced by a new political order. In Morin's view, its constitutional and financial powers permitted the federal government to move into new areas of governmental action almost at will. The system has become centralized, and Ottawa wields the principal levers of power with respect to such matters as manpower, regional development, the environment, urban affairs, foreign investment, and the like. The provincial governments have become mere regional branches of a centralized federal government, with neither the autonomy nor the financial resources to plan their own futures. In his speeches to the Conference of First Ministers, in December 1976, and later to investors in New York, Lévesque gave a similar analysis. Ottawa had continually usurped provincial powers; the only answer was for Quebec to recuperate full decision-making and taxing powers.

The present position of the federal government with respect to possible changes in the constitution has not been fully elaborated since November 1976.

While Prime Minister Trudeau did say in his speech to the Chamber of Commerce in Quebec City that the whole constitution, aside from the respect for individual and collective human rights, is open to challenge, in later speeches he backed off from this position and talked much more of accommodation and modification. He has indicated that decentralization could be considered but it cannot go much further without destroying the central government. In any case, no amount of decentralization would satisfy the Parti Québécois. During his speech in Saskatchewan on 17 April 1977, Trudeau stated: "Canada is not divisible. We will not discuss it—ever." The health and welfare minister, Marc Lalonde, stated in an interview that special status for Quebec is not a realistic solution and that the breakup of Canada would be preferable.

At a more concrete level, it would appear from federal government documents and its negotiating stance during the last ten years that its main interest is in the patriation of the constitution, finding an amending formula, and establishing a bill of rights and entrenching language rights. Beyond this, the federal government believes that in any redefinition of the federal system it must retain control of the major instruments of economic policy including the capacity to stimulate and regulate the economy. It must have the economic resources necessary for the redistribution of income between the wealthy and the poor provinces in Canada as well as between individuals. It would also require full responsibility for Canada's foreign policy. It would not be excluded from areas of cultural and technological development by the provinces.

Ottawa agrees that new methods must be found to improve cooperation between the federal and provincial governments. It would not frown on proposals to have some senators named by provincial governments and to give the Senate increased powers with regard to nomination of Supreme Court judges, ambassadors, and heads of cultural agencies. However, the Senate would no longer be able to maintain its veto power over legislation in the House of Commons.

If this still represents the basic general position of Ottawa, it would hardly satisfy the English-speaking provinces, let alone Quebec. Nor does there seem to be an alternative choice in the positions of the two major opposition parties. Both have stressed the need for a strong central government. The leader of the Progressive Conservative party, Joe Clark, has said that the provinces could be accorded more control and powers in the fields of industrial development, culture, immigration, urban affairs and communications. He contends that we must search for a further alternative, between the status quo and independence. Ed Broadbent, leader of the New Democratic party, finds even the Progressive Conservative policies too decentralizing, especially in economic powers. He also attacks the Liberal party for turning over medicare, hospitalization, university education, exclusively to the provinces. His party believes that to decentralize economic powers strengthens the rich provinces, weakens the poor, broadens the gap between east and west, and lessens English Canada's capacity to understand and accept changes in Quebec. However, the NDP, traditionally the most centralist of the federal parties, has recently sought to adapt to the increasing force of Canadian regionalism.

Two strong stands have been taken by provincial premiers on the Party Québécois proposal for sovereignty with association. In speeches to the Canadian Club of Toronto in January and the Canadian Club of Montreal in April, and at his subsequent interview with *Le Devoir*, Premier Allan Blakeney of Saskatchewan gave a fair representation of the reactions of western Canadians. He believes that the answer to the current problem is a more flexible federalism which would not redistribute major economic powers needed to defend the country, but would give the provinces more powers to meet their own cultural, social, and economic aspirations. In particular, he believes there are areas in which the country can move towards greater decentralization, such as communications, culture, and immigration, and that in some areas there could be special arrangements between individual provinces and the federal government. He would expect to see greater representation of the provincial governments in certain central institutions such as the Senate and the Supreme Court. However, Premier Blakeney bluntly stated that association after independence was not of interest to western Canadians. The western provinces, he said, were dependent on the stability of the eastern manufacturing economy to stabilize the ups and downs in the western resource-based economy. For this reason, they were willing to pay higher prices for products from the east that are protected by a tariff. But, should Quebec separate and no longer provide its manufacturing economy, the West would no longer see any reason for a common system of tariffs or other aspects of a common market.

A similarly strong position has been taken by Premier Bill Davis of Ontario who said in a speech to the Empire Club of Toronto that "it would be absolutely foolhardy for the government of Quebec to believe that it would have both independence and economic associations with the rest of Canada." Davis suggested that if the Quebec government was responsible for the termination and closing off of options, they would be very naive to believe that the same spirit of understanding and cooperation would continue after political independence.

This then is the situation as it now stands. There has been little advance in constitutional thinking since the Quebec election. The provinces are calling for a shift in some jurisdictions to the provinces, more concurrent fields of jurisdiction, a disentanglement of administrative arrangements between the two levels of government, and a greater participation of the provinces in central institutions. Neither the western provinces nor Ontario are willing to contemplate a common market with a politically sovereign Quebec. Leaders of the Atlantic provinces have simply exclaimed that a possible Quebec separation would be a traumatizing experience with disastrous consequences. Clearly, there is a vast gap between the current Quebec government and the government in Ottawa and those in the other provinces. While Quebec has been talking in terms of sovereignty-association since the November election, all the other political leaders have been talking not only of their dedication to a Canada of which Quebec is a willing partner but of their determination to maintain a reasonably strong central government. There have been a good many proposals for constitutional reform on the table for a number of years. However, in comparison with either the demands of previous Quebec governments or the current proposals of the Parti Québécois, the reform proposals may be qualified as incremental innovations to a generally status quo situation. None of the propositions of the federal government or the provinces comes anywhere near satisfying the desires of any of the governments that have held power in Quebec during the last decade or more.

Is there room for reconciliation? This will depend on a balance between diverse circumstances. It seems clear that if the Parti Québécois leaders maintain their prime political objective, there is no possibility of compromise with the current leaders of the federal government and the English-speaking provinces. However even with the Parti Québécois in power there are a number of possibilities. It is possible that the leadership is mainly intent on maximizing its potential for negotiating the strongest possible position for Quebec, even though PQ cabinet members have denied such an intention. In the longer term, economic conditions in Quebec, constantly negative reactions from the other Canadian provinces, and a "no" vote in a referendum on independence could all persuade the Parti Québécois leadership that the politically wise solution is to negotiate for maximum autonomy and equality within Canada.

These possibilities aside, the only other path is an approach to the Quebec people above the head of its government and the provision of support to the federalist opposition parties in Quebec and the various voluntary associations which are supporting the federalist option. However, if the history of the last ten years tells us anything, it tells us that René Lévesque's image of the French-Canadian nation and its role in federalism is strongly held by elites in all sections of Quebec population. In addition, all the Quebec governments of this period have demanded autonomy, equality for the French language, and guarantees for both. No effective appeal to the Quebec people and its federally oriented parties is likely to succeed without a dramatic demonstration on the part of the other provinces and the federal government that significant changes can be made to the Canadian federation which will go far beyond proposals for maintenance of the status quo or merely incrementalist reforms. Since the Quebec election we have heard many calls for unity, and many professions of sympathy and understanding for the Quebec position. We have not as yet heard of dramatic proposals for change, the creative ideas for new institutions which can assure both provincial autonomy and cultural equality. In other words, we do not have in hand either the political forces or the ideas which can win the referendum for the Canadian option. The current crisis in the Canadian political system may produce such ideas. It may also produce something much worse.

What Alternatives Do We Have If Any?

EDWIN R. BLACK

Don't rock the boat and don't upset the applecart are just two of the many sayings illustrating how unpopular change often is. Most of the resentment behind the English Canadians' reaction to the rise of separatism stems from opposition to too much change in our lives. Even out-and-out reformers begin acting rather conservatively when René Lévesque threatens to alter the whole basic economic and political makeup of the country. Debates about what is involved are both confused and confusing. This is mainly because we discuss basic changes not in terms of the practicalities such as which government should do what and why but in terms of symbols. We use ideas like "two nations," "balkanization," and "special status" without ever agreeing on precisely what we are talking about. Many of us, for example, were brought up to believe that "fairness" meant exactly the same treatment for everyone regardless of their different needs or situations and we thought that "Canada" necessarily meant a country that stretched "from sea to sea" without interruption. Both symbols saved us from worrying much just what it was we meant by justice or what it was we wanted by way of a country. Now that we are trying to sort out these ideas, some of our symbols are getting in the way.

It seems clear that we must accept some significant reorganization of our constitution if we want to keep Quebec within Confederation. What are our alternatives? At first blush, the answer seems fairly easy: change the constitution, change the way in which we divide up the powers of government between Ottawa and the provinces in some way that keeps everybody more or less happy. Three objectives have to be met in this exercise. First, we need the minimum rearrangement which will satisfy the majority of those Quebecers who really want to stay in Confederation if at all possible. (This means ignoring the wishes of the confirmed separatists altogether.) Next, we need to maintain a government at Ottawa that is strong enough to get on with the job of national development, and, finally, we need a system which will help settle the disputes between the West and central Canada as well as keep the Atlantic provinces satisfied. As soon as we spell out all this, though, and as we realize how little time we have left for the job, the task begins to grow almost unmanageable. The legal part of the problem is probably the easiest. Rearranging governmental powers and sharing out the different taxes has already been worked out on paper many times in this country. The difficult part has to do with the way these new proposals are dressed up, and what will be the labels and symbols that will be attached to them by the supporters and opponents of change. It also has to do with who will sell these new ideas to the Canadian people, and whether we have a majority of English-speakers as well as a majority of French-speakers who will buy the same vision of a new or slightly revised Canada.

Constitutional rearrangements sometimes involve redrawing boundaries, they often require reorganizing the central political institutions like Parliament, and they certainly mean changes in the powers exercised by different types of government. Although there are many theoretical possibilities the range of practical alternatives is much smaller. In talking about constitutional alternatives, however, we must remember that by themselves they cannot be expected to satisfy complaints rooted in economic disparities, regional jealousies, cultural differences, and so on. To be workable, our alternatives must reflect social realities. Those realities, however, are themselves in the process of change—both in Quebec and elsewhere in Canada. That makes the problem doubly difficult. The solutions we debate come out of what we now think we know about the social changes that have just taken place. But we need more. We need constitutional "solutions" that will also let us deal with the new changes taking place today and tomorrow.

What do we expect from constitutional change? Much of the argument over the various proposals for such changes comes because people make assumptions about what is involved. Some will argue that constitutional change is merely tinkering, and does not mean very much. At another extreme are those who expect changing the constitution will mean Canadians will start changing their attitudes and behaviour. It would be unwise to expect that any constitutional redrafting exercise is going to end all our difficulties. That is impossible. We would never arrive at any decisions and the country would soon break up if we paid attention to those who refuse to approve any constitutional changes unless they incorporate solutions to all our problems.

Those attitudes prevailed too often in the past and were responsible for most of our constitutional logjams up to now. The most we should ask from constitutional change is a generally acceptable framework for decision-making within which we can grapple more effectively with the disputes among the major language groups and those among the different parts of Canadian society.

The best-known constitutional alternatives can probably be disposed of fairly quickly. However good they might be at heart they are so passionately disputed that they are impractical and unrealizable. The first and least likely alternative is greater centralization. By that, people mean trying to increase Canadian unity by giving the Ottawa government the "final say" over everything that is done in this country. Under a centralized system, provincial governments would no longer have legal ground for not doing what Ottawa wished with respect to schools, taxes, labour relations, language of work, rights for separate schools, petroleum prices, expropriation of industries, and so on. All those abilities to pass laws, impose taxes, and tell people what to do that the provinces now possess exclusively, or which they now share in some way, would be put in Ottawa's hands. If provincial governments remained, they would be stripped of all effective independence and turned into administrative arms of the central government. Greater centralization of this sort is popular with some English-speaking Canadian nationalists and especially with those who resent granting special status to any kind of minority whether based on language, culture, or region. Canada would gain the appearance of greater political unity and provincial premiers would stop competing with federal politicians to win the voters' approval. Other people like the centralization idea because Canada would have a government much more able to deal with foreign economic or cultural threats, and because it would be easier to move Canada toward a more egalitarian society and possibly toward a more class-based politics. The idea has particular attraction for those yearning for government that is easier to understand. A constitutional system in which political power was much more centralized than it is today would certainly deny any future possibility of ready access to power by minorities based on language, culture, a single economic interest, or odd notions of banking and money supply like those of the Social Crediters.

A unitary government, or even a much more highly centralized one, is not feasible today. The absence of any major group pushing for unitary government together with the absolute certainty of uncompromising opposition from a host of important power groups in our society make it useless to pursue the idea much farther. Certainly, if centralization were to be successful, it would put an end to any prospect of a peaceful Quebec secession. But it would not be successful, and even an attempt by an important English-speaking group would make the secession of Quebec much more likely. Greater centralization might also inspire some western provinces to try going it alone.

A second theoretical alternative also calls for a great centralization of power but at two capitals rather than one. Best known as the "deux nations" approach, its modern version first came up in an intellectually respectable form twenty years ago in the report of the Tremblay royal commission in Quebec. During the late Sixties, sponsors as different as the Union Nationale party of Quebec and liberally-minded English-speaking professors floated different versions of the two nations idea. Most of them promptly sank from sight. The approach depends on one crucial assumption: the overwhelming importance for political purposes of a Canadian's membership in one or the other of the official language groups. The assumption comes easily to those who think language is the most important determining factor of culture. Those of us who do not hold to that assumption and reject the idea include many English-speakers of diverse ethnic origins and varied economic interests. If the point is conceded, however, the two nations idea enjoys a certain logic as a means of reorganizing political power within Canada. Under it, all French-speakers, who are said either to live in Quebec or identify with it, would be citizens of the French-Canadian nation whose government would have all powers relevant to its present and future health concentrated in Quebec City. Similarly, English-speakers would give all important political powers to their single "national" government in Ottawa. Representatives of the two "nations" would bargain with each other and decide on a basis of perfect equality whatever matters they wished to conduct jointly like a customs union or monetary system.

Although the two nations alternative to the status quo comes in different versions, they share one thing in common: the outright hostility of politicians as diverse as John Diefenbaker, Pierre Elliott Trudeau, René Lévesque, and most English-speaking provincial premiers. A thorough criticism of the notion is easy to make but it is unnecessary. The voters may not have known what it was they were doing in 1968, but almost every commentator says that Canadians decisively voted against anything like the two nations theory at the 1968 general election. For English-speakers, the concept marries the worst aspects of Quebec independence to a tightening of Ottawa's control over the western and Atlantic provinces. The 1968 campaign has discredited the symbolism of "two nations" for a long time.

Giving Quebec a status that was constitutionally different from that of the other provinces first became popular in some Quebec circles during the early 1960s. Such "special status" proposals meant that the federal government would withdraw not only from all conditional grant programs but from all activities whatever they were in the health and social welfare fields. Quebec would get and enjoy exclusive legal authority in these areas as well as enough money and taxation compensation from Ottawa to pay for equivalent activities at the provincial level. Quebec's right to make international treaties within its own areas of authority was to be recognized and her government was to receive extensive rights to consultation and some influence in federal economic policies such as tax levels, international trade, tariffs, and the supply of credit. This particular "special status" school of argument had nothing to say about the other provinces. Presumably they were to remain equal in status to each other but inferior to Quebec. Neither was anything said about possible changes in the influence of Quebec's MPs in the federal cabinet and House of Commons. Effectively, this would have meant that Quebecers would have two channels of influence over federal government policies while citizens of other provinces would be limited to one, their federal members of Parliament.

A federal offer that was made to all provinces during the Sixties but accepted only by Quebec has since resulted in what is in fact a special status for that province. There can be no doubt now that the relationship between Quebec residents and the federal government is quite different from that existing between Ottawa and citizens elsewhere. Twenty-nine joint Ottawa-Quebec programs were terminated after one agreement and the federal government has been steadily reducing its involvement in further health and welfare fields. Quebec's new "special status" is one recognized in the working constitution rather than in the formal British North America Act. The more general recognition of that special status which exists today might make possible a larger-scale reorganization along such lines than was once considered possible but that possibility depends on finding an acceptable name or "symbol" for a new system which acknowledges that every province needs and demands special treatment.

Eliminating the power of one of two squabbling parties is a simple means of ending the intergovernmental rivalry and discord which characterize Canadian politics. One of the logical alternatives—the unification of our politics through centralization of all authority in

Ottawa—we have already examined and rejected because it is politically unacceptable in British Columbia and Alberta as much as it is in Quebec. Why not try another route: if not the elimination, then at least the considerable reduction of the central government's law-making powers by giving many of them to the provincial governments? That might also cut out most of the regions' complaints about the way the country was run—with a few important exceptions. While all the provinces have complained at some time or other about Ottawa's uses and abuses of power, the provinces individually have a different interest and a different stake in the various federal powers. Not everybody would be happy to see their sister provinces wielding the same powers Ottawa now does. Ontario, for example, wants a large, tariff-protected market for its manufactured goods. Many of its present customers, however, would prefer to buy on the same free world market on which they depend to sell their own goods. The wealthy provinces would like to eliminate all federal taxation within their borders, but the poorer provinces depend on that same federal taxation to get the transfer payments and subsidies which support their educational and welfare systems. There are many other similar conflicts of interest between the provinces.

Although the "compact theory" does exist in our history, it is only marginally relevant, and we really do not have any carefully worked out Canadian blueprints suggesting the shape and possible workings of a fully decentralized system of government. Some clues can be found, however, in international organizations and in the history of other countries. Curiously, the most accurate name we can find for a loosely organized set of independent or nearly independent states is one which we already apply—mistakenly—to the Canadian union: confederation. That word, when used analytically by a political scientist, does give strong though superficial support to those who argue that in Canada the provinces really should have the final say in all matters, with the central government only carrying out those chores assigned to it by agreement of the provinces. Such was the nature of the American organization which followed the Declaration of Independence. (Part of George Washington's famous troubles over supplies to fight the British resulted from the inability of the central institution—the Continental Congress—to raise troops and money except through the independent state governments.) In a "pure" confederation, only a few, limited powers are assigned to the central government, such as defence and a common currency, with the sovereign provinces left largely to govern themselves as they see fit. Whether the central government in such a system would always have to perform its duties through the provincial governments without any direct contact with the citizens (as in international alliances like the North Atlantic Treaty Organization), or whether it might deal directly with the citizens in a few, limited areas, has not been much explored by advocates of greater decentralization in Canada. (Most commentators seem to imply simply "more power" for the provinces without denuding Ottawa and without spelling out how it could be done.) We can only imagine what powers would be left to the central government in a "pure" Canadian confederacy: defence, currency, and a common tariff seem to be the minimal requirements. Even here, the history of fighting over the tariff between the "inner" and the "outer" parts of Canada challenges such a presumption fundamentally. A highly decentralized arrangement should satisfy all but the most separatist residents of Quebec and most of the residents of the wealthy provinces. Nearly all the important things that governments do would be decided by politicians who were close at hand, easy to influence, and no longer troubled by the need to make "national" compromises. The façade of a united Canada would remain so there might be no serious challenge to treasured symbols. But it would please neither the citizens of the poor provinces nor those who feel we should be trying to make the lifestyles of all Canadians more equal rather than less, or who seek national standards and a "national" attack on problems. Theoretically, it must be admitted, Ottawa could be left with enough taxing powers to allow continuance of the existing money transfers to the poor provinces, but in political practice it could not survive.

Those who worry now about the weakness of the Canadian identity would have even greater concerns under a highly decentralized system. If Ottawa were not left responsible for at least some functions which most Canadians valued highly we would end up with a political system which was even more fragile than the one we have now. A central government whose "beneficial" activities were few or nearly invisible to most voters could do very little toward increasing Canadians' slender sense of community. Turning Ottawa into little more than a taxing and redistribution agency would create a government that would always be hardpressed for popular support and whose future would always be in doubt. The route of extreme decentralization, taking virtually all power away from Ottawa, is not a fruitful alternative.

Trying to make the present constitution work better is yet another alternative. Some would argue, of course, that that has already been tried and has failed. But only one or two roads in that direction have been tried, and others should be explored. If we are to try making it work better, we need some agreement on what the "present constitution" means. In practice the ten provinces do enjoy a large measure of political independence; they can and do bargain with others from positions of considerable strength; and their governments exercise complete policy discretion in many of the most important areas of state activity. So does the central government, although its independent powers are different from those of the provinces. Most remarkable about the status quo or the "working constitution" is the thorough intermixing of the fields in which both provincial and federal governments are active. Some of the most notable areas of overlap include the taxation of both individuals and corporations, the regulation of some business profits and employee incomes, marketing controls over agricultural products, transportation policies, planning natural resource development, health and social security, stimulating the economies of depressed areas, and so on.

Many of the federal government's activities add up to a form of constitutional trespass on the provinces' rights. Although those activities are not spelled out in the British North America Act, the central government does have extraordinarily wide powers to spend money and collect taxes. The use of these and other powers in the B.N.A. Act has allowed Ottawa to buy and bully its way into almost any area in which it wanted to do something. It has been the exercise of these powers and a growing refusal by provincial politicians to be bullied or "bought off" in some areas that has contributed so much to the recent worsening of federal-provincial relations. Other disputes arose because in some sectors both federal and provincial governments were legally entitled to take action (or thought they were) and they wanted to implement conflicting policies. Controls over natural resource companies in petroleum, potash, and other mineral areas, for example, were the subject of federal-provincial quarrels over which policies would be best for province and country.

The constitutional status quo clearly means that our governments will continue to be entangled in each other's activities. Much "reform" talk involves earnest but futile attempts to restructure things to reduce or prevent such entanglements. Futility arises because the more active governments become, the more entangled they get, not only in the citizen's affairs but in those of other governments as well. As it is hard to predict what governments will even be doing five years from now, so it is even harder to provide for the effective separation or nonentanglement of their often conflicting activities in the future.

So far we have dealt with the substance of the constitutional status quo. Few citizens, however, understand the details of this complex web of activities, and most substitute for such knowledge the convenient shorthand of representative symbols—not all of which are closely related to the "facts". Thus, for some, the present constitution must not be changed because it represents the battle-proven superiority of their "racial" group over another, while for some others the constitutional status quo is intolerable because it represents their humiliation and exploitation by another group. Still other population groups have comparable emotional stakes in the different symbolic contents which they attribute to the constitutional status quo.

Effective changes in the structure of government activities can readily be brought about without the elaborate rebuilding of constitutional castles in the sky. As it has been interpreted by the courts, the formal constitution provides us with great flexibility to arrange which governments will do what. Over the past forty years, Canada has undergone three very significant shifts in the jurisdictional emphasis of our working constitution. We have moved from relatively inactive, decentralized government during the Twenties and Thirties, to highly unified wartime and postwar regimes, and lately to highly-involved, interactive, and aggressive governments at all levels. The most significant factors in bringing about these changes were shifts in public and politicians' attitudes. The most important means were agreements between governments and the vigorous exercise of the central government's powers to spend and tax virtually without restraint. Very few amendments of the formal constitution were required and quite possibly none at all was really essential to the process.

It would not be nearly as easy to change the way Canadians cling to their different and ambiguous constitutional images. The Parti Québécois government has proposed what amounts to a divorce from the rest of Canada followed by a new common-law relationship negotiated between equals. For most English-speaking Canadians, the key to minimum acceptability was that there be no formal divorce, and they argued that formal divorce would "obviously" incur high costs and that both parties would end up worse off. At times the dilemma appeared to be that Canadians outside the province were willing to give Quebecers whatever powers of self-government they wanted—so long as the resulting political status was not called sovereign independence.

Many French-speaking Quebecers on the other hand were willing to accept close ties, especially in the economy, so long as that was not called federalism. The symbols blocked the road to meaningful political agreement.

The cry for more glamorous and exciting leadership is a common response to this and other political problems. Too many Canadians consider public policy alternatives in terms of individual leaders, and look increasingly for a shining knight on a white charger to rescue them from their perils. Learning little or nothing from the subsequent failures of the shining knights who won the campaigns of 1958 and 1968, our commentators once again have been seeking a champion for the campaign of 1978. In vain did Prime Minister Trudeau object after the Parti Québécois victory that the national unity issue should not be viewed as some kind of cowboy shootout at the OK Corral involving only him and the separatist Quebec premier, René Lévesque; it was a problem to be worked on at all levels of political leadership, Trudeau said. As each TV generation has come to political semi-awareness in Canada, the hero emphasis of our mass media politics has been reinforced. Television excels in restructuring our perceptions to the point that we see the entire world through the entertainment concepts of stars and personalities, a development which has been television's particular, powerful, and quite irrational contribution to political life today. No wonder, then, that even the task confronting the sought-for saviour of Confederation is not at all clear. Should he deal harshly with all Quebec malcontents, putting the separatists firmly in their place (jail, perhaps?), and making sure that economic and (English-speaking) common sense prevail? Or do we want a Confederation crusader able to create and sell a new image of Canada to people of all persuasions, without much regard for the real shape or effectiveness of the decision-making structure which results? From a cynical point of view, the saviour some Canadians want looks like a new Sir John A. Macdonald who can talk out of both sides of his mouth at once—in both languages.

The tendency to demand political champions instead of political leaders is particularly strong in Canada. That we can blame on the concentration of mass media power in a very few institutions in three or four cities. The burden of public expectation placed on the premiers and prime ministers is extraordinary and the development of alternative and supplementary leadership is seriously inhibited by the denial of public attention to opposition parties at all levels and to spokesmen of many other social organizations.

Change in federal policies represents another as yet unexplored alternative to passive acceptance of the inevitability of Quebec secession. What steps might the governments at Ottawa and in the provincial capitals take which would persuade the majority of Quebec voters that Confederation still offered better prospects than separation? Here as in other places we must beware of playing into the hands of separatist leaders. Any easily-won increase in transfer payments or too-ready concession of the Quebec government's jurisdictional demands would be exploited by separatists as proof that Quebec has been defrauded by the federal relationship in the past and that even better things could be expected from independence together with a negotiated association. Such a situation would add further to our troubles by infuriating other provincial populations already unhappy with federal policies. On the other hand, the outright refusal of clearly justified requests runs the risk of separatists arguing successfully that Ottawa's inflexibility demonstrates the absolute hopelessness of staying in Confederation. The only course with the hope of some success is a hard one. It requires the central government to deal with all provincial governments far more sensibly than it did during the late Sixties and to execute its own range of responsibilities much more successfully than it has been doing recently. This it must do in ways which are highly visible and in areas seen to be very important by Canadians everywhere. Bilingualism, for instance, must be moved from its position as the cornerstone of Ottawa's national unity policy. Essential as it was, and still is, its flawed implementation has caused far more disunity than unity in the country. Then again, direct reimbursements to individuals in respect of expenses for medical care, hospitalization, and post-secondary education would build far more support for Confederation than the most generous of the complicated tax point and subsidy transfer plans on which Ottawa has relied so heavily.

Ironically, and dangerously, politicians in provincial cabinets and in local councils and school boards are in positions in which they can contribute little positively to the situation but could provide a good deal of ammunition to Quebec separatists. Most significant is the provision or deliberate nonprovision of services in French wherever there are substantial French-speaking populations. Such services and, most importantly, the attitudes underlying them are essential if meaning is to be given to the counter-separatist claim that all of Canada and not merely one province is the legitimate homeland of Quebecers.

Much of the country's business is carried out through the mechanisms of intergovernmental relations. The changes taking place in this field demand attention if only because many of the proposed solutions to the national unity crisis will be tested there during the many negotiations that take place annually. At one time, most arrangments between governments were settled by specialists from the different federal and provincial bureaucracies. As the provincial governments became stronger and better coordinated, and as the problems began changing from the technical to the more value-oriented, the federal-provincial discussions have become highly politicized. The foundations for most basic social services having been laid in the provinces, their governments tend to diverge more and more in terms of their priorities; they have fewer shared policy objectives. The "quiet diplomacy" of the specialists sharing similar professional values is necessarily being replaced by the meetings of heads of government who alone can settle the thorny political disputes. Unfortunately, the various heads of governments perceive the problems differently. They disagree on the diagnoses of problems, and so they disagree on the appropriate prescriptions or solutions. The stakes in these negotiations now include sizable chunks of almost every government's political program: mineral development and taxation, petroleum product flow and price control, revenue sharing, communications regulation, and so on. On every issue, the province of Quebec comes into conflict with the government of Canada—as do the governments of the other provinces as well. One predictable result is increased mass media attention to these meetings together with the hardening of public stances and more negotiation in private. While it has been our intergovernmental negotiating mechanisms which has made our federalism work, this accomplishment has been at the considerable cost of much reduced public accountability. The operation of cabinet governments in this country gives the cause of democracy a difficult enough time as it is. Premiers and prime ministers are forever holding important negotiating conferences in secret because they see the political costs of making concessions in public as much too high. They return to their capitals with veritable "treaties" wrapped up and there is no way they can allow them to be meddled with even by their own cabinets. The chances of government caucuses, legislative assemblies as a whole, or the public in general having any influence over particular agreements of this sort are close to zero. The stakes of these intergovernmental conferences are becoming more important all the time, not less, and soon they may be thought to include the very future of Canada as a state. The preoccupation with national unity will have the effect, even more than in the past, of diverting the attention of both citizens and governments from the important economic and social problems that remain with us and which, if continually subordinated to constitutional questions, will pose equally serious threats to our social fabric.

Could we improve the situation by changing the structure of government at Ottawa? Some would argue yes, it needs to be made more "democratic." By that they mean our government needs to be more responsive to the different values and demands of the East and the West, of the city and the farm, and so on. Certainly some blame for our present troubles does attach to the way in which we have organized our system of Parliament, the courts, and the bureaucracy. Most obvious is the misrepresentation or nonrepresentation of different sectors of the country within the House of Commons. For those distortions and others we can blame our election and party systems. It seems ludicrous that ten of the most important politicians—the provincial premiers—should have no say at all in decisions made at Ottawa. To deal with that and other problems, the Senate could be reorganized in a number of ways to make it more representative of the provinces than it now is. The governments of other federal states have more regionalized Senates and so could we, if it were not for the dependence of every Canadian cabinet on its strength in the House of Commons. What is needed is not a reasonable plan for Senate reform or for incorporating federal-provincial conferences into the Ottawa government, but a strong will on the part of federal politicians to bring it about. That has been missing since Confederation.

Bureaucratic reform is, perhaps, more important and more difficult. For more than a decade federal cabinets have been trying to change the bureaucracy to make it more representative of both language groups; the purpose has also been to make it better able to respond to citizens of either language group. The cost has been very high and the degree of success low. From time to time, demands have been made that other groups must also have more representation in the bureaucracy; Indians are needed in the Department of Indian and Northern Affairs, labour people in Manpower divisions, and small businessmen in Trade and Commerce. While these claims might be met (and are to some extent), it is much harder to build in and maintain the representation of regional feelings. Almost the entire bureaucracy is organized along the professional lines of specialists and practitioners of the various types of government activities: medicine, economics, engineering, defence, transport, etc. The policies of the federal government arise in or are given substantial shape by these galaxies of experts and few of them have much time or patience for the sensitivities and particular problems of the outlying regions. It is only during the last stages of policy-making when the politicians get fully involved that these concerns receive much consideration. By then, it is usually too late: the politicians' amateurish presentations can seldom stand up to the overwhelming expertise of the professionalized bureaucracy.

While the attention given to structural reforms has varied widely, from a great deal for the Senate proposals to none at all for the bureaucratic question last raised, two more important questions arise. Would such changes make any real difference and is there really enough time to implement these or any other reforms? We might well press for structural reform because of the changes we hope they might eventually bring about, but we can have little faith that the East-West and Ottawa-Quebec tensions would be substantially eased by the mere fact of altering the structures of our central government. Like bilingualism and other policy innovations, formal structural changes are expensive to come by in political terms and, then, often too late in the coming. It takes time to change the working behaviour of those who govern us and even longer for that changed behaviour to persuade Canadians everywhere that Ottawa does govern in the interest of everybody regardless of language or region.

The difficulties facing those seeking viable alternatives to Quebec's secession are formidable. The least of them is constructing workable rearrangements of the constitutional division of powers between Ottawa and the provinces. That is readily done. The most promising of such schemes add up to abandoning the effort to impose uniform solutions all across the country, and treating the provinces differently from each other in some rough harmony with their varying needs and wishes. Our central government already does this with respect to the Canada Assistance Plan (providing for quite different sets of federal-provincial welfare arrangements), and so too with family allowances, regional economic development programs, agricultural activities, and even some types of taxation. The newly promulgated communications policy appears to be a further step in this direction. The result of these and other provisions is that every province is already treated somewhat differently from the others. How far this can be carried safely depends not on some theoretical constitutional calculus but on the efficiency and visibility with which Ottawa carries out its own support-building programs among the citizenry as a whole. An extension of such special relationships can probably be devised to suit at least nine of the ten provincial governments. Despite the range of their dissatisfaction with various central government policies, few governments other than that of Quebec have pressed for constitutional changes in the allocation of jurisdictions. At most, they have wanted federal leaders who were more sensitive to differences in their situations and more disposed to consult and to inform before acting unilaterally in areas of great importance to them.

Even if a special status relationship could be developed which would please those provinces with largely English-speaking populations, could any of these alternatives possibly satisfy Quebec? The simple answer is no—not if by Quebec we mean a government determined to achieve sovereign independence. The majority of Quebecers, however—even the majority of French-speaking Quebecers—could well be satisfied with a set of changes drawn from the more moderate alternatives suggested here. Those changes would necessarily include a high degree of "cultural sovereignty" for the province: final authority over matters such as language use (which might further imperil Ottawa's already weakened national bilingualism policy), over broadcast and cable communications, and, of course, education. So long as the *institution* of separate schools is not touched, the province seems constitutionally free (as was Ontario half a century ago) to prescribe whatever language of educational instruction it wishes. Apart from financial involvement, the central government has already virtually withdrawn from the social welfare field in Quebec. Greater symbolic independence can probably be provided in other areas, especially those of divided jurisdiction like immigration, labour, and agriculture—provided freedom of movement of all Canadian citizens is assured and that agreement could be reached on protection of fundamental individual liberties, on revisions to the Supreme Court of Canada Act, and on removal of the federal powers of disallowance and reservation. Most of these latter changes could be accommodated even within the fairly rigid form of federalism which Mr. Trudeau was advocating during the late Sixties and early Seventies.

The economic powers of government provide the biggest stumbling block. Many Quebecers, not all of them separatists by any means, are persuaded beyond any rational demonstration otherwise that they have suffered economically from their association in the Canadian union. They believe their province to be equally as well favoured by nature as was Ontario and they believe their people to be as capable, intelligent and hard-working as those of Ontario. When they compare their unemployment rates, standards of living, manufacturing industries, agricultural sectors, depressed areas, income and municipal tax rates, and the burden of public debts like that for the Olympics to the situation in Ontario, they are convinced they have been cheated. It does not matter that people in other provinces make the same and even worse comparisons; the relevant comparison is taken to be Ontario. The economically discontented of Quebec are many and they blame their lot on the English-speaking who they believe have used their control over the central government to exploit Quebec and the French-speaking for Ontario's special benefit. The provincial attempts to redress the balance somewhat through regulation of business enterprises have proved inadequate in the eyes of many Quebecers. To set these matters right, it is argued that Quebec requires control over all the great economic levers to government: tax rates, credit and the money supply, the treatment of foreign investment, and the ability to manipulate the total economy.

Here is the major sticking point for even the most flexible of federalists. Some important influences over the economy are essential if any central government is to perform effectively. Without some such control, Ottawa would be trying to navigate the ship of state with unpredictable engine power and a broken rudder. It could not possibly work. If a majority of French-speaking Quebecers believe that their province must have full economic sovereignty if they are to receive economic justice, then no number of constitutional proposals for special status and no number of charismatic leaders selling shiny new political symbols can possibly provide workable arrangements for Quebec within Confederation. That "economic justice" might not be so easily attained outside of Confederation either. In any form of economic association which might follow her withdrawal from Canada, Quebec would still have concerns about credit, money supply, tariffs, and tax arrangements. These matters would still have to be negotiated with a larger, more powerful group of English-speakers who would be more foreign than ever. That point, unfortunately, is likely to be neglected in the debates ahead.

Whatever its attractions, our constitutional status quo is bound to be disrupted. How significantly and how soon are major questions. The new Quebec regime does not have completely clear sailing. Despite the "no win" situation in which many believe it has the Canadian government, the Parti Québécois has still to demonstrate its political and administrative competence and until it shows what it can do with the economic powers it now has, the possibility exists that shrewd Quebecers will resist the oratory and withhold any approval for separatist adventuring on unknown economic seas. Meanwhile, those who would save Confederation face the herculean task of finding and selling options which offer at least minimum satisfaction to both the majority of Quebecers and the majority of Canadians outside Quebec. For its part, the central government must do more than simply improve its economic management. It must be more flexible in dealing with the provinces, more willing to discuss constitutional change in symbolic and substantive terms, and more adept at building political support for federalism all across the country. Its record so far is not encouraging.

Liberté, Egalité, Efficacité:
Respecifying the Federal Role

WILLIAM P. IRVINE

Two questions always arise in political discussions between French and English-speaking Canadians: What does Quebec want? What does English Canada want? These are fair questions, and the answers are confused. Some common ground may be found, however, if we examine the interplay of four fundamental political forces central to the well-being of both language groups. These are *liberté*, *égalité*, and *efficacité*, along with the growing thrust toward regional or provincial society-building. Together these concepts point the way toward a respecification of the roles of the federal and provincial governments.

The problem of society-building is what chiefly differentiates Quebec politics from that of the rest of Canada. The metaphor an English-speaking Canadian most often uses to describe his society to a foreigner is that of the mosaic. There is no single Canadian identity, no conception of an "un-Canadian activity," except the absence of patriotism towards national Canadian institutions. The cultural mosaic is a very liberal conception. It implies that a Canadian should have access to all the cultural products he can afford to consume, either by himself or in cooperation with others to form a market. Only recently, hesitantly, and in the face of evident opposition in some quarters, has the Canadian state directly challenged the operation of the cultural market by proscribing access to some cultural products and by underwriting the costs of others. For the French-speaking Quebecer the freedom to colour one's particular chink of the mosaic is meaningless unless it admits the possibility of mobilizing both legal and economic power to build institutions that will promote and reflect his unique culture. The market is a threatening force, and many Quebecers believe the only reliable instrument by which to challenge it is the state of Quebec. Quebec is not alone in using its institutions to reflect and promote local cultural values. Monarchical symbols are much more in evidence in some provinces than others. New Brunswick and Ontario may be evolving a set of truly bilingual institutions. Many provinces may insist on unicultural institutions and this, too, should be their right.

All Canadians have a long tradition of using their governments to challenge markets and it is not here that the basic conflict arises. Alberta is currently attempting to build an economy that will sustain itself after its oil and gas has disappeared. Saskatchewan has taken many innovative steps towards building a "commonwealth" for its residents. Many provinces feel that their economic priorities, if not their total economic future, have been ignored by the central government. Quebec has not been alone in arguing for a greater decentralization of power—away from Ottawa, towards the provincial capitals. Canada is increasingly a collection of regionally based societies of which Quebec is simply the most advanced in that respect. Any successful political rearrangement of Canada will have to reflect this fact. Indeed, we can posit that a new constitution, if it can be negotiated at all, will concede to all the provinces the preponderant power to shape its particular culture and to regulate most institutions within its territory. In terms of new powers for the provinces, this means, specifically, control over communications media of all sorts and more access to the primary levers of economic development. Some of these would be turned over to the provinces, others would have to be shared with them to a much more significant extent than at present.

While the existence of this trend to the accumulation of society-building powers at the provincial level cannot be denied, neither can we deny the persistence of powerful forces, both within and outside Quebec, which want a strong national community. These forces are partly rooted in the loyalty of English-speaking Canadians to a society extending from "sea to sea" and partly in forces which seek a continent-wide economy on which to base their capacity to function in the world economy. Here lies the interest in *efficacité*.

In building an economic base, provincial governments want more control than they have at present over the housing market, over industrial location and investment strategy, and over the major social programs which shape and reflect cultural values, and which constitute the major determinants of the size of the government budget. With respect to economic powers, it seems undeniable that in their own interests the provinces would have to support a central authority capable of preventing a ruinous competition of policies which might leave all provinces worse off. Ten different currencies managed by ten different authorities would all be lower in value, or more volatile in value, or both, than a single currency. The central authority would also have to be able to make sure that all provinces bore their fair share of goods provided in common, such as in the area of defence. In order to prevent beggar-my-neighbour policies, the central authority would need to have the capacity to coerce individual provinces and would therefore have to be a central government, not the secretariat of an interprovincial conference.

What powers might the federal government claim in the interests of *efficacité*? Virtually all, including the Parti Québécois, recognize that there would be a common interest in a Canada-wide monetary policy and the maintenance of an internal and external market. Defence and foreign policy would be primarily federal concerns, though the provinces would retain the external representation that they now have. Many common services—such as postal delivery, air and train services—could continue to be provided mainly by the federal government. The promotion of basic research, and the testing of products for safety and wholesomeness, could remain under federal control even while decisions on the use of the results of this research could be left to the provinces. There is no reason why provinces could not be responsible for dispensing such controversial substances as Laetrile or saccharine, though they might seek to accommodate each other by restricting purchases of such substances to residents of their own province. The federal government would have to retain predominant control over foreign investment. Because the exercise of these federal powers would affect not only the national community but also the strategies of province-building, much more effective processes of consultation would have to be developed. For example, a much greater provincial voice is needed in transportation.

While efficiency requires that the rules of the economic game be Canada-wide, it is probably not necessary that control of the actual spending of money for public purposes be retained in Ottawa. In industrial location policy, for example, the federal government could develop rules of allocation and convey the money directly to provincial agencies dealing with the problem. Analogous solutions in the area of housing could be sought. With respect of manpower training, both the federal and provincial governments ought to retain the right to subsidize training in various skills. Provincial expenditures would presumably focus on those skills needed within the province. Federal training programs would be offered primarily in areas of labour surplus or where needed skills were in short supply.

Part of what it means to be a Canadian is to have access to a certain minimum standard of living, whatever one's age, family size, health or employment status, and to have access to certain government services without having to bear a tax burden excessively greater than that of similarly placed Canadians resident elsewhere. These are the components of *égalité* which will have to be retained in a new constitution if the notion of a national community is to have any meaning. Through its government-to-government equalization of tax revenue, Ottawa already plays a substantial redistributive role while leaving the provinces control over the shape and substance of policy.

The federal government has also made direct payments to individuals, but these would be given up. This would place a burden on provinces with high unemployment rates. A province with 10 per cent unemployed would have to tax its remaining workers and employers more heavily than would a province with only 2 per cent unemployed. However, it should be possible to ease the burden through normal equalization.

To ensure a measure of *égalité* among individual Canadians, governments could cooperatively devise a form of negative income tax on provincial benefits to individuals. A federal-provincial conference would have to define a list of recognized beneficiaries: dependent children, disabled people, people over 65 years of age, others permanently unemployed, temporarily unemployed, and so on. The same conference would approve, and assign monetary value to, a list of modes of provincial benefits to individuals. These modes would include direct payment, housing subsidies, tuition payments, supplies of drugs or other goods etc. Provinces would annually supply each family unit with a statement of provincial benefit received. These could be declared on a return to Ottawa which could calculate a national average personal benefit from government for each class of recognized beneficiary. Where any person or family received less than the national average for that class, a direct payment from the federal government would follow. The totals of the payments paid to residents in each province would be established and the sum deducted from the equalization payment paid to the province. Some scheme such as this would not dictate to the provinces *how* they must provide benefits to their populations but would prevent any province from discriminating excessively against any class of recipient. One consequence of this scheme would be that provinces would have no incentive to dump their welfare problems onto others. Let us suppose, for example, that a province chooses to discriminate against unmarried unemployed people (a highly mobile class) in its social payments, in the hope that they might move elsewhere. Under the scheme just proposed, a province could still do so, but only by sacrificing some of the equalization money it might have drawn. The implication of the goal of *égalité* is that the Canadian government would retain a substantial fiscal capacity, but little of it would be spent directly on the welfare aspects of society-building. Provinces would get the tax room together with equalization, and they would provide the services and benefits. The federal government would remain as the final equalizer through its tax system. Such a federal withdrawal would clearly remove a significant popular constituency from the federal government, but this seems inevitable in a system where provinces are to be recognized as agents of community-building. In any case, the list of recipients and benefits would have to be renegotiated periodically, and groups would still find it worthwhile to lobby the federal government. One doubts that the withdrawal would seriously affect federal capacity for economic management through fiscal policy. Large sums of money would continue to pass through federal hands before being redistributed through equalization. There would still remain the discretion to raise the sums needed through taxation or through deficit financing.

I have already implicitly defined the *liberté* aspect of the federal role, which consists of assuring to all individuals access to alternative institutional structures through which the individual can express his personality. Liberalism in this sense is a direct negation of the view that society has a right and a duty to limit access exclusively to institutions reflecting the dominant image, and these two values must be traded off against each other. No Canadian state could insist on less, though the precise dividing line could be negotiated.

The institutional presence of the Canadian state should reflect its reality—it should be bilingual from coast to coast. This feature will respect and partly reflect the host society for each institution. Federal bureaux in Quebec would have bilingual signs (with the French in larger letters). The language of work would be French provided that service could also be given in English. In the interests of institutional diversity, the federal government should continue to administer cultural agencies such as the CBC and the NFB and to make their products available in both languages throughout the country. The federal government would cease to regulate communications media but would continue to support cultural products and to distribute them.

Most contentiously, the federal government should be allowed to operate "minority language" schools, that is to say, English schools inside Quebec and French schools outside Quebec. Since this power would inevitably appear to the Québécois as a direct attack on their society-building aspirations, some acceptable trade-offs will be needed.

Canada has had a good deal of experience with the total immersion language teaching of young children. It might be possible to get expert agreement that a language so taught is "fixed" after four or six or ten years of exposure. It would then be perfectly appropriate for the host society to specify that the minority language could only be taught exclusively up to grade ten, after which teaching would have to be bilingual.

It must also be recognized that the host society, through its provincial state, could indirectly affect the curriculum of minority language schools by defining standards of performance necessary to accredit the graduates of those schools. The schools should not go beyond the secondary level and it would be up to the host province to decide whether graduates could attend any post-secondary institution in the province, whether they would be eligible for provincially supported apprenticeship manpower training programs, and whether they could qualify for a provincial licence in whatever occupations the province is licensing—automobile mechanics, for example. This same power to set admission standards would give all provinces some influence on the minority education curriculum outside its borders. Students in French high schools in Manitoba would want to be assured that their degrees would gain them admission to universities in Quebec. English students in Quebec might want to attend university elsewhere. Such matters would require interprovincial cooperation.

A less satisfactory trade-off, but not one to be rejected out of hand, would be to specify that these minority language schools would have to charge fees equal to some percentage of the real cost of running the national program, say 20 or 25 per cent. The province would retain the power of discretion in awarding scholarships. This discretion would extend to the number and value of scholarships to be made available, and even, though I would view this with some reluctance, to the selection of recipients of scholarship aid. In practical terms, the only change in Quebec's Bill 101 under the latter trade-off would be to specify the conditions under which a student was eligible for scholarship aid rather than the conditions under which he or she was eligible to enrol in an English school.

Since the last-mentioned proposal could be carried out in a fundamentally illiberal and inegalitarian way, I would hope that the provinces could be persuaded to limit their influence over the minority language schools to the first two modes.

What would be the institutions of the new Canada? Clearly there would have to be a new constitutional document, redefining the powers of the federal and provincial governments and including a bill of rights which would define individual freedoms, the agencies for their protection, and the role of the federal government in assuring access to alternative institutions and in specifying the bilingual character of federal institutions. The document might also state the principles of equalization among provinces and individuals. The jurisdiction of the Supreme Court might be limited to constitutional matters, including those concerned with human rights.

Under the new dispensation, the whole role of the central government would be to achieve those goals—economic, egalitarian, and liberal—which smaller societies do not necessarily have the capacity or will to achieve for themselves. If there exist such goals, in which we all have an interest as Canadians, it would be unacceptable for any smaller society to have a privileged position in their definition. This requirement has deep roots in the political culture of English-speaking Canadians.

We would have to take great care to avoid even more closed and technocratic government than we now have. Moreover, if we wish to encourage the delegation of additional tasks to the central government, we would have to arrange for parliamentary committees, composed of representatives from the delegating provinces, to have effective authority over those tasks. Party responsibility as currently practised would not apply in these cases. The Senate might be the appropriate house for such committees. Finally, since the minorities whose protection fall to the federal government may not all be territorially concentrated, some form of proportional representation would be in order.

These proposals may be politically impractical or may have undesirable consequences for some of the very values I wish to promote. I hope both disadvantages might be overcome. Canada's claim to continued existence has to be based upon more than economic convenience. It must rest upon the commitment of all Canadians to securing certain welfare benefits and rights for all citizens. If this cannot be achieved, then the goal should be as amicable and civilized a separation between Quebec and the rest of Canada as is possible. Future relations would then be based upon mutual advantage but would seek this through normal processes of international law, diplomacy, and economics.

If the proposed reforms have any chance of success, it is because they seek to accommodate the economic interests of all the provinces. The main economic initiatives would clearly come from the provinces and the federal government would have a coordinating and service role.

Choices would still have to be made at the federal level and there could still be a party battle about them, but the cost of defeat to any province or region would be less.

By reducing the salience of the federal government, the divisive effects of federal bilingualism policies would also be reduced, diminishing one of the most severe current tensions.

The intended compromise between the liberal patriotism of English-speaking Canadians and the *dirigiste* nationalism of many Québécois has the strength and weakness of all compromises. It cannot give either side all that it seeks. It can give both much of what they want. The primary intention is to facilitate society-building by provincial governments. The proposed changes or something like them would retain the economic advantages of union and the liberal goals in which Canadians have invested so much of their emotions and feelings.

One increasingly attractive approach to the problem of Confederation is to ask what are the powers which the federal government would need to exercise in order to maintain the essential characteristics of a national community, while allowing for the individual development of the various regions. The foregoing proposals suggest an answer. Ottawa must remain the essential guarantor of a national common market and of cultural diversity at the national level. It must be an agent of redistribution, redressing the persistent imbalances of resources and wealth among the regions. It must regulate competition among the regions and perform certain common services. It must retain responsibility for overall fiscal and monetary mangement. But it must exercise these powers in greater cooperation with the provinces. It must recognize that provincial governments will be the source of most innovation, change, and development, and the central providers of services to citizens. Ottawa will become the balance wheel in the system, exercising its power through regulatory activities and the tax system. It will become a much less pervasive force than it is now.

Fundamental to the success of any proposal, however, is its capacity to draw on resources of *fraternité* among all Canadians. I believe these exist and can survive any short-run political tactics designed to exploit polarization. It is for this reason that one can remain optimistic about the prospect of respecifying the federal role in Canada.

Reaching the Lifeboat:
The Roles of Leaders and Citizens

RICHARD SIMEON

It is one thing to suggest some of the alternative constitutional arrangements by which the Canadian communities might rearrange their affairs. It is another to suggest the strategies by which they should be advocated, and the procedures by which they could be negotiated. The willingness of Canadians to consider far-reaching changes does not seem in doubt. Ardent supporters of the present federal system are few and far between. While "selling out to Quebec" is anathema to many, others are anxious to explore possible accommodations, especially if those could simultaneously deal with some of the other sources of grievance and discontent. Similarly, on the Quebec side many are anxious to examine the possibilities.

But how can this process begin? On the one hand, leaders of the present Quebec government appear adamant in their refusal to contemplate negotiation within the federal framework. On the other hand, English-Canadian leaders are reluctant to offer concessions to Quebec, for which they could be attacked as "selling out to the separatists."

Moreover, the record of Canadians' search for constitutional change offers little hope for the future. Repeated attempts have failed to find agreement on how to patriate or amend the constitution, much less on substantive change. The commitment of Quebec's Union Nationale government under Daniel Johnson to fundamental change led in 1967 to the Ontario-sponsored Confederation of Tomorrow Conference, and then to a drawn-out process of constitutional review, culminating in the Victoria Charter of 1971. This document demonstrated how deep the disagreements were—how limited the consensus—and it was not enough. The Liberal Quebec government of Robert Bourassa rejected it. The dilemma was clear: lack of consensus ensured it would fail. How, it might be asked, could we possibly do any better now?

One answer might be, we will do better because we must: because the urgency is now so much greater, and the costs of failure so much higher. Governments may now, in the name of unity, be willing to contemplate changes which a few years ago they felt were intolerable. Its opponents argued in the 1960s that special status could only lead down a "slippery slope" of ever-increasing demands, and ever fewer links between Ottawa and Quebecers, resulting eventually in separation. But we have travelled the slippery slope anyway, and one of the more troubling questions is whether an alternative strategy in, say 1968, would have avoided our present difficulties.

Let us assume a willingness now to explore new avenues, to start with a clean slate, and let us assume many Quebecers are willing to explore such alternatives. How to proceed? Several alternatives have been suggested, ranging from a renewal of formal federal-provincial negotiations on the constitution, to the convening of some form of constituent assembly charged with the drawing up of a new constitution. Two issues arise: who is to negotiate with whom? And in what forum?

First, who is to speak for English Canada? The obvious candidate is the federal government. But several theoretical and practical questions stand in the way. For Ottawa to negotiate with the PQ government on constitutional change already assumes something like a "deux nations" position, in which the predominantly English provinces are seen to be essentially homogeneous, and willing on a matter such as this to subordinate their governments to Ottawa. Both assumptions are unlikely. Moreover, Ottawa's ability to speak for the country as a whole is gravely limited by the virtual absence of representation of the West. The present Ottawa government's commitment to existing strategies suggested in the first months after November 15 an unwillingness to generate new alternatives. The high proportion of Liberal seats from Quebec was both an advantage and a disadvantage here: it ensured Ottawa could make a credible claim to speak for Quebec, and it suggested its ministers should have a considerable understanding of Quebec affairs. On the other hand, as Peter Desbarats pointed out during the 1970 October Crisis, it gives the conflict some of the characteristics of a "family quarrel" in which the very familiarity and emotional involvement of the opponents fosters a particular inflexibility and bitterness.

So the participation must be broadened. The most important participants are the other nine provinces. Several provincial premiers —among them William Davis of Ontario and Allan Blakeney of

Saskatchewan—seem to have greater credibility in Quebec than almost any federal cabinet minister or opposition leader. Provincial leaders' involvement in these issues in the past has varied considerably as has their willingness to contemplate constitutional change. Yet precedents such as the Confederation of Tomorrow Conference and initiatives such as Ontario's sponsorship of the Destiny Canada Conference in June 1977 suggest a strong commitment to responsible action. Provinces share many of Quebec's grievances with federal policies, and perhaps increasingly, also see themselves as representing highly distinctive regional communities. Hence there are considerable grounds for greater agreement between Quebec and the other provinces than between Quebec and Ottawa. Such agreement, however, is much more likely to lead to a general decentralization than to acceptance of "deux nations."

Interprovincial discussion is likely to focus the debate very strongly on issues of *intergovernmental* concern, such as tax-sharing, rather than on broader issues. And, as politicians with a vested interest in the importance of regionalism, provincial government participants are likely to stress the significance of regional diversity. Through them, the possible "national" concerns are likely to be neglected. In choosing participants in the debate, one is also choosing how the problems will be defined and what alternatives will be considered. Nevertheless, the provinces will undoubtedly play a central role in any negotiations and they should be taking the initiative.

Constitutional change in recent years has been the preserve of largely secret intergovernmental negotiation, part of what D. V. Smiley calls "executive federalism." Many objections have been raised to this pattern. It is marked by a preoccupation with status and political competition, secretiveness, an arcane language of debate, and the freezing out of public participation. Perhaps now another, more fundamental objection can be raised: in dealing with the issue of Quebec, intergovernmental negotiation has demonstrably failed; our leaders have not been able to find accommodation.

Perhaps no one can, but one fascinating result of the Quebec election has been a widespread view that the politicians and existing processes have failed and that constitutional discussion must now be carried to the people. Solutions, if they exist, are more likely to well up from the grassroots than to flow down from above.

Broadening the debate in this way to encompass more participants and more perspectives has considerable risks. Canadian political leaders have long had a fear of mass involvement, which suggests a fear that this debate could fly out of control and the extremists take the floor. Nevertheless, it is clear that we must seek wider forums, not for formal negotiations and decision, but to explore the new possibilities and to indicate the source and breadth of support for various alternatives. The formal institutions and processes cannot simply be bypassed; whatever their weaknesses, it is through them that adjustments must ultimately be made.

How can we widen the debate? First, one might consider the role of the federal official opposition. Indeed, shortly after the Quebec election, the *Toronto Star* actually suggested a new Government of National Unity, including both opposition leaders and some nonparliamentary "Great men." This implied, of course, that there was only one issue in Canada, and it would be our sole preoccupation. This view is premature. Nevertheless, it is imperative to integrate the opposition into discussion of the issue, if only to bring more views to bear and to give federal action greater legitimacy. Some consultation can go on informally. Some can take place in fuller parliamentary debate about Confederation. In addition, both Ottawa and the provinces should establish permanent standing committees on federal-provincial relations to parallel the cabinet committees and departments most governments have already established.

There must also be greater citizen participation. The mobilization of concern since November 15 has been startling. Both inside and outside Quebec, existing groups have been revitalized, and a host of new groups and movements have been born, reflecting as many different strands of opinion. Forums, seminars, conferences, symposia, speeches, workshops, have proliferated, no doubt causing massive indigestion for that small group of experts widely thought to hold the key to the future or to be able to interpret one language group to the other. Such widespread mobilization does seem to demonstrate the "will to survive" which Prime Minister Trudeau invokes so often, and which is, indeed, a necessary condition of survival itself. Yet it is clearly not sufficient. Survival also requires a search for concrete alternatives and the creation or revitalization of structures and mechanisms through which debate can be channelled.

Disillusionment with the ability of traditional leaders and institutions has produced a large number of proposals for alternative mechanisms. Claude Ryan, editor of *Le Devoir*, has urged creation of a task force of eminent Canadians to review fundamental constitutional arrangements and prepare the ground for a formal constitutional conference. A political scientist, Léon Dion, has elaborated a similar proposal for a federally-appointed group of English and French Canadians who share a commitment to Canada and an understanding of Quebec to examine all possible constitutional options. Jack McClelland, the publisher, calls for a task force of 100 to 200 "people of known excellence" from any background *except* politics to diagnose the problems and draw up proposals to be submitted to a national referendum.

A group of English-speaking intellectuals has also suggested appointment of a constitutional commission—half nominated by Ottawa and half by Quebec— which would seek out opinions and report within a year. The report would go to a popularly elected constituent assembly which would draft a new constitution to be submitted for public ratification.

Such alternatives have many attractions, especially the view that any final settlement should be publicly voted on. But they have their pitfalls. It would be exceedingly difficult to draw up a means of appointment or a mandate for a task force or commission which everyone would accept as legitimate. Indeed, it might be as difficult to get agreement on the structure and membership of a constituent assembly as it would be to get agreement on a new constitution itself. Neither is it clear that either a group of "wise men" or an elected assembly would be any better able to find a new consensus than more established political mechanisms. Finally, there is a practical objection. Almost certainly, none of the governments, in Quebec, Ottawa, or the provinces, would be willing to delegate their authority in such a crucial matter.

The role of "experts" can and should be only advisory. While public involvement is necessary, it is best achieved through informal processes which channel opinions through the regular political mechanisms. We are now perhaps paying the price of the historic underdevelopment of representative political institutions in Canada; the remedy, however, is not bypassing them for untried mechanisms. Better would be a more informal, unofficial process of debate and discussion, especially if it brought together diverse groups from across the country. As with Ontario's Destiny Canada conference, these may be government-sponsored. Such meetings would have the great value of canvassing wider alternatives than are likely to emerge from governments. They would provide governments with a catalogue of alternatives, and, what would be of most value, with an indication of which policies were likely to be feasible and which would encounter major opposition. Finally, in the present atmosphere informal gatherings are more likely than intergovernmental negotiations to ensure a dialogue between independentists and federalists, which is essential to any future accommodation. Thus public discussion is an essential prelude to formal negotiation. Debate should proceed in two stages—from the widest possible canvassing of public opinion, to discussion by more formal bodies.

One such forum is the seven-man Task Force, chaired by former Ontario Premier John Robarts and former Liberal minister Jean-Luc Pepin, which the federal government established in July 1977. The Task Force's mandate is to support groups and individuals working to maintain national unity, to publicize their activities and promote contacts among them, and to advise the federal government on the strategy of public relations, the study of possible constitutional changes, and other matters related to the issue of unity. Its main role appears to be to advocate and support federalism rather than to explore in depth the possibility of major specific changes in the shape of Confederation. This follows the general strategy of the federal government since the Quebec election, which has been to minimize the possibilities of radical change, and instead to concentrate on building support for its bilingualism strategy and to promote the "will to survive" through increased understanding and a fundamental commitment to unity. However, it is now crucial to translate this generalized "Save Canada" feeling into more concrete and specific proposals for change. Many of the 500 participants in the Destiny Canada Conference in June 1977 demonstrated their willingness to do so, as the discussion evolved from a stress on the need for goodwill and understanding to a desire to deal directly with "What should be done" and to consider far-reaching changes.

Assuming the possibility and desirability of "Re-Confederation," a renegotiating of the federal bargain, how might it be achieved? A negotiation requires at least two parties. The Parti Québécois seems determined not to negotiate from within the federal framework; for it, the signal to begin negotiations is the referendum. In an interview in the *Montreal Star*, Premier Lévesque was asked if there must be a referendum before negotiations begin. He answered:

> Negotiations in the sense of truly formal negotiations ... yes. Because there is no reason why we should go at it piecemeal after the experience of the last something like 30 years of federal-provincial relations on that score. ... There is no percentage there, and it is a waste of time. If there should be any kind of constitutional conference, there's no reason why we shouldn't attend it. But certainly not to negotiate outside our option until such time as the people in Quebec give their mandate, by referendum.

Claude Ryan suggests the federalists would also face a dilemma: how to negotiate with somebody we already know will be satisfied with nothing less than independence? How does one make concessions when one knows that each will be followed by others, even more costly?

These are real problems, but, given the uncertainty of a referendum result, and the immense difficulties of relationships afterwards, the argument for an attempt at renegotiation is powerful. However, it is equally clear that such formal negotiations cannot be rushed. The debate is not yet far advanced within Quebec. Federalists outside Quebec have only just begun to explore the options and are far from agreement as to what is either desirable or feasible. Opinion varies sharply from group to group and especially from region to region. The first task remains to explore the limits of support for and opposition to many possibilities. Similarly, there may be opportunities for compromise with Quebec which are now best pursued informally. To engage in formal negotiations prematurely is to increase the risks of failure; and there can be little doubt that to fail again in the search for constitutional revision is to make independence almost inevitable. René Lévesque is right—the piecemeal discussions of the past have borne little fruit. Before formal negotiations begin, all sides must be confident that success could be achieved.

On the other hand, it is important that federalists in all parts of the country develop a set of reasonably clear and definite proposals *before* the Quebec referendum. If such proposals were acceptable to the Quebec government, then the referendum could become simply the ratification of a new Confederation. That appears most unlikely. But it is vital that in the referendum, the alternatives presented are not just the status quo versus independence, but rather some alternative to the status quo versus independence. In the internal Quebec debate, federalists are hampered by not knowing whether their options would be acceptable elsewhere—hence they cannot provide a credible alternative to the PQ. If, however, the Quebec people could be presented in a referendum with a clear indication of specific changes, then the chances of a federalist victory are much increased.

One possibility is as follows: after an initial developing and testing of possibilities through widespread public discussion, consultation with experts, and informal contacts among governments, a formal constitutional conference would be convened by the federal government, or, if it were unwilling, by the provinces acting together. Quebec would, of course, be invited. It might refuse to participate. If so, the conference would continue, with an empty chair, and the remaining governments would attempt to draw up a set of proposals which, in effect, would be the federalist alternative to the status quo option with which Quebec voters would be faced. If Quebec did not participate some means would have to be found to represent federalist opinion within Quebec, probably through a federally-appointed delegation. It would also be important to give the conference the widest possible legitimacy and for that reason the delegations should include representation from opposition parties in each government.

It would be far better if the Quebec government were to be represented, and it might well be possible to overcome its reluctance. If other governments displayed a clear willingness to make major adjustments well in advance, then the PQ might see the possibility of achieving their major goals in the federation. Politically, in Quebec, the charge that the PQ had spurned one last chance at substantial reform in order to embark on an unknown venture would be telling and could well force the government to the table. The risk for the other governments is that if the conference failed, then the PQ would itself be in a very strong position in the referendum campaign. Even so, the people of Quebec might be persuaded to accept a reform package even if their governments had rejected it. Thus the conference would agree on a series of proposals for change. Whether or not the PQ agreed to them, they would constitute the federalist case in the referendum. If the package included major change, it would also be valuable to submit it for approval by the citizens of the rest of the country as well.

In this debate it must also be recognized that the range of possibilities, from status quo through "sovereignty with association," represents not a series of fundamentally opposed options but in fact a continuum. The symbolic weight attached to "federalism" in English Canada and to "independence" by the Parti Quebecois, together with the looming of the referendum as the sharp dividing point in the debate, obscure the possibility of agreement on many matters of substance. Symbols are important but we should try to see beyond to the substantive content underlying them. This is especially important in the dialogue with Quebec federalists, for most of whom the status quo is unacceptable, and who accept the logic of Quebec as a distinct society without extending it to the need for outright independence.

The discussion of alternative institutional and constitutional forms is, of course, only one of the levels at which the debate will take place. Dialogue in many other forums is vital. The policies pursued by the federal and provincial governments will send important signals to

French Canadians. English Canadians may not be able to play much of a *direct* role in the referendum campaign, but they can and should have an important indirect part. Their participation in a heavy-handed manner could easily backfire.

Some may argue that this strategy gives the game away before it starts. It may also turn out that non-Quebecers will, ultimately, not be prepared for change. The corollary of that is the virtual certainty of secession. Again it might be argued: so be it. Not only is this a counsel of despair and defeat, it ignores the costs of failure. If we do fail, we must be able to tell ourselves that we tried.

IV
The Longer Run

Scenarios for Separation

RICHARD SIMEON

Canadians have entered a period of decision whose outcome is un-known, and which is fraught with the danger of rapid polarization and escalation of political conflict. Divorce is notoriously a messy, ac-rimonious process, in which both parties may act vindictively or irra-tionally. The breakup or disintegration of countries has likewise sel-dom been achieved peacefully. Yet that is the prospect before us. Can it come about amicably? What would be the consequences if the cause of Quebec independence is defeated? What are the chances of working out the kind of economic association advocated by the PQ? What steps might be followed from the present period of skirmishing, through a referendum campaign, to the post-referendum period? What out-comes are most likely? Let us assume a choice about independence has been made, and examine the political dynamics likely to accompany and influence the decision and its aftermath.

Accepting Quebec's independence and agreeing to economic associ-ation are two distinct questions. It is not hard to imagine English Canada accepting the first, but refusing the second. The spokesmen for the Parti Québécois sketch a plausible and beguiling scenario, in which the choice for independence is "normal," indeed inevitable, and in which a future association could easily be arranged to the mutual benefit of both Quebec and English Canada. On the other hand, others outline much more frightening scenarios. One envisages the refusal of English Canada to accept a referendum result, followed by increasing hostility and tension, strong appeals from federalist Quebecers to "save us," and a general pattern of mutually reinforcing tension leading to a spiral of escalation beyond anyone's control, culminating either in official repression or in civil disorder of the type which has convulsed Northern Ireland. This scenario also contemplates armed intervention from outside, massive economic collapse, and indefinite chaos. Others, while not sketching such bleak prospects, do nevertheless argue that Quebecers who look to future association are deluding themselves: it just would not be accepted in English Canada.

These two scenarios are the extremes; neither the prediction of tranquil transition to independence, implied by the PQ, nor that of grim civil war is likely to be fulfilled. Yet in looking at some of the factors which might make each more plausible, and in trying to fit into this framework some indication of how these factors would take shape, we can usefully speculate on the possible outcomes. The intention is not so much to *predict* events but rather to show how different possibilities might come about.

We must take several kinds of factors into account. First are the participants. In Quebec they include government, opposition leaders and parties, and other social groups such as the business world, the non-French-speaking, and the militants in the PQ. Outside Quebec, they include the federal and provincial governments, opposition leaders, non-government groups including business and other interests, and the general public.

Other actors may become deeply involved, especially if conflict mounts in Canada: the United States government, foreign multinational corporations, and perhaps some other countries, such as France. Second, events will be conditioned by some broader background factors: the most important is the general economic climate in Quebec and Canada. Third, we need to take account of the sequence of steps leading up to and immediately following independence. The critical pivot here is the referendum itself. It is the focus of the independence campaign, and of federalist arguments against it. The chief questions turn on the timing of the vote, the wording of the question, the ground rules for the campaign, and, most crucial of all, the interpretation of the result: the more ambiguous it is, the greater potential for disorder. Finally, there is the post-referendum stage, in which the issues will either be how to bring about independence and whether to adopt economic association, or, if the referendum fails, what other changes might occur. At each of these stages, earlier experiences will shape and condition what comes later. It is a dynamic process, not a series of unrelated snapshots. Whether the result is continued federation or fragmentation, the reworking of French-English relations is likely to involve a protracted period of uncertainty.

How does the PQ model envision the peaceful accession to independence? The details, including such vital matters as the wording, timing, and ground rules for the referendum, have not yet been fully sketched, but the general outlines are clear. One of the surest recipes for violent conflict, both within Quebec and between it and English Canada, would be some wholly illegitimate decision, such as a coup d'état. But the PQ has stated with undeniable clarity that independence can and must be achieved "strictly through the democratic process."

Premier Lévesque asserts that "all Quebecers of voting age, without distinction as to their origin, will share equally in this historic decision." Early PQ manifestoes assumed that a duly elected PQ government would have a mandate to move directly to the central goal. For example, the 1973 party program said that independence would be negotiated directly after a proclamation by the National Assembly. It explicitly opposed any federal intervention, especially through a referendum which was then seen as a tool to bar the way. The issue divided the party leadership from the more militant activists, but electoral tactics won, and in the 1973 election PQ literature proclaimed: "Today I vote for the only team ready to form a true government. In 1975, by referendum, I will decide the future of Quebec. One thing at a time." This was the strategy which worked so well in 1976. Nevertheless, the rank and file hostility to the referendum might well re-emerge if it were unduly delayed, or if the result were negative. Inded it has been suggested the party may decide to reverse itself and call an election on the issue instead.

However, Lévesque's commitment to a referendum before the expiry of the PQ term seems ironclad. Most predictions suggest it will occur within two or three years of the 1976 election. The question has not yet been chosen, but it appears likely that it will ask for a mandate to negotiate sovereignty with association, instead of an outright declaration of independence. Jacques Brossard, a constitutional lawyer who has analysed the separation process in detail, suggests the question could be "Are you for or against the principle of the legal accession of Quebec to sovereignty within an economic association with Canada?" The great difficulty with this formulation is, of course, that association is in the gift of English Canada, not of Quebec alone, and it leaves open what Quebec would do if English-Canadian cooperation was denied.

PQ spokesmen have said little about such questions, or about how to interpret the various possible referendum results. They have said the referendum would not necessarily be definitive: a defeat would not preclude another try. In the discussion of association they have argued that Canada, especially Ontario, would simply be forced by economic circumstances to accept association, since not to do so would risk loss of markets, massive unemployment, and other dislocations.

What would happen after the referendum has not been spelled out, but presumably the National Assembly would then give the government a mandate to negotiate the details with English Canada. This would take some time. As Vera Murray notes, in *Le Parti Québécois*, for the PQ independence has become less an *event* than a *process*.

Despite the vagueness of the PQ scenario on many key points, the general outline is not in doubt. In the optimistic Lévésque strategy the decision to separate is made in an orderly, legitimate fashion; it is broadly accepted as fair by the governments and people of English Canada, as well as by Quebecers themselves; the referendum vote is followed by correct and polite discussion of how to carry out the transfer of sovereignty, convey to Quebec the required powers, draw up the plans for association, and place the final seal of legitimacy on the agreement.

Under what conditions might such a scenario be plausible? How realistic is it? It depends critically on the willingness of English Canadians to accept the legitimacy of Quebec independence itself. Lévesque suggests that they will for several reasons. He argues that they will come to see separation as preferable to seemingly endless squabbling between Quebec and the rest of Canada within Confederation. "Tomorrow," he writes in *An Option for Quebec*, "English-Canada would be grateful to Quebec for bringing it [separation] about." He also argues that in the period leading up to independence, English Canadians would undergo a "psychological development" through which they would come to accept the idea as inevitable and would thus be willing to "sit at the same table without too great a gap between us."

In some ways, events since the publication of his book have borne him out. Few English Canadians regard Quebec's separation as desirable. Most see it as both impractical and as a fundamental blow to their own sense of national identity. Yet after many years of discussion, and after the 1976 election results had sunk in, it does appear that most articulate citizens have accepted that it may happen. Quebec is already in many ways a separate society and many ties have already been cut. However much that is regretted, the idea that the province should take the step to formal sovereignty is no longer unthinkable. Few responsible persons have seriously suggested that a clear decision to separate must be flatly rejected and that Quebec should be forced to remain. The costs of coercion would be astronomical; "send in the troops" may be advocated in a bar-room, but seldom in serious argument. If force were ever used it would more likely be as a result of events going out of control, than of a calculated decision to stop separation. Whether or not a referendum is the appropriate means to reach a decision has also received little attention, but most discussion seems to assume it will occur. The focus is on how best to influence the result. This position implies acceptance of the *possibility* that the vote will favour independence, and to that extent the basic right of Quebec to choose its own destiny has been acknowledged, even by the most passionate defenders of Confederation. Similarly few have argued that a referendum asking whether Quebec should be allowed to go should be submitted to the rest of Canada.

This acceptance does not necessarily extend to the project of economic association. It is one thing to accept the right to secede; it is another to make further concessions felt to be imposing additional costs on the country left behind. Association seems to imply that Quebec, as one of two partners , would have a much greater voice in fundamental economic policy than it has now. Furthermore, for the West, the present Confederation bargain involves an implicit trade-off: the West bears the costs of tariff policies designed to develop and protect the manufacturing base of Ontario and Quebec in return for the benefits which flow from the ability of that protected economy to provide equalization and economic stabilization to the more volatile resource-based industries of the peripheries. That delicate balance would be upset by secession, so it would no longer be clear that association would be in the objective economic interests of the rest of the country outside Ontario and perhaps the Maritimes. PQ leaders too often act as if Ontario were the only other part of Canada they need consider. If the association part of the PQ scenario is to be achieved, there would need, at a minimum, to be a clear demonstration to English Canada of the advantages to be gained from it.

If Canadians have implicitly accepted that Quebec must make its own decision, the question still remains: what would be regarded as a legitimate decision? Here the conditions under which the referendum is conducted are vitally important. The more that English Canadians felt the question was "rigged" or biased, or that the federalist case was denied full expression, the less likely they would be to accept the results and to cooperate in bringing separation about. So it is essential to the PQ scenario that the campaign be accepted as fair and it appears that the government recognizes that. An election called to produce a mandate to separate would probably accord with past constitutional practice better than a referendum. By now, however, the referendum has been widely accepted as a *sine qua non* of legitimacy. To retreat from that commitment would be interpreted as an admission by the PQ government that it was going to lose the referendum. Federalists would cry foul.

Assuming the referendum is not abandoned, the result is crucial. If 95 per cent of the voters voted for independence it is hard to conceive of any major opposition to formalizing independence. But as one moves down the scale from unanimity to 90, to 75, to 60, to 55, to 50 per cent, the matter becomes ever more cloudy. The problem is further compounded by the ethnic make-up of Quebec: what if, for example, virtually 100 per cent of the non-francophones voted against and 60 per cent of francophones voted for? Although defeated by a narrow margin, PQ supporters could claim that the majority of "les vrais Québécois" had voted in favour and independence should therefore follow. At the moment, such an outcome may be the most likely. It is also the one which would provoke the greatest tension, since English Canada would almost certainly regard it as insufficient, while many of the more ardent nationalists in Quebec would take it as a signal to proceed. Even if the referendum were to pass, but by a small margin, the result might be disputed, since it is often argued that such fundamental political choices should be made by some "special majority" such as two-thirds. This has not been formally proposed, and one factor which would influence whether it would be is the intensity and articulateness of the anti-independence voters. The stronger their sense of threat, the greater the likelihood they will call on English Canada to reject the secessionist option.

The strength of such feelings would in turn depend on the other actions of the Parti Québécois government. It can be argued that independence itself may not be the primary fear for many, though for many anglophone Quebecers with deep roots in the province but a strong sense of Canadianism, it is a fundamental concern. For others, the reaction could turn on different grounds. Fears could be reduced if the PQ were to make further concessions to anglophones in the form of guarantees of linguistic rights, especially in the schools. A very important *quid pro quo* in any separation agreement would be an exchange of mutual guarantees for minorities. Such an agreement might also include assistance to those who wished to leave.

On the side of Quebec business, reactions are likely to be varied. Canadian businessmen may feel very differently from owners of foreign-based firms, since the former would share the personal response of English-Canadian citizens generally, while the latter are more likely to make calculations based on the cold facts of the balance sheet. Multinational firms already have much experience working in many countries and languages. Certainly business opposition to the PQ stems from fear of its social and economic policies as much as from its desire for independence. If it were felt that an independent Quebec would undertake large-scale nationalization and other such policies, then the business voice would undoubtedly be raised in strong opposition to a positive referendum result. The PQ's policies so far have recognized this danger, and much effort has been expended to demonstrate the responsible character and administrative ability of the government, and its receptive attitude to private investment. Assuming such reassurances are believed, the primary business viewpoint —especially of the externally-based firms—will depend on which outcome is regarded as the more disruptive of economic life in general, and trade with other areas in particular. If it is believed that to sharply oppose independence, even if only a bare majority support it, would increase uncertainty, or strengthen the more militant sections of the PQ, then the business sector will probably argue that it is better to be a midwife to peaceful separation, and to a renewed relationship, than to oppose it.

Similar considerations apply to the rest of the country. If English Canada is convinced the referendum is fair, that the secessionist movement is not out to punish opponents, and that the movement is not a threat to other fundamental political values, then it is difficult to conceive of strong opposition. Just as PQ conduct will affect the federalist reactions during and after the referendum campaign, so the tactics of the federal government and others will influence the behaviour of the PQ. Many Quebecers, including federalists, argue that this is primarily a domestic Quebec affair, and that it is illegitimate for "outsiders" to try to influence the result. But obviously the federal government would be a participant and so should other English Canadians. The problem is that the more intense the referendum campaign, the higher the perceived stakes, the greater the tension, and the greater the difficulty of amicable post-referendum relations. A federalist campaign which emphasized the dire economic consequences of an independence vote, especially if accompanied by actual or threatened withdrawal of capital, could have severe consequences. If it succeeded in frightening Quebec voters into voting for federalism, the frustrated advocates of independence would make charges of blackmail and coercion, and this could fuel a very bitter and perhaps violent campaign in which other means to independence would be sought. If, on the other hand, the referendum succeeded, the Quebec government would be tempted to act against those who had tried to sabotage the democratic process.

If English Canada did accept the basic legitimacy of a decision to separate, and if that were seen not to be extremely disruptive of their own interests, then the Lévésque scenario in the post-decision phase is plausible. Negotiations, however strained, would follow. Both sides would have strong incentives to do so in good faith. For Quebec the need would be greatest, since it would stand to lose most if satisfactory arrangements to maintain access to the Canadian market were not achieved. The English-Canadian incentives would include the desire to preserve economic relationships and established markets, the desire to protect minorities, and the need to maintain the St. Lawrence Seaway and transportation links with Atlantic Canada. On both practical and moral grounds, both sides are likely to wish to reduce the chances of armed conflict. English-Canadian and foreign capitalists, especially those with fixed assets in Quebec, would wish to minimize possible threats to their property. Arguments made against independence do not necessarily imply that there would not be rapid accommodation to the new reality in the event of separation. The incentive to negotiate would also be enhanced by the probable vagueness of the referendum question. Federalists will want to know how much of the benefits of Confederation can be rescued.

Different groupings within English Canada would react in various ways to a decision to separate. Mass surveys taken so far do not suggest widespread sentiment to keep Quebec in at any cost, though there would be some such pressure. It is also possible that those English Canadians with the greatest commitment to a bicultural Canada which includes Quebec are the same people whose values would be most opposed to coercion. Nevertheless, English-Canadian leaders could be under some pressure to be tough and uncompromising, especially in the tense atmosphere of a vote. One factor, therefore, which would favour the Lévesque scenario is the ability of those leaders to control or restrain their followers.

The same is true on the Quebec side. In the heady aftermath of an independence vote there would be intense impatience to achieve the New Jerusalem as quickly as possible and to cast off the shackles of federalism. If English Canada appears reluctant to begin negotiations, pressure for a unilateral declaration would grow. Similarly the prospect of discussions with English Canada in which Quebec would be compelled to make concessions, or of an independence agreement which placed limits on Quebec's real independence, could rapidly lead to demands to cut the whole process short. The PQ leadership today seems firmly in control, but there have been sharp internal tensions within the party about the process of achieving independence and about the closeness of the links with Canada which should follow. Moreover the rapid process of social change has eroded the authority of all Quebec elites, including government. To manage these volatile forces while engaging in orderly discussion with English Canada will not be easy.

A clear vote for separation and its acceptance in principle by English Canada would almost certainly mean that the United States would remain aloof. Various elements in France may give moral support to the movement; American government and business are likely to give similar support to federation. Neither is likely to intervene directly unless grave disorder threatens within Canada. With strong interests in Canada and Quebec to protect, the American response is more likely to support an orderly transition than to block independence. The fear of foreign intervention will be an additional incentive for both sides to negotiate.

Finally, a peaceful separation will depend in part on economic conditions. Continued economic deterioration—itself in part a result of political uncertainty—between now and the referendum would gravely embitter relations. English Canada might blame Quebec for its woes; Quebecers might allege that actions by English-Canadian capital designed to frighten them into staying were to blame for their problems. Similarly an economic panic after a positive referendum would make discussion of the modalities extremely difficult. Again, the possibility of creating self-fulfilling prophecies is obvious.

The peaceful transition to an independent Quebec is by no means implausible. But it does depend on some difficult conditions: acceptance of the legitimacy of the idea itself; agreement that the specific procedures followed are fair and the results relatively unambiguous; the advocacy of economic, social, and cultural policies by Quebec which are not seen as a fundamental threat either to the political values or to the economic interests of other parts of the country; the ability of both the Quebec and federal governments to restrain their more extremist followers; nonintervention by outsiders; and a relatively stable economic climate. All these conditions could be met, but it would not be easy. Even if they were, the negotiation of a separation agreement would be complex. It would try patience on both sides, as English Canadians faced daily the cutting of links, dismantling of much of the federal bureaucracy, the need to remake many government programs, and the like. The blow to self-esteem would be immense. Many issues might quickly blow up into major disagreements. In Quebec there would be haste to get the matter done with, and an intolerance of delaying tactics. But, difficult as it would be, it *could* be done.

Economic association would be another matter. It is one thing to grant Quebec the right to go its own way; it is another to facilitate its departure or to conclude a separation agreement that is seen to give an independent Quebec even greater influence over English Canada's basic economic policies than it now has. The closer the economic association sought, the more this would be the case, since the model implies that Quebec and Canada would make joint policies as equals. A likely result is a rapid increase in economic conflicts within English Canada. One irony in the current situation is that while Ontario and the other eight predominantly anglophone provinces are a cultural unit, they are not an obvious economic one. Ontario and Quebec, conversely, are not a cultural unit, but they are an economic one. Negotiating an association would reopen all the old economic grievances of Confederation and make it extremely difficult for English Canada to develop a position. The implications of this for the independence project are unclear: some Quebec leaders might argue, "if we cannot have association then we had better give up independence." Such voices would likely get swept away. Already many in the PQ argue that close association may not even be desirable, and some, such as Rodrique Tremblay, argue that Quebec should search for other links anyway. The western premiers, the premier of Ontario, and many businessmen have asserted that a common market is simply "not on." These may just be bargaining positions taken to disabuse Quebecers about the prospects; they may change, especially if association is seen to be necessary to prevent economic turmoil. Nevertheless, public pressure on politicians to avoid a "sell-out" would be hard to resist.

The "pessimistic" scenario is largely the reverse of the optimistic one, and can therefore be examined more briefly. Violent conflict would arise if the proposal to separate were approved in the referendum but English Canada refused to grant the right to independence, or if the proposal were narrowly defeated and the more extremist supporters of independence turned to extra-parliamentary means of achieving their goal. There would be a lesser but still real risk of sporadic violence by some non-French-speaking Quebecers directed against the new regime in an independent Quebec.

Minority violence if the referendum is defeated—even if this happens resoundingly—is a distinct possibility. Many spokesmen have expressed the hope that the referendum will be definitive; if the PQ loses, they suggest, the party should abandon the field at least for the time being. René Lévesque argues that a no decision would have to be respected, but nothing would bar putting the question again later. If that were the case, our future would remain uncertain for a very long time. One hopes that a result such as a close negative vote would be followed by an immediate attempt by the leaders on both sides to

negotiate the differences within an altered Confederation. It is un-
realistic to believe that a referendum defeat would cause independentists to abandon their goal. The vast majority would accept the verdict
for the moment, but other elements in Quebec might not. The commitment to independence is intense; expectations have been built up
over a long time; they would not be lightly abandoned. Radical impatience with the democratic method is not new to Quebec, as the FLQ
movement showed. In retrospect we now know that it was a tiny group
of almost pathetic proportions—yet even this ragtag army was able to
create much turmoil, inflict violence. and incite massive repressive
measures in October 1970. The experience of many other western
countries, with groups such as the Weathermen and others in the
United States, the IRA in Britain and Ireland, and some Basques in
Spain, demonstrates that widespread violence and disruption can be
caused by a few urban guerillas. Denial of independence, even by a
majority vote, could provoke the view that democratic procedures will
never permit separation and that federalists must be taught that the
maintenance of federation is not worth the cost. Only a tiny minority
would be tempted to violence, but they could do much damage. Once
started, there is a familiar scenario: provocation creates repression,
which leads to further provocation, the growth of sympathy for the
rebellious groups, increased repression and so on up the escalator. The
challenge of defusing such rebellion without stifling the broader
movement with which the rebels identify is one that few governments
have met.

A similarly violent movement by English Canadians opposed to
separation is also possible. Outside Quebec it seems unlikely, since the
issue has not provoked anything like the same passion and because the
vast majority of English Canadians have little contact with Quebecers.
The youngest and least mobile of anglophone Montrealers provide the
most obvious base for anglophone violence. That possibility cannot be
discounted, but it is unlikely because such a small rebellious group
would probably gain little public sympathy.

Among the more general conditions which would minimize the
chances of a peaceful outcome, the most obvious is an outright rejection by English Canadians of *any* form of decision by Quebecers. That,
I have argued, is most unlikely. More probable is a situation in which
the Quebec division is seen to be indeterminate or undemocratic. The
PQ government could be accused of muzzling the opposition, or of
using its official power unfairly to help the independence cause.
Federalists could be accused of scare tactics, economic blackmail, and

so on. In either case, the losing side could argue that the vote was unrepresentative or meaningless. In such a campaign, too, the stakes could become so high that neither side was willing to talk to the others. This would be no ordinary debate. Hence the importance of at least tacit agreement on the rules of the game.

An overwhelming vote for or against independence is not likely to provoke argument about its legitimacy. But a close vote, especially one in which a majority of francophones were for independence, would be extremely difficult to deal with. Both sides could claim victory. An ambiguous result could lead to a call for another referendum almost immediately. Or the federal government could call an election—and the mind boggles at the prospect of Quebecers electing a strongly federalist Liberal government at virtually the same time as it votes narrowly for independence. The fact that Trudeau and Lévesque are the two most popular leaders in Quebec suggests the possibility of such an outcome. One hopes that any such indeterminate result would lead not to turmoil and bitter recrimination, but rather to recognition of the fact that Quebecers are not only divided one from another, but are also divided in their own minds. Again this implies the need to seek new accommodation.

The "worst case" scenario might involve the overthrow of the present PQ leadership and its replacement by those who say "les vrais Québécois" are for independence, so let it go ahead. This would likely provoke widespread disorder in Quebec, and not only from anglophones. There would be a widespread demand for federal intervention, augmented by similar pressure from English Canada. Ottawa would invoke the War Measures Act and send troops into the province, though constitutionally that requires a request from the province. Battles in the streets would inevitably follow, as would general economic panic. Voices of moderation would be swept away. Frightened by disorder on its northern border and by threats to its property, the United States would almost certainly intervene, ostensibly as "peace-keeper," though probably in support of one side or another. Both other countries and probably many Canadians would ask for United Nations intervention to keep the peace. Whether the UN would be neutral, or would support Canada as a member nation, is unclear. The eventual outcome—partition or reconquest—would be unpredictable, but in any case the turmoil would be long-lasting.

To describe such a scenario is to be appalled at its plausibility—and to be determined at all costs to avoid it.

What else might make it more likely? On the Quebec side, government policies which fundamentally threatened the property rights of anglophones would soon produce appeals for federal intervention. Similarly widespread expropriation of American or Canadian-owned industry would provoke further appeals and rapid disinvestment. American businesses and government could, on the Chilean model, try to "destabilize" the Quebec regime, assist dissidents, and the like. Such measures seem unlikely, except under extreme provocation, which the PQ government in power will certainly avoid. One also hopes that both the federal government and English Canadians generally would resist any foreign intervention. However, under most circumstances, one would expect the US to argue for moderation and stability, and the Quebec authorities to be careful to avoid policies which would attract fundamental opposition from business.

The demand from Quebec anglophones to "save us" also seems somewhat unlikely. In a sense it is language policies, not independence, which poses the greatest threat to them, and Quebec can implement those even within the federation. In addition many anglophones will vote with their feet and others will decide to make their way as members of the Quebec community.

One of the surest recipes for disorder is a massive pull-out of capital surrounding the referendum vote. It is not hard to imagine severe economic collapse, which could in turn feed any number of extremist movements. There would no doubt be some withdrawal, but we can expect businessmen to limit such actions in order to avoid collapse which would further endanger fixed assets in Quebec. Once started, however, the capital exodus from Quebec could soon become a torrent. Ironically, English-Canadian refusal of association could hasten economic decline, and the resulting tension could produce more anti-business Quebec policies. This in turn could stimulate pro-business intervention from Ottawa and Washington.

It is, of course, one thing to suggest what various actors might do on "rational" grounds, and quite another to predict what they might do in the heat of the moment. For example, even if it were "objectively" within the interests of English Canada to negotiate an economic association, resentment and hostility may well prevent those benefits being perceived—or even provoke a deliberate beggar-thy-neighbour response. Similarly, in the complex, drawn-out negotiations following an independence vote there could be many points at which frustrations would build up and lead to their termination, or to mutually damaging unilateral action. Just as it is hard to envisage leaders who have devoted years to the drive for independence quietly accepting a defeat for their cause, it is difficult to imagine English-Canadian leaders coolly bargaining away the federation.

Pessimistic scenarios of disorder and escalating conflict can plausibly be sketched in the event of votes both for and against independence. The PQ emphasizes that the process of decision is perfectly normal, to be debated in much the same way as one might a rise in family allowances. But, of course, it is not. The issue touches the most fundamental chords of national identity on both sides; potentially, it drastically affects material interests as well. Some statements from both sides suggest that rhetoric is already escalating rapidly, perhaps giving a foretaste of much more bitter discussion to come. Some federalist politicians have increased their attacks on separation and stressed its allegedly dire consequences. The PQ in turn has interpreted such remarks as blackmail and propaganda. Neither side regards the other's arguments as legitimate; each accuses the other of sabotaging the democratic process.

Against these intimations of a breakdown in communication must be set other factors. The Canadian democratic process has held up. It has, as it should, permitted the PQ to develop, to win power, and to promote its central goal. The PQ has not tried to muzzle its opponents. Words like "traitor" are seldom heard, and strong voices for moderation quickly condemn those seen to use the issue to provoke ugly hostilities. The issue is legitimately in the political arena and is being handled by legitimate political processes.

It might, of course, be replied that it is all very well to discuss the matter relatively dispassionately now, but that if the decision to seek independence is made such moderation will vanish. Certainly the democratic procedure is fragile, and one can find in Canadian history events—such as the hanging of Riel, the quashing of the Winnipeg General Strike, and the internment of Japanese-Canadians—which indicate racial and linguistic intolerance and a willingness to use official power to stifle dissent. It is always possible that demagogic leaders will play on such passions with considerable success. But, on the federal side, none of the major federal parties, nor any of the provincial governments in power today, appears to want to play such a role. Quebec politics in recent years has been somewhat more volatile, but here too the overwhelming weight of leadership appears unequivocally committed to an open process of choice. Perhaps one of the most distinctive Canadian traits is a fear of disorder and of unrestrained conflict, based in part on the perceived fragility of the national fabric. Reinforcing it are more concrete incentives to stress the need for maintenance of order. On the economic side, for workers and owners alike, the major threat is not so much independence itself, which if achieved peacefully is not likely to have severe economic consequences. The turmoil that might accompany separation, or its denial, poses a far more real economic danger. Hence another strong group of pressures for moderation.

We have identified several flash points which could spark off the pessimistic scenario: economic depression; a hostage or siege mentality among federalist Quebecers; impatience among frustrated independentists if the referendum fails; a disputed referendum result. Several other factors which a few years ago might have been expected to lead to a breakdown of political order may now be set aside. There is no outright rejection of even the possibility of independence by English Canada; a hasty unilateral and manifestly undemocratic declaration of independence by Quebec is improbable; a secessionist government which had a set of additional goals fundamentally repugnant either to anglophone economic interests or to their political values is not expected. These are no longer realistic fears, and for that reason there is hope of reaching an outcome without large-scale violence or repression. It will not be easy. To facilitate a free and open choice will require a high degree of moderation, restraint, openness, and political skills in leaders on both sides. The tragedy for federalists is that the greatest test of Canada's commitment to freedom of choice might result in the fragmentation of Canada itself.

Disengagement

HUGH THORBURN

There are two major problems to be considered in dealing with the question of the disengagement of Quebec from Canada. The first is concerned with the process of decision making, and the second with the means of carrying out the decision once made. It is easier to find a solution for the first problem—a reasonable and fair process for the people concerned to reach a decision—than for the second. If the decision is that Quebec should remain within Canada, the question of disengagement does not arise. Should the decision go in favour of independence, an examination of the issues then to be confronted —even under the most optimistic assumptions about the willingness of both sides to negotiate—demonstrates in a frightening manner just how difficult it would be to disentangle two highly integrated communities.

Let me make clear my assumptions and biases. My preference is for Quebec to remain in Canada, although I recognize the need to adapt to the changed situation in Quebec and the rest of the country. However, I also consider it essential for Canadians to think through processes for effecting separation well in advance of that eventuality presenting itself as an urgent problem. We are now in a position to consider the modalities in a dispassionate and deliberate manner. If we fail to do this, we shall expose ourselves to the risk of having to react suddenly in an atmosphere of crisis. We should act like a general staff, and prepare contingency plans for all eventualities.

There is all the more need to avoid conflict in this situation, because of the very high degree of vulnerability of this country. Conflict could produce economic breakdown and political turmoil, even disorder or civil war. The country is also vulnerable to outside interference. Therefore a high priority must be placed on the need for the political leaders concerned to discuss the issues among themselves, so as to work out means for settling the question democratically. If this is not done, the country will be exposed to extreme risk and possible catastrophe.

DISCOVERING THE WILL OF THE PEOPLE

Prior to the referendum promised by Premier Lévesque there will be, indeed there already is, a political campaign, involving policy pronouncements and governmental acts calculated to influence opinion in the referendum. Passions will be aroused on both sides, making accommodation by politicians difficult. This is the time, then, when foreseeable risks are greatest; and therefore there is more than usual reason for discussion.

It is essential that there be at least tacit agreement on the modalities of the referendum, and the steps to be followed afterwards. But how can the federal government, committed as it is to the defence of unity, lay aside its commitment, and in cooperation with its opponent plan the dismemberment of Canada? Even to permit subordinate officials to plan scenarios for separatism is to admit to a less than total commitment to the integrity of the country. The peremptory rejection of this suggestion in the past by the Trudeau government is ample testimony to the prevalence of this attitude.

But the situation is more serious now. Even the most devoted federalist must admit that the separation of Quebec might happen. The responsible course of action is to plan for all possible contingencies.

The problem is: how is it to be done? Should *everything* be done in secret, to avoid causing alarm? Or should the fact that the planning is being done be made known? The answer is for both governments to make known, clearly and emphatically, that they are deeply committed to the democratic means of making decisions. This commitment must come before any preference for a given result, because any result achieved by manipulation or duplicity is likely to be a subject of contention in the future—perhaps a cause of conflict. If this position is made clear, then, and only then, will the electorate in all provinces understand and support the essential consultations between Ottawa and Quebec that are needed to prepare for the plebiscite and its interpretation.

The difficulty remains great. How can the leaders of the two sides cooperate to facilitate the determination by the Quebec electorate of the great issue which divides them? What is required is a degree of trust

and magnanimity on both sides that it is hard to conceive of in circumstances of acute friction such as prevail at present. This is a procedure
for saints, and not for ordinary men. If it comes to pass this country is
blessed indeed, and the solution arrived at (whatever it is) will be the
right one, because it will be the will of the people concerned, given
freely without manipulation.

However, we are not likely to witness such an event. More likely, we
shall see cautious manoeuvring by both sides, edging towards their own
advantage but trying to avoid violent confrontation. This will involve
contact between the two governments, but the federal government will
fear to let it be known that contingency plans for implementing the
separation of Quebec are being made, especially if they involve consultations with the Quebec authorities. This would seriously undermine
the federalist cause and sap the morale of those who were trying their
best to defend federalism.

The Canadian government could begin talks with its Quebec coun-
terpart openly, with a view to cooperating honestly in ascertaining and
implementing an acceptable procedure. This initiative could hardly be
refused by Quebec. The content of the exchange would, of course,
have to remain secret. Once under way such talks would provide a
useful contact for elaborating contingency plans to meet all eventualities. They would also permit the general conditions of the referendum to be discussed. Since the referendum has to be interpreted
by both the federal and Quebec authorities, such discussions could
prove useful.

The problem for the federal government is in the construction
public opinion would place on such talks. In order to avoid the imputa-
tion of "planning for separatism" or "negotiating the dismemberment
of Canada," they would have to be clearly understood for what they
were: the laying of plans to carry out loyally the will of the people
whatever the outcome.

Here we encounter a further problem. The government of Quebec
could not avoid discussing the modalities it contemplates for conduct-
ing the referendum, but would not wish to surrender its initiative or its
right to choose the time and wording for the referendum. This is a
crucial power and its trump card. However, it should be willing to
discuss these together with the method of implementation. In return
the federal government would have to agree on rules for interpreting
the results.

It is likely that the actual question will be a loose one, asking not for separation but for a *mandate* to *negotiate* independence with association. Such a question leaves the governments concerned great latitude in negotiating the new arrangements, and takes virtually all power of determination away from the people. It does offer a means of permitting the government of Quebec to pursue its objective of independence with economic association. It would enable the PQ to claim a victory, and would put the federal government on the defensive; but it would leave the field wide open for the negotiation of many different forms of association.

THE PROCESS OF SEPARATION: OPTIMISTIC SCENARIO

Once it is clear to all that Quebec has opted for independence, it will be in the interest of all that this be effected as quickly and harmoniously as possible. Both sides should agree on the sequence of events, so that an orderly transition occurs. This suggests an agreement of separation, laying out the terms of the settlement in detail, the timetable of events with dates for the beginning and end of the transition period, and the date for the proclamation of the two successor states. What follows are suggestions for such a document, which would have to be worked out between the two successor states, with the federal government acting for the English-Canadian one. The two basic possibilities to be considered are separation with agreed-upon continuing association and a complete severance between the two states. Both should be prepared for. We begin by considering sovereignty-association, and then deal with the "pessimistic scenario."

Machinery for disengagement. A federal government faced with a clear majority decision by the Quebec voters to seek independence would be in a difficult situation. Could it possibly take the position that it has a mandate to negotiate independence? If the government were Liberal, its legitimacy would be even more precarious, since such a high proportion of its members would themselves be Quebecers. A dissolution, followed by an election, would cause further crisis. It is frightening to imagine the outcome of a campaign in which one party fought on a platform of 'No" to independence, and another fought for a negotiated independence. It would even be possible, judging by the pattern of past elections, that Quebecers who had just voted for independence might re-elect committed federal Liberals to Ottawa. The most likely response to an independence vote, however, would not be an election, but an attempt to broaden the legitimacy of the federal government through the formation of a crisis coalition, which would include representatives of the opposition parties, and perhaps a few other notable Canadians.

But let us assume this hurdle is surmounted, and a government in Ottawa convenes a conference, in which, together with the other nine provinces, it sits down to negotiate with Quebec. The result of the deliberations would be an agreement to separate, stating the terms in general outline. These would then be turned over to teams of experts representing both sides, to work out the details.

The federal-provincial conference might decide that the risks of holding a country-wide referendum on the agreement of independence are too great, and that the federal and provincial governments together possess complete sovereignty. What for example would happen if non-Quebecers rejected it? Therefore they could conceivably decide to bypass the referendum of ratification and assume the full responsibility for Quebec's exit from confederation. On the admittedly improbable assumption that the conference agrees to an elaborated document of separation, and that it is approved by a majority in both Quebec and the nine provinces, let us persist with the optimistic scenario. What are some possible steps?

The transitional period and the control commission. During the transition period, there would have to be a joint control commission appointed in equal numbers by both governments, with a neutral, presumably foreign, chairman. It would supervise the carrying out of the agreement of separation. It would have the supreme control of the armed forces of both successor states, which would be used for security and supervisory purposes. Naturally, at the end of the transitional period the armed forces would return to the control of their respective governments. This arrangement would see Canadian servicemen doing, in their own country, the kind of peace-keeping and overseeing duties that they have performed so well abroad.

Obviously the separation of such a highly integrated state as Canada into two separate states would be complex and time-consuming. There would have to be a defined period, say one year, during which the old structures would be dismantled insofar as they affect Quebec, and new Quebec ones created and put in operation.

The changes would involve considerably more than name plates and titles, and would involve personnel and institutions. Since many government services are essential and others important, they would have to continue during the transition period without interruption. Clearly this assumes a high degree of good will and cooperation. Also there would probably have to be no-raiding agreements to prevent competitive bidding for desired categories of civil servants.

The boundary. The first problem is agreement on the boundary. To accept the existing territory of Quebec is certainly the easiest solution, and it is probably the best. However, there are problems that must at least be mentioned. French Canada and Quebec are not one and the same; and there could well be agitation from Quebec to permit parts of New Brunswick and Ontario to join the new country. English-speaking communities near the border may well seek to join the neighbouring provinces. There is also the long-standing dispute with Newfoundland over the Labrador boundary, which was determined by the Judicial Committee of the Privy Council in the Twenties but is still contested by Quebec. Then the Hudson's Bay territory in the north which was added to Quebec in 1912 could well be claimed by Canada if Quebec becomes independent. There is the possibility of numerous disputes if there is any departure from the present boundaries, so that Quebec can be expected to stick by Premier Lévesque's position that no right of secession will be recognized for communities smaller than the province. English Canada's reaction is harder to predict, but the need for discussion between Canada and Quebec on these questions is obvious.

Required guarantees. Both sides in a tense situation are bound to feel insecure, especially about their supporters in vulnerable or isolated situations. Therefore it seems sensible for both sides to exchange guarantees for the freedom and security of such persons. Most obviously the rights of the English-speaking minority in an independent Quebec and of the French-speaking minority in English Canada would have to be guaranteed by both sides. These would have to include the continuance of schools in the minority language, at least for the transitional period and maybe permanently. These arrangements would be reciprocal—so both sides would exchange assurances.

Equal rights to employment and to hold and use property should be exchanged. Guarantees for fair compensation for property required for state purposes should be given (mainly to reassure the business community).

Presumably both states would offer guarantees of the conventional civil rights and fundamental freedoms in order to reassure their citizens as well as the international community. If they were similar, a general atmosphere of security would be created. Such statements would be particularly valuable, given the inevitable atmosphere of tension that would accompany separation, and would serve to allay fears and encourage both successor states to respect fundamental rights, in the knowledge that any violation would expose their own minority to possible retaliation.

Both successor states would begin their lives with the corpus of law that they presently possess. For English Canada there would be no reason for change as both federal and provincial governments would for the moment continue as before. For Quebec the federal government would disappear, but the existing federal laws would continue unless and until changed by the Quebec National Assembly. To do otherwise would be to create chaos and uncertainty. Naturally Quebec would be free to make whatever changes or innovations it sought after independence.

Civil servants. The problem centres on two groups: the federal civil servants working in Quebec, and Quebecers working in Ottawa and elsewhere. Some of the former will wish to remain federal government employees, and would therefore have to leave Quebec to do so. Ohters may prefer to remain, especially if they could retain their jobs under the new regime. Good sense dictates that these wishes be respected, and that they be guaranteed in the agreement. Then there are the federal civil servants working elsewhere in Canada who may wish to return to their native province of Quebec to work there in French. They too should be similarly covered by the agreement.

However, the issue is more complex than this. People want more than the guarantee of a job; the question is what job, where, at what salary, and under what conditions? Each must be free to solicit offers and make his or her decision on the basis of clear options, within the transition period.

It is to be hoped that the migrations and changes caused by these free choices would produce appropriate numbers of the required skills on each side of the border. If not, the costs and difficulties will have to be absorbed by the respective governments.

An independent Quebec would have to build up its post office, customs and immigration service, armed forces, and so forth from scratch. Persons experienced in these areas would be particularly precious to the new state, which might be tempted to entice such personnel to join the fledgling service by offering promotions to them. Therefore this is an area that should be discussed before the separation procedures begin. The ultimate choice will naturally be made by the individuals concerned, but cooperation would be desirable.

The armed forces. A most delicate and dangerous area concerns the armed forces. The suggestions above for civil servants should apply to the armed forces as far as possible. However, the situation offers greater complications. Forces are inherently mobile, so that current location is irrelevant. Since the service is federal it seems appropriate for the government of Canada to offer a free choice to all personnel to opt for the Quebec services during the transition period.

These conditions would probably leave the vast majority of the current armed forces in their present units, although some of the French-speaking service personnel might opt for Quebec, which presumably would agree to recruit them into its forces but should not be obliged to do so. This sharing of personnel by permitting the persons concerned to choose is probably the only possible arrangement, because of the integrated nature of the forces.

Since the armed forces are now federal, and the majority English-speaking, no doubt a substantial majority would opt for English Canada. Quebec should be willing to accept this, provided the *matériel* concerned was assessed and Quebec compensated for any loss in the property settlement.

The real problem concerning the armed forces is the fact that they would be needed for security duties. This suggests that the opting of personnel, and the remustering (which would not in any case be very extensive), should be done at the beginning of the transition period. Then the reconstituted units would be available for duties promptly. Naturally some formations would have to be available for duty while others are being reconstituted. Troops stationed overseas would have to be returned to Canada for reconstitution and possible security duties. Canadian commitments abroad would have to be reduced drastically during the transition period.

This arrangement is not likely to be acceptable to Quebec unless it has some assurance that the Canadian forces will not be used to its disadvantage. Therefore it seems sensible for a joint Quebec-Canada army council to direct the forces of both countries during the transition period. This would assure that neither side would be in a position to take advantage of its control of the forces for its own purposes. The ultimate control of the forces should, of course, pass to the joint control commission which would be committed to employ them even-handedly to maintain order and secure sensitive installations.

The problem of military equipment poses a difficult question. Probably the best solution is for it to be assessed at replacement costs or "market" value, with each successor state to claim its entitlement according to the general accounting agreement. This process could be time-consuming and subject to disagreement.

The financial settlement. If this complex and contentious issue is to be resolved amicably, some general features of the agreement should be settled in advance. Here are some suggestions:

1. The obligations for the national debt should be apportioned between the two successor states on a proportion of population basis, with Quebec accepting the obligation to its own residents, and Canada for its.

2. Government installations such as office buildings, military facilities, harbour, railway and canal works, airports, etc., should be transferred gratis to Quebec, on the ground that as a former part of Canada the province can be assumed to have paid its share of costs, and should therefore receive those facilities situated within its borders. (There may have to be special compensation given to Canada for the large and costly administrative complex recently constructed in Hull.)

3. Installations belonging to Canadian federal crown corporations should pass to new cooperative state organizations to be operated jointly by the successor states. Air Canada and Canadian National are the obvious main examples. There would be no need to apportion equipment between the states, or to break up ongoing operations.

4. The St. Lawrence Seaway would operate as a cooperative state enterprise without debt. (The federal government has recently proposed writing off this debt.) Any deficit would be apportioned between the successor states on the basis of a formula based on the relative tonnage of shipping consigned to and dispatched from the ports of the two states.

5. Radio Canada would of course be transferred to Quebec, although its personnel would of course have the same option as the regular civil servants. The installations situated in Quebec would pass to the new state, but if their value exceeded Quebec's entitlement, based on its proportion of the population of Canada, then Canada should be compensated for the difference.

On this basis a joint financial settlement commission, appointed equally by the governments of Quebec and Canada, with a mutually agreed-upon neutral chairman appointed from outside Canada, should meet as soon as possible during the transition period and continue until both governments are satisfied that its work is done.

There should be no appeal from the commission's financial rulings. Other matters could be referred to the general commission.

A subcommission charged with settling the disposition of military equipment, supplies, and moveable equipment belonging to the federal government departments, but situated in Quebec, should follow the same general guidelines. In the interests of agreement it might be expedient to apply them to determining the extent of the federal government's share of the outstanding deficit for the Montreal Olympic Games.

Currency and the Bank of Canada. One of the crucial powers of a sovereign state is the control of its currency. Since any independent state of Quebec will begin life in conditions of economic adversity, its government will be concerned to have full control of its currency. The Parti Québécois has made clear its desire to maintain the Canadian common market. If this is the case one might ask, why not begin by keeping the common currency—the very objective that the European Economic Community has set itself, so far unsuccessfully? Here there are problems. A common currency implies a common economic policy—and Quebec may choose, or be compelled by events, to follow a course divergent from Canada's; for example, Quebec, with a militant trade union movement, may decide on a policy of high wage settlements and rising prices; whereas Canada may favour controls on prices and wages. If so, a common currency would be impossible, and trade barriers may be necessary to prevent an unacceptable flight of money. Since it is probable that Quebec would choose policies divergent from Canada's, it is sensible not to count on a common currency, at least in the short run. After all, one of the most evident manifestations of sovereignty is a separate currency, since it confers real independence as well as responsibility. The problem comes in creating confidence in the new unit. This could be done by following sound policies (in the monetary sense), or by pegging the Quebec currency to Canada's.

If it were to opt for its own currency, Quebec would have to have its own central bank to assume the role of the Bank of Canada. A date would have to be fixed for the issue of the new currency and a rate of exchange announced for conversion to it. After the transition period Canadian currency would cease to be legal tender in Quebec. The problem of the transfer would be delicate, e.g. how to prevent people apprehensive of the new currency from hoarding Canadian money, how to induce people to have confidence in the new issue, and so on.

The problem of retiring the Canadian currency from Quebec is not easy. As Quebec exchanges the Canadian for its new currency it comes into possession of vast amounts of Canadian dollars. If it sells them it would push down the value of Canadian funds. If it holds them they act as a reserve or backing for its own currency, but at zero interest. It is to be hoped that there would be agreement between the two central banks, so that both currencies would retain their value.

The idea of a common market suggests some form of currency relationship similar to the European currency arrangements, which permit sufficient stability for a free exchange of goods, and for long-term economic relations, yet leave each country master of its own currency. If this worked successfully, then it would be time to contemplate a common currency.

On the other hand, since the common Canadian dollar already exists, both sides might decide to keep it, provided they could concert their economic policies sufficiently. And the result could well serve as a valuable discipline assuring the soundness of the financial policies of both countries.

Communications with the Atlantic provinces. If Quebec secedes Canada would be cut in two by a foreign state, and the problem of continuous contact between the two parts of the county would have to be faced. Road, rail, and waterborne transportation would all be affected. The solution will depend primarily upon the relations between the two successor states. If they are good, then simple, informal arrangements will suffice. If not, then more burdensome regulations and safeguards will be needed.

Much the best arrangement would consist simply of assured rights of passage for all persons and goods by all means of transportation. If there is to be a common market in any case, there would be no need for controls at the border beyond the simple oversight existing among members of the European Community. The same could apply to persons as long as the immigration arrangements of the two states were sufficiently integrated.

If these conditions did not apply, then much more complex arrangements would have to be made, providing for goods to travel in bond through Quebec, for passengers to travel in sealed trains and buses, and for all cars to be checked at the border.

There should be no recourse to such arrangements as the land bridges that characterize the access routes to Berlin from West Germany. These merely cause suspicion and encourage harassment.

We must presume, of course, that there would be two separate citizenships, Canadian and Québécois. Therefore some border checks are to be expected. The hope is that they could be kept to a minimum, if the proposed common market were to have any meaning. However, since Canadians have no obligation to carry official identity papers, the border check would have to take the form of personal inspection such as currently occurs when Canadians enter the United States. A less time-consuming and irksome arrangement would involve the showing of some such document as a border crossing card or passport. However, given the North American aversion to carrying such papers, the personal inspection would probably be preferred.

The Port of Montreal and the Seaway. Canada's main port for ocean-going vessels and for overseas air communications is Montreal. Quebec would probably favour arrangements for the city to continue to play this role, in order to retain this lucrative business within its borders. The problem is: what should the arrangments be? There are many examples of such arrangements elsewhere, but probably no single prototype would serve in all respects. The desired conditions are easy enough to identify. The seaport would have to be free to continue to serve both successor states, and additional formalities would have to be kept to a minimum. This would require the stationing of both Quebec and Canadian customs and immigration officers in the port, to clear passengers and goods destined for the respective states. The actual title to the facilities and control of their administration might be a problem. A preferred solution would be to have a joint crown corporation responsible to the two states own and operate the facilities. This is the same form as suggested for the CNR and Air Canada. Arrangements similar to those at the seaport could apply to the international airport (presumably Mirabel). The controls required for Dorval Airport which handles North American flights would depend on the amount of freedom of movement to be permitted between Quebec and Canada, but its ownership and administration should, for simplicity's sake, be through the joint crown corporation.

If such amicable arrangements could not be agreed upon between the two states, the way would be open to protracted deadlock, causing the port to lose the bulk of its business to Toronto and other ports. This could happen very easily; indeed, in the case of air traffic there is already a trend in that direction.

The St. Lawrence Seaway poses special problems. Basically it is the result of agreement between the American and Canadian governments, although the riparian states and provinces gave their agreement to aspects affecting them. All Canadian costs of construction were born by the federal government. The Canadian assets in the seaway itself were valued in 1968 at over $500 million, with $220 million in installations located in Quebec. In addition the federal port facilities in Quebec were valued in the same year at $265 million. Clearly we are dealing with a difficult and delicate matter. It would be preferable for simplicity to leave present arrangements undisturbed, because to re-cast them would open the door to intractable problems involving not only Canada, but the United States as well. The best solution would be for a joint crown corporation (Quebec-Canada) to take over from the present St. Lawrence Seaway Authority, with agreement to share the costs and benefits on an equitable basis. This is easier said than done, given the complexity of the matter and the conflicting interests. English-Canadian ports, both in the Great Lakes and the Maritimes, would be anxious to exploit the opportunity to drain traffic away from Montreal. As an independent country Quebec could be expected to assert its sovereignty over its coastline. On the other hand, as a succes-sor state it would surely assume the treaty obligations of Canada that had become legally its own, especially since they would be mainly with the United States, which has many levers to pressure a recalcitrant Quebec.

If Quebec were unwilling to agree to the cooperative operation of the seaway with Canada as suggested above, and decided to claim its rightful control over navigation in its territorial waters, Canada could be expected to seek financial compensation for its share of the installations. This could lead to a dispute as to the amount of compensa-tion, since Quebec would claim some rights as a previous member of Confederation which had paid its share of Canadian taxes. How this relates to such costly installations as the seaway, which was largely financed by loans, is another matter. In these negotiations Quebec has some good cards too. For example, the threat to stop Canadian ship-ping in the St. Lawrence could mean that Canada would have to seek expensive communications through the American east coast ports. On that account the Canadian negotiators could be expected to be reason-able in their demands, rather than get caught up in competitive threats to raise tolls on their respective parts of the waterway, stop navigation, etc. Essentially, the functioning of the seaway demands close coopera-tion, and this would continue to be the case, especially since it involves the United States, whose good will both successor states would covet.

The Native Peoples. While the federal government has had primary responsibility for the native peoples, it is difficult to see how, if Quebec were to separate, it could do other than to turn this responsibility over to the Quebec government. It could, and should, ask for guarantees to safeguard the acquired rights and privileges of these people. The one which is particularly conspicuous is the right to schools in the language preferred by the parents. If the present proposals of the Quebec government are implemented, the children of persons educated in English in the province will be able to opt for English for their children. Presumably this would apply to the native peoples; however, the federal authorities should ask for guarantees against any diminution of their rights.

As for the native people themselves, it is difficult to know what they are likely to request. It is safe to assume, however, that they would seek to guard the privileges they already have. Since many have already been taught in English, they might well ask that this schooling be continued. Naturally they would be concerned about the rights to their lands, and about traditional hunting and fishing rights. Since Quebec has recently reached agreement on some James Bay land claims, the situation appears superficially promising. But the settlement was far from universally acceptable to the native people, and must cause concern about traditional rights in other areas.

Both the Inuit and Indians are under the British North America Act the responsibility of the federal government. Only some of their rights and privileges are stated in federal legislation and in treaties with the crown; others are diffuse and difficult to define. Now if they should decide that they prefer to remain as they are, the responsibility of the Canadian government, presumably they could so insist, and a serious situation would arise. The vast northern area known as New Quebec is largely populated by native people, and was federally held territory until 1912, when Quebec and other provinces had their boundaries extended. Disagreement over native rights might jeopardize the claim of an independent Quebec to these territories. As to the rights of the Indians living on reserves in southern Quebec, or as assimilated people there, their rights would be much more difficult to protect. They could well be faced with a *fait accompli*: accept the terms agreed upon by the two governments. However, the federal government could be expected to insist that Quebec accept the obligations towards them that the crown in right of Canada had undertaken. If relations were good, Quebec would probably agree, and the transfer could be made to the crown in right of Quebec.

Reconstituting the Federation. One other vital set of questions would remain: the reconstitution of the federation without Quebec. Would Ottawa's position vis-à-vis the remaining provinces shift, and in which direction, towards centralization—as *péquiste* writers have assumed—or towards decentralization? At the moment, the trends suggest the latter, but the searing experiences of negotiating independence might well lead English Canadians to rally around a stronger central government, if only to forestall the spectre of other separatist movements appearing elsewhere. There can be no doubt, however, that soon after negotiating independence, the federal bargain would have to be rewritten for the other partners as well.

THE PROCESS OF SEPARATION: PESSIMISTIC SCENARIO

There is scarcely any limit to the possibilities of disastrous confrontation that might occur, and there is little to be gained by elaborating them in detail. Suffice it to outline briefly the most probable general course of events, should understanding break down between the governments of Quebec and Canada.

The danger is likely to stem from the two governments dealing with each other at arm's length, like two foreign powers, each pressing every advantage to crowd the other into accepting its position. This is the road to confrontation, which is fraught not only with the danger of violence, but of economic and political deadlock, producing mass unemployment and uncontrolled inflation. This is the kind of situation that tempts outside actors both governmental and private to undertake self-serving adventures.

How is such a confrontation likely to develop? It could begin over a disputed interpretation of the plebiscite results, leading the Quebec government to take steps in the direction of independence which are resisted by the federal government. Or it could come as a result of some Quebecers protesting against some of the nationalist policies of the Quebec government, such as the question of English language schools. This could produce confrontation, and perhaps violence, with the minority group protesting to the federal authorities, and asking for protection and the guarantee of what they see as their rights.

The law at present requires the provincial authorities to call on the military for "aid to the civil power," but clearly the Parti Québécois government is not likely to do this. It is difficult to imagine the federal authorities standing aside if, in their view, the English-speaking minority is being oppressed. Indeed the pressure from the other nine provinces would surely not permit it to do so. Yet intervention would probably mean confrontation between provincial officials (e.g., the provincial police) and federal ones (probably the RCMP or the armed forces), possibly in a setting of riot and disorder. This sort of situation is what civil wars are made of, as the situation escalates, aided by the acts of extremists and rising passions on both sides.

The flash points in such a situation are largely in Quebec and the confrontation would likely be between Quebecers in the first instance. The federal involvement is likely to be secondary—a response to a call for help or for protection. However, it is the federal intervention that would have the more serious consequences. There would be casualties and property damage, concentrated in the cities of Quebec but not confined there. There would have to be martial law or its equivalent in those places, and general repression throughout the country. There would be economic breakdown in the directly affected areas, and serious economic dislocation elsewhere. No doubt the bulk of the armed forces would remain loyal to the federal government, but some French-Canadian formations might side with the government of Quebec. This would be an extremely dangerous situation, whose results are entirely unpredictable.

Let us assume instead that Quebec proclaims its independence and closes its borders; and that the federal government decides against forceful intervention. This would lead to the sort of nonviolent war currently obtaining between Great Britain and Rhodesia. It would mean closed borders, economic boycott, and other economic measures by the one government against the other, in order to bring it to terms. In a highly integrated state such as Canada, this would bring instant ruin to businesses on both sides of the border, mass unemployment, and therefore sudden and unpredictable political instability. The probability is that strong pressure would be brought upon the federal government by the business community, the nine provincial governments, the trade unions, and others to take decisive action to end the ruinous emergency situation caused by Quebec's unilateral action. Events in Quebec would be far from tranquil, and disorder is likely, since the economic crisis there would be more acute than anywhere else, and the confrontation between the two positions more intense. Either the provincial government would resign, or some sort of breakdown would occur, with violence and repression a likely result. At this point even if the Quebec government were to give up, the emotional climate, and the feeling of outrage among many PQ supporters, could well produce a rash of violent incidents. Such conditions often produce small terrorist organizations like the FLQ in 1970. For such commandos to go into action could well produce another Ulster.

One point of clarity emerges. Unilateral action should be avoided at all costs. The governments concerned must preserve their willingness to deal with one another. The costs of doing otherwise in a highly integrated country such as Canada are simply unacceptable.

The major consequence of such a disruptive event as the secession of one of the central provinces of Canada could not really be planned for; and that is the emotional upheaval with its unforeseen physical effects. There would be many bitter incidents as the fabric of the nation was taken apart and reapportioned. Business confidence would be seriously undermined. Investment would come to a halt, and capital would, where possible, leave the country for more secure havens. As a result, there would be serious unemployment, especially in eastern Canada, with its attendant frustration, anger, and bitterness. To cope with a serious economic depression during the transition period, and perhaps beyond, would require policies of deficit financing, heavy welfare payments, and extraordinary efforts by governments to maintain employment, even in the face of deep budgetary deficits. Here the cooperation of both Quebec and the other provinces would be vitally important but one wonders whether such a situation could possibly call forth such cooperation. It would be hard to prevent people from blaming their misfortunes on one or other of the political elements, or on the other language group. Such volatile reactions, especially if they are widespread, can produce political instability and spawn extremist political movements.

These dangerous times would probably justify exceptional security arrangements, but what should they be? Concerted efforts would be needed to keep the peace, and prevent inflammatory rhetoric designed to turn one group against another. There would have to be special arrangements to protect community leaders from attack, and the media would have to be restrained from using provocative material. Care would have to be exercised to prevent unwarranted interference from outside the country. We should have to be watchful lest democracy itself be sacrificed in the disruption. Certain security arrangements over time reduce freedom, and the lack of trust and community solidarity occasioned by such a struggle are themselves a threat to democracy.

These considerations should also lead us to ensure that the transitional period is as short as possible, so that the country can get back to normal quickly. The longer the transition goes on the longer will be the accompanying depression and period of tension.

A particular danger is that elements in English Canada may come, in the transitional period, to blame Quebec for their economic ills, and refuse to go along with the common market after independence. After all, they may say, why should we continue to pay artificially high prices for textiles, shoes, clothing, etc., when Quebec, for whom these sacrifices are being made, is opting to leave Confederation? The tariff is one of the major reasons given for western alienation, and many westerners resent it deeply, even now. Admittedly opinion in Ontario would be less negative, because it also benefits from the tariff, particularly in the case of its labour intensive and/or inefficient industries. However, the internationally competitive industries, plus agriculture, could well join the chorus against the common market; and if in fact it is refused there would be serious economic disruption in Quebec, and not insignificant problems in Ontario and the Atlantic provinces.

I raise these possibilities not because they are inevitable, but rather to show the darkest dangers in the hope that all our efforts will be bent to avoid them. If independence for Quebec were realized, both states would have a full agenda before them. They would have to work out their external trading patterns, their relations with the United States, Britain, and France, the role of the state in relation to production and distribution, the form of government (parliamentary monarchy or some sort of republic), and so on. The Quebec government would have to determine the degree of socialism to apply in view of the Parti Québécois' electoral program on the one hand and the realities of North America on the other. Specifically, is the PQ to risk interference from outside by nationalizing the operations of some multinational corporations, or is it to risk the disenchantment of its left-wing supporters? English Canada would have to decide on the means of integrating its economy and making it competitive in the modern world, on how to handle the problems of ethnicity and language, given the diminished saliency of bilingualism and other devices of accommodation. It would be many years before the two successor states had settled into a routine, and recognized who they were and what they stood for. The old myth of a bilingual Canada would have to be replaced by new ones.

In this transformed situation the country might well develop a new sense of purpose, which clearly it has lacked while its energies were absorbed in the struggle over Quebec. The long neglected questions of economic planning could then be faced. Constitutional change would not only be possible, it would be forced upon the country by the disruption over Quebec. But all this assumes that the basic constitutional system and the union of the remaining provinces survive the disturbance. No one can predict the outcome—but if it comes to this, we shall have no choice but to soldier on.

Association After Sovereignty?

CHARLES PENTLAND

The Quebec independence movement, as many observers have noted, has much in common with the multitude of nationalist, anticolonial, and secessionist movements the world has experienced in the last half-century. In at least one respect, however, the attitudes and expectations at the core of the Quebec movement differ strikingly from the usual pattern. In most instances, the advocates of independence pursue as their overriding goal the formal achievement of political sovereignty, and assume that economic independence will accompany or flow from it. Even where continued economic interdependence after political sovereignty is a fact of life, it is rare to find the leaders of independence movements actually proposing formal economic associations with their erstwhile compatriots or colonizers. And yet, such a proposal has been central to the program of the Parti Québécois from its inception almost ten years ago.

From the creation of the Mouvement Souveraineté-Association in 1967 to the capture of power by the Parti Québécois in 1976, it has been a constant theme of René Lévesque and his colleagues that Quebec's political independence should be accompanied by the creation of a new, mutually rewarding set of economic relationships. It is not surprising that so far the PQ has chosen to concentrate on the meaning and mechanics of "sovereignty" or "independence," and its opponents on the traumas and irrationalities of "separatism." Even so, it is remarkable how little thought has been devoted by any party to what form the putative economic association between an independent Quebec and the rest of Canada might take.

In his manifesto of 1968, *An Option for Quebec*, René Lévesque briefly sketches his conception of a Quebec-Canada relationship modelled on the Nordic Council, Benelux, the European Economic Community, and the Central American Common Market. Some sort of "New Canadian Union," he argues, seems "made to measure for the purpose of allowing us, unfettered by obsolete constitutional forms, to pool our stakes with whatever permanent consultation and flexible adjustments would best serve our common economic interests: monetary union, common tariffs, postal union, administration of the national debt, co-ordination of policies, etc." The partners to such a union, he adds, could even cooperate *as equals* on questions such as the treatment of minorities, and on foreign and defence policy.

Elaborating somewhat on the concept of a Quebec-Canada monetary union, Lévesque proposes a five-year treaty to cover a trial-and-transition period during which, ideally, the dollar would remain the common currency, monetary management would be undertaken jointly, and capital markets would remain linked. If such a readjustment of the existing system cannot be negotiated, Lévesque argues, then Quebec will have to create its own currency and instruments of monetary management. The Canada-Quebec common market, too, would require negotiation of a long-term agreement between the two partners. Such an agreement would embody both continuation of the present free trade arrangements between the two, and "new or amended tariffs on goods from the outside world . . . set through regular consultation between the two ministers concerned."

Beyond these provisions, Lévesque sets out proposals for fiscal coordination and for "joint or parallel planning" in such fields as transport, communications, citizenship, and labour. The whole would be overseen by a series of mixed permanent committees, a secretariat forming "the highest administrative authority of the association," a court of arbitration, regular meetings of joint councils of ministers, and parliamentary exchanges—all of these, needless to say, constructed on the basis of parity between Quebec and the rest of Canada.

Perhaps we should not expect too much in the way of substance, specificity, or intellectual rigour in what was, after all, not a treatise on forms of economic association but an opening shot in the political struggle for independence. The fact that Lévesque invoked the widely divergent examples of Norway and Sweden (following their separation), the European Community, the Benelux, and Central America to illustrate his case suggests uncertainty, confusion, or deliberate ambiguity about the form he then saw the Canada-Quebec association taking. Subsequent statements, howver, have done little to clear up these difficulties or to develop the central themes further.

In the *Programme Edition 70* of the Parti Québécois (1970) the emphasis is overwhelmingly on sovereignty and independence—why they are necessary, how they will be achieved, how they will be used in the interests of the people of Quebec. Four pages (in ninety-six) are devoted to the question of the economic association. Here too, the language is tough and uncompromising—agreement on an association is not an absolute necessity for an independent Quebec, and if negotiations founder on one point or another the idea can be abandoned for the time being at least. The point is underlined (p. 27): "Il ne faut jamais oublier que si le mouvement d'intégration économique au niveau des continents est un phénomène moderne très puissant, la poussée des peuples vers l'indépendance en est un encore plus fort."

The common market and the monetary union remain the twin pillars of the proposed association, although they are discussed in terms which suggest a growing concern lest the rest of Canada mistake Quebec's interest in such arrangements for a willingness to let go certain levers of economic control. In the first place, it is observed that while a common market could exist without monetary union, the reverse is not true. And if monetary union were to prove infeasible, Quebec would seek, not a full common market in which all factors of production moved freely across the border, but a simple customs union allowing for greater national control of capital, labour, and raw materials. Secondly, the point is stressed that while initially the common market would reflect existing complementarities and interdependencies in the two economies, in the long run it would have to evolve according to Quebec's needs for independent development. And thirdly, to scotch any suspicion that Quebec was unusually eager to give up control of monetary matters, the Parti Québécois argues that in today's international monetary system no state has much autonomy in such matters anyway, and that, therefore, union with Canada is immaterial from that perspective.

In the 1973 program the emphases change slightly. The customs union, in which each partner agrees not to put up tariff barriers against the other after political separation, is preferred to the common market. More stress is placed on the harmonization and coordination of economic policies and on functional cooperation than on monetary union, although the latter is still mentioned. These changes undoubtedly reflected factional shifts then occurring in the Parti Québécois and changes in its leaders' perceptions of English Canada's outlook. On the one hand, Jacques Parizeau's preference for a customs union over a common market was gaining influence, as was his more decentralized conception of monetary union. On the other hand, after the events of 1970, more radical members of the party apparently had growing doubts as to how far English Canada would go to accommodate an independent Quebec economically, while others felt that in any case their socialist Quebec would sit uneasily in such a framework.

In the 1976 electoral campaign, since little was heard from the Parti Québécois on the question of independence, even less was heard on the issue of association. But in the summer of 1976 René Lévesque restated at least the main lines of party policy in the authoritative American journal *Foreign Affairs*.[1] As envisaged by Lévesque, the independence scenario "would call, as a decisive first step, for a customs union, as full-fledged as both countries consider to be mutually advantageous . . . For indisputably, such a partnership, carefully negotiated on the basis of equality, is bound to be in the cards. Nothing prevents one envisaging it, for instance, going immediately, or at least very quickly, as far as the kind of monetary union which the European Common Market . . . has been fitfully aiming at for so many years. And building on this foundation, it would lead this new 'northern tier' to a future immeasurably richer and more stimulating than the 109-year-old bind in which two nations more often than not feel and act like Churchill's two scorpions in the same bottle."

Looking back over almost ten years of the Mouvement Souveraineté-Association and the Parti Québécois, then, one cannot help but observe that apart from subtle variations on certain themes, there has been remarkably little alteration, elaboration, or conceptual development in the idea of an economic association between a politically independent Quebec and the rest of Canada. Since it is such an important matter, why has it been so little analysed and debated?

One explanation, to which Premier Lévesque would no doubt subscribe, is that those with whom he most wished to discuss the question were not willing to accept the premise of separation, let alone construct blueprints for the aftermath. The idea of a Quebec-Canada customs union succeeding the present federal system, therefore, met with "the most resonant silence in all orthodox federalist circles."[2] Constructive debate, which would in turn have forced the independentists to develop their ideas, was just not possible.

More important, perhaps, is the psychological milieu of the independence movement which, like its counterparts earlier in history and elsewhere in the world, concentrated its political and intellectual energies on attaining political sovereignty. There were those in the Parti Québécois expert enough in the matter of international economic relations to feel confident that the post-independence options were reasonably clear and sure. In the meantime, there was the political kingdom to be sought first.

We must also consider the argument that the idea is not really taken seriously by many independentists. One view, the most cynical, is that it is merely a sop, a reassurance to liberal opinion in the rest of Canada and to waverers in Quebec that after secession all will go on as before. In reality, once the symbols of sovereignty and the levers of government are in hand, other options may begin to look more practicable. Another variant is simply that as the party becomes infused with an increasingly youthful membership, and as its socio-economic program becomes radicalized, the association option will grow less attractive and be de-emphasized.

In addition, there may have been good tactical reasons for not sketching the post-independence model in detail—even if the model were clear to the Parti Québécois planners. For one thing, there was always the possibility that the party's post-independence economic arrangements would look rather like the present ones. To the extent that they could be so interpreted, then independence would seem little more than a symbolic act and, as such, less defensible electorally. Moreover, all those economic arrangements in their myriad of details were to be negotiated with the rest of Canada. It would be impossible to be specific about objectives and modalities until the two sides had actually sat down across from each other.

Finally, there is considerable disagreement within the higher councils of the Parti Québécois over the form post-independence arrangements should take. Some look beyond the rest of Canada for more, or different, partners, while others differ on what should be done about tariffs, money, and cooperation. To go beyond the generalities of Mr. Lévesque's public statements and the party platform was therefore to risk open division. Not surprisingly, now that the issue is of some urgency, the new Quebec government has appointed a committee chaired by economist Bernard Bonin to explore different models of economic association, no doubt as a prelude to reconciling the different positions within the party that have become evident since last November.[3]

Whatever the best explanation, the fact remains that the Parti Québécois' concept of the economic association between an independent Quebec and the rest of Canada is not yet in a form which allows for much detailed, critical analysis. In order to explore the concept we shall have to work with a few relatively familiar recent examples of economic association elsewhere which might bear upon the Canadian situation.

Let us, for the sake of argument, accept what seems to be the dominant scenario for Quebec's independence as presented by the

Parti Québécois. It would be useful, first, to explore the assumptions on which that scenario rests, and then to see what sorts of issues would arise in the subsequent attempt to negotiate an economic association of some kind. In discussing those issues we shall have to keep in mind, first, what the experience of other economic associations like the EEC might tell us, and, secondly, what the pattern of interests in Quebec and the rest of Canada would suggest about the outcome of negotiations.

The first assumption is that the economic association will be negotiated between two sovereign entities, not within the existing federal structure. In other words, there will have been a complete collapse of the Quebec-Ottawa dialogue (whether willed and engineered by Quebec or not), a referendum on independence whose results are accepted generally as unambiguous support for secession, and some sort of formal procedure in which Quebec establishes itself as a widely recognized sovereign state. This assumption must be stressed, since it is unclear from some Parti Québécois pronouncements whether or not the new arrangements sought can be negotiated within Confederation. If they can, then we are in a different realm of analysis from that of customs unions and monetary unions as generally understood and, more important, in a completely different psychological milieu. It is indeed possible to contemplate something like an "economic association" emerging through devolution in a federal system, but for simplicity's sake, and to respect what seems to be the dominant Parti Québécois assumption, we shall adhere to the "sovereignty-first" view.

A second assumption is that the rest of Canada accepts the fact of Quebec's secession with some equanimity if not enthusiasm and takes a broadly positive attitude toward a new form of association with it. There must be acceptance of the idea in principle and a willingness to bargain long and hard about the details. Again, this is not an assumption to be made lightly. As noted already, some independentists are actively questioning their long-standing view that Anglo-Saxon economic rationality will necessarily push the rest of Canada to accept Quebec's separation and the arguments for a customs union. And already some important English-Canadian voices have warned that bitterness has always been the fruit of secession and that Quebec cannot expect English Canada to be an exception to the rule.

There is probably no way of knowing whose assumptions are correct here. It is plausible that both emotional reaction and economic calculation will drive some English Canadians to look inward or southward, while others will find the case for new ties with Quebec more persuasive. But it is not unreasonable to expect that there will be some pressure in the rest of Canada pushing for, at a minimum, discussions with Quebec about certain kinds of economic cooperation and liberalization. Since provinces like Alberta can be expected to show less enthusiasm than Ontario for the idea, and since in a truncated Canada power will have shifted westward, it will not be easy for the nine provinces to reach consensus on whether to talk to Quebec, let alone about what.

A third assumption is that the new economic association will embrace the newly independent Quebec and the rest of Canada exclusively. That this is the official Parti Québécois position to date should not blind us to other possibilities, some of which have already been canvassed by prominent members of the party. Among the alternatives to a Quebec-Canada linkage—alternatives which will no doubt take on a fresh colouration in the euphoric atmosphere of a newly independent Quebec—the following at least deserve mention.

Quebec goes it alone. The argument here is that in addition to a certain isolationist tradition still carried over from the period prior to the Quiet Revolution, Quebec has great need of tariff protection. High tariffs would make it an unacceptable partner to the rest of Canada, the United States, or any other candidate. These economic arguments would presumably be reinforced by pressures toward nonalignment (i.e., withdrawal from NATO)—a goal more easily realized if Quebec takes its economic distance from NATO members.

There is no denying the existence of some support for relative economic isolationism in the independence movement. On balance, however, the forces favouring association of some sort are likely to prevail.

A Quebec-European Community link. That an independent Quebec would be theoretically an attractive partner for at least some members of the European Community—especially France—is undeniable. As the French interest in enriched uranium has already shown, Quebec is perceived in Western Europe as an important source of raw materials and energy for a group of states now heavily dependent on Africa and the Middle East. In principle the Community's needs, and those of Quebec for investment capital and markets, could be met either by an association agreement similar to that enjoyed by a number of Third World countries or by a trade and economic cooperation agreement like that signed by Canada with the Community last year.

While some such arrangement is in principle possible, and has certain economic attractions for each side, it does not seem to be in the cards politically. Even assuming France and Quebec both wanted it, it is most unlikely that France's partners would be willing to jeopardize their relations with the rest of Canada by encouraging it. But we should not dismiss out of hand the possibility that some Québécois and some Europeans will promote the idea, if only for bargaining purposes with other states.

A Quebec-U.S. common market. This alternative has the advantage of having been promoted by a number of prominent economists in the liberal wing of independentist thought, most notably by the new minister of industry and commerce, Rodrigue Tremblay.[4] It represents a viewpoint—often viewed as paradoxical by English Canadians—in which close ties with the United States are seen as less exploitative, more profitable, and less threatening to cultural identity than similar links to an economically smaller and culturally less self-assured English Canada. From the Quebec point of view, the attractions of an association with the United States lie in the huge market for raw and finished products, and in the expected influx of investment capital, while for the U.S. the attraction—as for Europe—would lie in energy, especially hydro-electricity, and raw materials.

What makes this option less likely to prevail is the presence of fears in other wings of the Parti Québécois about the eventual "Louisianization" of Quebec or, at the very least, the establishment of a situation of dependency on the American industrial heartland. An additional inhibition would be strong pressure against this policy from the rest of Canada, combined with a reluctance on the part of Washington to offend or intervene.

A North American common market. A further extension of the liberal economic thesis sees the future not only of an independent Quebec but also of Canada and possibly Mexico as best assured by a free trade area or customs union with the United States.[5] Like the previous option it holds that Quebec's economic and cultural independence will be less threatened if English Canada is rivalled or replaced as an economic partner by the United States. In this version, however, there is assumed to be an additional security in numbers and diversity, rather analogous to that enjoyed by the smaller Western European states in the European Community.

Presumably, this model would appeal to like-minded economic liberals in the rest of Canada, many of whom have been advocating Canadian-American free trade for years. Others would undoubtedly argue that the combination of having to negotiate new economic arrangements on the basis of equality with a seceded province *and* adopt free trade with the Americans would be altogether too much. In any case, this seems the least likely of all the currently mooted alternatives.

Having reviewed three necessary assumptions to this whole exercise—that the economic association will be negotiated after Quebec secedes, that the rest of Canada will be in a mood to discuss it, and that the Quebec-Canada combination is not only the most workable one but also the one Quebec is in fact likely to favour—we cannot but remain sensitive to the difficulties each contains and accept them with some circumspection. After 15 November 1976, many things became conceivable or possible which were not so before. After a future secession the intangibles and the unknowns will loom even larger than they do now. But let us accept for the moment that the "souveraineté-association" scenario works as Lévesque seems to expect, and try to see what issues will emerge, what political forces will set to work, and what the experience of other economic associations might suggest about the negotiations and their outcome. If in fact one or more of the central assumptions proves wrong, some of this analysis may still be applicable.

A CUSTOMS UNION?

As we have seen in examining the evolution of independentist ideas from 1968 on, the minimum objective in negotiating a new economic arrangement with the rest of Canada seems to be a customs union. Of course, in most historical cases where two or more independent nations have entered into such arrangements, they were agreeing to a progressive dismantling of tariff barriers between them and a progressive elimination of the differences in their respective tariffs vis-à-vis the rest of the world. The best recent example is the European Economic Community, where from 1958 to 1968 the original six members reduced the tariffs between them, in annual steps, to zero on almost all products. In the same period they created around them a common external tariff, sometimes by moving gradually to the arithmetic mean of the former national tariffs, sometimes (on very sensitive products) by political negotiation. When Britain, Ireland, and Denmark joined in 1973 they entered a similar transition period in which their tariffs against the other six members were reduced (in five stages to 1977) and their external tariffs brought into line with those of the Community as a whole. There are numerous other cases of states undertaking this sort of commitment—if rarely with the same striking success as in the Community—such as the *Zollverein* of the German states in the early nineteenth century, the Benelux, the Central American, Andean, and Caribbean Common Market schemes, and a variety of attempted customs unions in east, central, and west Africa.

The Quebec-Canada case differs from all these in at least one important respect. Since a customs union already exists within Confederation, what is proposed in effect is to continue it after secession. A significant part of the present economic arrangements, then, would survive whatever break occurs in the formal political and constitutional ties. What, then, would negotiations between Quebec and the rest of Canada be about? Presumably there would be at least three interrelated sets of issues. First, what, if any, tariff rearmament would be permitted between Quebec and the rest of Canada? Secondly, would there in fact be a customs union, or just a free trade area with no common external tariff? And thirdly, if there were to be a common external tariff, at which level would it be set on particular products (in other words, to what extent would it differ from the present one)?

The question of introducing tariffs on certain products between Quebec and the rest of Canada has rarely been discussed by the Parti Québécois. Clearly, however, if great obstacles were to be raised by the rest of Canada to some of Quebec's negotiating points, the implicit threat to use the tariff weapon could always be made explicit—the assumption being that the rest of Canada, and Ontario in particular, has great need of Quebec's markets for manufactured products. At present, it is true, a tariff war is barely conceivable; both sides, it is recognized, would lose enormously. But the fact that after secession there would exist for the first time in Quebec City a government with the full range of protective instruments at its command (subject, presumably, to the restraints of the GATT) can be expected to change the pattern of political demands in Quebec. Firms feeling threatened by Canadian (or American) competition would put heavy pressure on the Quebec government to use these instruments. The government, in turn, might in the short term find the selective deployment of protection very useful electorally, while in the longer term the requisites of

Quebec's economic development and social transformation might be taken—especially by the more radical wing of the Parti Québécois—as requiring a broad range of protective devices.

But what of the rest of Canada? Can we assume that there will be no pressure there for any sort of tariff rearmament vis-à-vis Quebec? Broadly speaking, only in Ontario and some Maritime provinces is there much potential demand for protection for particular industries from Quebec competition. Ontario, like Quebec, has been the main beneficiary to date of the Canadian customs union, and is unlikely to want to risk its overall position by reverting to a selective protectionism which could escalate in future. It would seem, then, that on the whole the threat of tariff rearmament is not a strong one outside Quebec, although we should not rule out differences among the remaining provinces on this question, or the growing use of sophisticated non-tariff barriers within any new economic association.

A more important issue concerns whether or not this new association would be a full customs union, complete with common external tariff. Many groups of states have, after all, found it economically advantageous to remove trade barriers between them while retaining their individual tariff structures in relation to the rest of the world. The most successful recent instance of this is European Free Trade Association formed in 1960 between Britain and six smaller West European states not members of the European Economic Community. Less successful has been the Latin American Free Trade Association, also formed in 1960.

Although this has not been the preferred alternative for the Parti Québécois, its attractions might become greater in the course of negotiations following the achievement of sovereignty. Having, on the one hand, free access to the Canadian market and, on the other, complete control of its tariffs and its commercial options in relation to the United States and other external partners, might seem to many Québécois the optimum solution. Ontario would, on past performance at least, be less likely to embrace this option: not to continue the common external tariff would, in effect, be to lose Quebec as an ally against the low-tariff provinces. (Inside Confederation this coalition has been explicit; in a new customs union Quebec's veto-power on external tariff and commercial policy would presumably continue to aid Ontario, offsetting the latter's weakened position within the rest of Canada.)

A major complication in any free trade association would concern treatment of goods coming from outside, since those entering the lower-tariff part would obviously gain a competitive advantage in the free Canada-Quebec market. In EFTA and other free-trade areas the solution to this problem has been to elaborate a complex system of rules of origin, whereby goods are accorded the benefits of internal tariff reductions if a certain agreed percentage of their value has been added within the free trade area or if a certain process of transformation has been applied to imported materials. To negotiate these percentages and to administer the system would, judging from the EFTA record, be a very complex and time-consuming task requiring the creation of some common bureaucratic machinery.

If, however, Quebec and the rest of Canada managed to agree in principle to maintain not just free trade but a common external tariff as well, would the tariff continue to have the same structure and level as the existing Canadian one? In the discussions on this matter the existing Canadian tariff levels would have the virtue of already existing and of no doubt reflecting the current balance of domestic pressures and external constraints. But now there would be two governments negotiating as equals about whether and how to change the tariff. The Quebec government, we might expect, would be pulled one way by a coalition of traditionally protectionist forces like the textiles industry and its more radical economic autonomists, and in the other by its influential economic liberals who see the way forward passing through the exposure of Quebec's economy to international competition. On the other side of the table would be a Canada in which the balance had shifted in favour of the traditionally low-tariff provinces of the West. Even Ontario, some economists now suggest, might feel ready to reduce protection in certain sectors. While it would be foolhardy to try and predict the outcome, the rearranging of the constitutional furniture might structure the debate more in favour of a lower collective tariff posture than has been possible under Confederation.

If a common external tariff is maintained, regardless of its structure, it will have interesting implications for general trade policy. The lesson of the European Community seems to be that once the common external tariff is in place it is economically, administratively, and politically difficult for the partners not to have a common commercial policy toward the rest of the world. For the Community the beginnings of this were evident in the Kennedy Round negotiations of the mid-1960s. Two years after completion of its customs union, the Community had a common foreign trade policy, which meant that its members were no longer free to conclude new bilateral trade agreements with non-member states. Since then, trade policy has become a matter for negotiation, first, within the Community (among the member-states and the Commission), and secondly, by the Community (represented by the Commission, sometimes alone, sometimes with the Council of Ministers). It is possible to exaggerate the "logic of integration" in all this, to be sure. But it certainly seems likely that Quebec and the rest of Canada would find themselves, by virtue of the common external tariff, under severe mutual constraints in their foreign trade policies and would be forced to harmonize or even integrate them to some degree. That, in turn, is bound to limit each partner's freedom of action in general matters of diplomacy.

A COMMON MARKET?

One stage beyond the customs union in the economist's lexicon is the common market where, in addition to internal free trade and a common external tariff, there is free movement of the factors of production—labour and capital in particular. In the Quebec-Canada case this concept raises at least two questions. First, are demands for such an arrangement, in whole or in part, likely to arise in post-independence discussions? Secondly, would the existence of a simple customs union lead—regardless of anyone's original intentions—to growing pressures for a common market?

As we have noted already, the language of the Parti Québécois programs shifted from common market to customs union in the early 1970s. A number of leading figures in the new Quebec government, among them Jacques Parizeau, are reported to be wary of engaging in too much in the way of liberalization or of common policy-making with the rest of Canada. Nevertheless, others have called for free movement of labour and, less frequently, for free capital movement, to be encouraged by monetary cooperation and fiscal harmonization.

Provisions for labour mobility would likely be attractive not only to Quebec but to those Canadian provinces with similarly high—or higher—unemployment or with significant numbers of seasonally migrant workers. For Quebec, the attraction would lie in the expedience (for the short term anyway) of being able to export some unemployment, having ensured through its language policies that the reverse flow is much smaller. But what would the provisions for free movement actually be? Presumably they would have much in common with the existing arrangements in Canada—absence of work permits and the like, and portable pension and social security benefits. By 1968 the European Community had installed a system along these lines, as well as a modest Social Fund to finance relocation and retraining of workers, although, of course, the scale of labour migration in Western Europe is much larger than anything a Canada-Quebec common market is likely to generate.

Free movement of capital is a much tougher proposition if we consider the divergence of interests among the Canadian regions as well as the experience of other common markets. Not even in the European Community has it proved possible yet to remove from national governments the various means they have of controlling the flow of capital in and out of their territories. Nor has much progress been made in harmonizing tax policies—a major determinant of where investment goes. It is quite possible that the tax systems, investment regimes, and currency regulations of the new Quebec and the rest of Canada will diverge, not converge, since investment has been one of Quebec's main areas of grievance against the economics of Confederation. If the divergence goes too far it might jeopardize the customs union by upsetting the distribution of economic power and the division of labour on which it was built.

A common market, at least with respect to labour and capital, is thus bound to be an important focus of any post-independence discussions. Even if it proves to be only secondary at that point, it will almost certainly come to the fore once the customs union is in operation. The experience of Western Europe is illustrative here, too. It does not, contrary to some beliefs, show that countries which have entered simple customs unions are forced inexorably on to more complex common markets and economic unions. But it does suggest that groups and countries feeling disadvantaged by competitive conditions and the "rules of the game" in the customs union will raise constant demands for piecemeal change. Even if some of these demands do result in the glimmerings of a common market, their main effect would likely be the familiar federal-style paraphernalia of further studies, joint committees, unimplemented reports, splendid rhetoric, and a great deal of tension, confusion, and frustration. Premier Lévesque might find himself wondering whether life really was simpler and less aggravating outside then inside Confederation.

MONETARY UNION?

To complement the customs union or common market, Parti

Québécois spokesmen have consistently proposed some sort of monetary union between Quebec and the rest of Canada. Like the trading measures, this would imply in great part the retention of existing arrangements rather than the creation of new ones from the ground up. The Canadian dollar would remain as a common currency or, failing that, a new Quebec dollar would make its appearance, fixed at parity to the Canadian one. There would be separate sets of financial institutions, including central banks presumably, although currency management both internal and international would require intense cooperation on a basis of equality between the two authorities.

Since the European Community countries are trying to create a monetary union where none has existed before, their experience may not apply in all respects to the Canadian case. But it is perhaps worth noting some of the problems which emerge when the currencies of increasingly disparate economies are tied together. In Europe the weaker-currency countries have been faced with the constant dilemma of either keeping their currencies tied to the stronger ones and thus being pulled upward out of their competitive range in trade, or cutting loose (as the French, Italians, and British have done) to drift downward, thus maintaining some competitive edge but at the price of inflation and, of course, of no longer being joined to a strong currency area in dealing with the rest of the world. Of these two choices it seems evident Quebec ought to prefer the first. But would the rest of Canada consent to joint management of manifestly unequal currencies on a one-to-one basis with Quebec? Would Quebec consent to anything less? Of course, it might be argued that whatever the formal arrangements, the interests of the strong-currency country will dominate policy in any case. Certainly the European Community's experience suggests this.

Perhaps even more basic to the Quebec-Canada relationship is whether it is possible to sustain a monetary union without a great deal of common economic planning and management. In Europe the "monetarists" argues that linking together their currencies would be not only an important symbol of unity and a source of strength in dealing with international monetary issues, but also an incentive to move closer on general economic policy. The "economists," on the other hand, argued that unless a great deal of common economic management and planning were first undertaken to reduce the fluctuations and the spread in economic performance between the states, no currency union could possibly hold up for long. It appears the "economists" were right. If so, it follows that a prerequisite for the kind of monetary union the Parti Quebecois wants would be a degree of common economic policy-making it might find unacceptable.

COMMON POLICIES

It is obvious that should Quebec separate a great many economic and technical matters would require cooperation between it and the rest of Canada. In some cases, this cooperation would be a function of unchanged interdependencies and essentially a continuation of the existing arrangements. In other cases, it would flow from the new fact of a customs union or common market between two equal partners.

Common policy-making, whatever the forms and contexts, can serve three kinds of purpose in a common market. In the first place, there is cooperation to manage what we might call loosely the infrastructure of economic life. This includes transport, energy supplies and prices, the environment, perhaps even research and development. Secondly, there is the harmonization or coordination of national policies so as to ensure fair competition within the common market and maximize the effects of liberalization. This means establishing rules of fair competition, harmonizing taxation systems, coordinating investment incentives and industrial development policies, and the like. Clearly some of the "infrastructure" policies—energy pricing for instance—also have effects here as well. And thirdly, there are common policies designed to redistribute resources in order to bring less advanced or less competitive regions or groups into a more equitable position in the common market. Included here are social and regional development policies, as well as aspects of agricultural, transport, consumer, and industrial policy.

Common markets and customs unions in Latin America, Africa, and Europe have all undertaken these forms of cooperation to varying degrees and with varying success. In the European Community enormous efforts have been made, in some cases for over twenty years, to establish common or at least harmonized policies in all the areas mentioned. These efforts have succeeded to a considerable degree in the fields of agriculture (whatever may be thought of the policy chosen), competition, and taxation. Besides agriculture, the social and regional policies are now endowed with modest Community funds to aid weak or marginal groups and regions. In other fields like energy, transport, industrial policy, and research and development the Community effort has not been impressive. But the pressures are there, and will increase, and even at its present level the Community represents a very complex and influential presence in its members' policy-making. Very likely its impact in harmonizing national policies and in redistributing resources from the richer to the poorer member-states will continue to grow.

For any Quebec-Canada economic association similar pressures must surely arise. A common external tariff, as suggested earlier, implies a common commercial policy. Monetary union points to a common policy in international monetary negotiations, as well as measures of regional compensation and harmonized investment policies within the union. Since free competition among unequals usually increases inequalities among firms, regions, and countries, free trade sooner or later raises demands for fiscal harmonization, competition policy, regional aids to development, consumer and environmental protection, and compatible welfare systems. On top of this there remain the special problems of agriculture. It is impossible to predict at this stage what precise pattern of demands and negotiations these various pressures will produce. But from Quebec there is bound to be some resistance to "harmonizing upward" to the levels of the richer parts of Canada, and perhaps some reluctance to become too embroiled in integrated policy-making in general. The rest of Canada—rich and poor parts alike—can be expected to dislike the more redistributive policies, which would probably produce a net gain for Quebec and which would seem to many to be merely the continuation of equalization payments, DREE and the like under new names.

INSTITUTIONS

International economic associations do not, by modern standards, require large bureaucracies and elaborate institutions, but they do require some. Free trade areas and customs unions rarely need more than a thousand officials to administer the rules of origin and regulate the internal market, while even the European Community, where much is made of the vastness and complexity of its bureaucracy, has altogether only about ten thousand international civil servants in its employ. But in Europe and elsewhere these administrators are delegated powers which can often impinge on the freedom of action of national governments and affect directly the activities of firms, interest groups, and individuals.

Any Quebec-Canada economic arrangement will clearly need some sort of bureaucracy—based no doubt in Ottawa-Hull—to ensure the effective working of the customs union, the monetary arrangements, and whatever common policies are established. In addition to the administrative staff there would need to be joint committees at the level of ministers or senior officials to set policy in matters like GATT negotiations, labour and capital movements, central bank cooperation, use of common funds for regional development, and management of the seaway, railways, and airlines. There might even be need for a court to arbitrate on disputed matters of policy or to adjudicate as between the administrators and the administrated. And no doubt the parliamentarians will seek, if not an assembly on the model of the European Community, at least some form of regular mutual consultations.

Whatever the eventual patterns they were to follow, these institutions would be the focus of some disagreement during negotiations for a new economic association. The issues would likely be, first, the degree of authority with which they should be endowed in areas of common policy, and secondly, the proportions in which Quebec and the rest of Canada should be represented in them. In the first place, giving the common institutions any degree of independent authority would be perceived by certain Québécois as giving the rest of Canada a veto power or at least avenues of intervention in fields vital to the building of the Quebec nation. In the rest of Canada, conversely, some might argue that to have Quebec leave is bad enough, but to see imposed on the remainder of the country yet another level of bureaucracy through which Quebecers can meddle indirectly in its affairs, would be intolerable.

As regards representation, Quebec would surely insist on the principle of parity at all levels and in all institutions, citing the model of the U.S.-Canada International Joint Commission and the rule of sovereign equality on which international organizations in general are based. The rest of Canada, while no doubt conceding parity at the formal intergovernmental level, might be expected to argue that staffing of the bureaucracy should follow quotas based on population and economic power, as in the European Community's Commission. Obviously, the more the economic association proceeds beyond a simple customs union to involve common policy-making, the more central the issues of supranationality and representation will become. Since these issues are highly symbolic as well as practical, and go to the heart of national sensitivities about status, any negotiations they do entail will be difficult.

Much of the foregoing discussion has been based on a set of assumptions which to many observers will seem extreme, implausible, unpalatable, or unthinkable. First, Quebec secedes from Confederation. Secondly, the Government of Quebec is willing and able to determine what sort of economic association it wishes to have, and with whom. Thirdly, the rest of Canada is persuaded, following the trauma of separation, to discuss such an arrangement. Many of us who believe that Confederation must and can be made to work will feel, on grounds of emotional commitment or tactical common sense, reluctant at this stage to consider alternatives to it. But perhaps we should remind ourselves that there is now in power in Quebec a group of able, dedicated people with strong popular support who are determined and to some degree equipped to change the context of political debate in Canada. Those who condemn thinking about the unthinkable as immoral, treasonous, or impolitic are obliged to show how not thinking about it is a more rational way for Canada to face its future. As Jacques Parizeau has said, "we, on both sides of the Ottawa river, are condemned to be reasonable."[6]

If we are prepared to accept the major assumptions underpinning the Parti Québécois' scenario, some form of economic association between a sovereign Quebec and the rest of Canada looks reasonable in principle and workable in practice. But our analysis has also suggested that even in the unlikely event that such an association were established on the basis of equality between the two partners it would have the paradoxical effect of placing major constraints on Quebec's freedom of action.

In the first place, a simple free trade area or customs union would not remain so for long. In addition to common policies desired for their own sake, there would be pressures for integration, harmonization, and redistribution flowing from the existence of the trading arrangements themselves. Such policy-links would not only constrain Quebec in important fields but also permit various kinds of Canadian intervention into its "domestic" affairs. Moreover, if such common policies are an inevitable consequence of interdependence and of the customs union, they would be a prerequisite of any effective monetary union. The result would in all probability be a relationship which would grate on some Canadians because of Quebec's sovereign and equal status, frustrate others who hoped it would lead to refederation through the back door and, most significantly, prove intolerable to those Québécois genuinely concerned to gain mastery over their own destiny.

The concept of "souveraineté-association," then, raises in acute form the classic question of the relationship between the symbols and the realities of sovereignty—a question constantly at issue in regional economic associations like the European Community, among ex-colonial states in the Third World, and in Canadian-American relations. Some Québécois will undoubtedly find satisfaction in capturing the juridical and political symbols of sovereign statehood while integrating Quebec's economy closely with those of Canada and the United States. Others will see association as the pragmatic exercise of exchanging the formal status of one-province-in-ten for that of parity so as to extract more from the rest of Canada, with which, willy nilly, Quebec would still be obliged to live and deal. Still others will see in association a betrayal of the fundamental ends of sovereignty, namely, to grasp the levers of economic, social, and cultural control so as to preserve and enhance the distinctiveness of the Quebec nation.

Every indication is that the first tendency dominates in the Quebec government, and that there are strong economic forces at work to reinforce it. It is perhaps the central paradox of the "souveraineté-association" idea that in the sorry event that Confederation proves unable to adapt and survive, Quebec would end up weaker and more dependant as a sovereign but associated state than it has ever been as a Canadian province.

NOTES

1. "For an Independent Quebec," *Foreign Affairs*, 54:4 (July 1976), 734–44.
2. Ibid., p. 741.
3. On the Bonin committee see *Globe and Mail*, 24 March 1977.
4. See R. Tremblay, *Indépendance et Marché Commun Québec-Etats-Unis* (Montreal, 1970).
5. As a long-term objective, this seems now to be favoured by Tremblay and possibly Parizeau as well. See R. Chodos, "The American Connection," *Last Post*, 6:1 (March 1977), 12–16.
6. Speech to the Toronto Chamber of Commerce and the Empire Club, Royal York Hotel, 17 March 1977.

The Battle of the Balance Sheets

PETER LESLIE and RICHARD SIMEON

The battle of the balance sheets has begun. Federalism, proclaimed Robert Bourassa, is profitable for Quebec. In this slogan he voiced what must now be recognized as the most telling argument within Quebec for federalism, that the province benefits from being part of Canada and that to embark on a separatist adventure would entail unacceptable financial risks. If the PQ can convince voters to the contrary, then the chief objection to separation is defused. Having played down the issue in the 1976 election the PQ is now engaged in a campaign to convince Quebecers that they would be at least as well off outside Confederation as within. Quebecers, it says, are not forced to choose between independence and a high standard of living. They can have both.

Debate about who gets what out of Confederation is as old as the federation itself. The West and the Maritimes have perennially argued that they have been the victims of policies designed to build the economy of central Canada, and Ontario used to describe itself as "the milch cow of Confederation." But the latest round of the old argument was touched off by the PQ government, four months after taking office, when it released the 220-page *Economic Accounts of Quebec*. The *Accounts* themselves are presented in a sober and cautious style, but the government's use of them has been less restrained. Rodrigue Tremblay, as the minister responsible, unveiled the document at an elaborately staged press conference in which he described Ottawa as "the major party responsible for the chronic economic stagnation which has prevailed in Quebec [in recent years]." Citing the *Accounts*, Tremblay said that between 1961 and 1975 the federal government had creamed off a surplus of $4.3 billion from the province, representing the excess of Quebecers' taxes over federal spending. Premier Lévesque added: "The very existence of a federal government which taxes Quebecers in exchange for services that it provides to them, has cost Quebec, in 15 years, the impressive sum of $4.3 billion."

The federal government was quick to respond. Its rebuttal argued that the Quebec ministers had misused and misinterpreted the *Economic Accounts*. Tremblay and Lévesque, said Ottawa, did not acknowledge that Quebecers benefit from federal spending abroad on defence, external affairs, and foreign aid. They also ignored the headquarters expenditure of those federal government departments located in Ottawa, even though the benefits accrue to all Canadians and a significant proportion of headquarters salaries are earned by Quebec residents who commute across the river. Moreover, the *Accounts* did not properly reflect the spending and employment provided in Quebec by crown corporations such as Air Canada. And finally, this time on the revenue side, the *Accounts* misleadingly included the full amount of customs and excise duties and sales taxes collected in Quebec, even though a significant proportion (indeed $4.2 billion over the 15 years) were ultimately paid by the residents of other provinces. The federal paper concluded that "The *Economic Accounts of Quebec* do not permit an evaluation of the impact of the revenues, expenditures and other financial operations of the federal government on the Quebec economy." It added: "The very existence of the federal government. . . is the source of considerable economic benefit to Quebec."

Ontario joined in with a paper accompanying its 1977 budget. It argued that the "Canadian federal system is working to redistribute resources from the rich to the poorer provinces to the ultimate benefit of all Canadians." Allowance was made for those items which the federal government had noted were omitted from the Quebec *Accounts* (or, conversely, were included but did not represent Quebecers' taxes). In this way the Ontario budget paper claimed to report virtually all federal spending and taxing in each province. The results showed that Ottawa redistributed funds from Ontario, British Columbia, and Alberta to the other provinces. The Ontario government especially emphasized Ottawa's revenue-equalization program, which has provided $6 billion to Quebec in the past ten years. This was, it suggested, "a rock-bottom and incontrovertible measure of Quebec's financial gain from Confederation."

But is it? Ontario has picked up only the most obvious of several questions one may ask about the economics of federalism. It has sidestepped the issue which was raised by Rodrigue Tremblay, who was not talking about fiscal redistribution but about the weakness of the Quebec economy which makes such redistribution necessary.

One cannot, however, determine who benefits from Confederation by looking only at public services and the flow of funds between governments. To get an overall view, we must distinguish three main kinds of question:

> Does each province get back in services what it pays for in taxes? If there is significant redistribution between provinces, do the rich ones subsidize the poor or do flows go the other way?
>
> What is the regional impact of federal economic policies—those aiming to stabilize the Canadian economy and which, like tariff and transportation policies, affect its overall structure?
>
> What benefits flow from having free trade between the Canadian regions, and which regions do the benefits flow to?

Any full balance sheet must answer all three questions. We do not try to produce our own version here, but we can suggest a few of the arguments.

DISTRIBUTION OF FEDERAL TAXING AND SPENDING

Regional disparities in wealth have been a persistent feature of the Canadian economy, and a frequent source of regional conflict. Especially in recent years, however, many federal programs have been designed to redress regional disparities to some degree by redistributing wealth from richer to poorer. Such redistribution is crucial to the idea of Canada as a national community. Since Quebec has traditionally been one of the have-not provinces, one would expect it to be a beneficiary of these policies. One of the surprises in the Quebec *Accounts*, therefore, was the assertion that over most of the last fifteen years, Quebec had in fact been a net loser: the federal government collected more funds in the province than it returned in spending.

There are several possible methods of assessing the regional distribution of federal taxing and spending, and each is likely to produce somewhat different results. The most straightforward method for our purposes is the "Public Accounts" method used by Ontario, which simply looks at the point of origin of each dollar of federal revenue and the point of impact of each dollar of spending. It considers only the initial effect, and does not examine whether some funds first spent in one province end up in the pockets of residents of other provinces. Funds not spent in Canada were allocated to the provinces on the basis of their population.

A clear general pattern does emerge. Overall, Ottawa does take funds from the three richest provinces and redistributes them to the poorer regions. In 1975–76, Alberta, Ontario, and British Columbia provided 64 per cent of all federal revenues, but accounted for only 50 per cent of federal spending. Albertans contributed $1.4 billion more than they received; Ontarians $1 billion more, and British Columbians $500 million more. The ratio of federal expenditures to revenues was .92 in Ontario, .89 in British Columbia, and only .68 in Alberta, many of whose oil revenues have been appropriated for the whole of Canada through such devices as the federal export tax. The big winners, as expected, were the Atlantic provinces. Federal spending there in 1975–76 exceeded revenue collected by more than two to one, a total of more than $3 billion. Atlantic Canada provided seven per cent of federal revenues, but accounted for 14 per cent of its spending.

Quebec has been much closer to the break-even point. In 1975–76 federal spending there exceeded revenues by about $2 billion—a sum which Quebec's own figures, derived in a different way, agree with. This large net gain is a recent development. Federal accounts for 1961–62, and Ontario's data, both show that Quebecers paid more to the federal treasury than they received. The shift from a deficit to a positive position appears to have occurred in the late Sixties and early Seventies, primarily because of the rapid growth of the equalization program and some changes in social security programs, especially the expansion of unemployment insurance. More recently, Quebec, along with the other provinces east of the Ottawa river, has derived large benefits from the federal oil import subsidy program, designed to equalize petroleum costs in Canada and cushion the eastern provinces from the effects of the skyrocketing price of imported oil. As Canadian domestic oil prices rise to meet the world price, this subsidy will decline. However, the effects of other policies will continue, and it is likely that Quebec will continue to be a net gainer, though to nothing like the same degree as the Atlantic provinces. The change in Quebec's position is well illustrated by these figures: in 1961–62 it contributed 24 per cent of federal revenue and received only 21 per cent of its spending; in 1976–77 the figures were almost exactly reversed. While Ontario and Quebec's figures are not the same neither are they fundamentally at odds with each other.

Saskatchewan and Manitoba are in much the same position: whether they win or lose overall in given years depends heavily on the vagaries of the prairie economy. Thus Ottawa is an equalizer but the greatest per capita transfers are not to Quebec; the Atlantic provinces are even greater beneficiaries. Large as the sums are, however, they do little to reduce Canada's large and persistent regional disparities. Like the

Canadian welfare system directed at individuals, they partially compensate for the disadvantages of the poorer provinces, but without eliminating the causes of those disadvantages.

By far the most important of the explicitly redistributive programs is the revenue equalization scheme by which Ottawa makes direct payments to the governments of the poorer provinces in order to bring their revenues up to the national average. In 1976 equalization transferred almost $1 billion to Quebec, about half the total sum involved.

Many other federal programs are directed at providing services or transfer payments to individuals. Some, like the Canada Assistance Plan, are implemented through sharing costs with the provinces. Others, like unemployment insurance, family allowances, and old age pensions, are provided directly by Ottawa. While not explicitly redistributive between regions, they may accord a special benefit to any province which has a high proportion of its population in the categories—young, poor, unemployed, etc.—to which the programs are directed. Such interregional transfers are substantial. For example, in 1975 the major transfer programs provided an average $519 to each Albertan, $561 to each Ontarian, $643 to each Quebecer, and $915 to each Newfoundlander. Combining transfers to individuals and to governments, one study estimates they eliminate one-fifth of the regional disparities in incomes. While the incomes of those in the poorer provinces are increased, the greatest benefits flow to Atlantic Canada: Quebec's gains are far more modest.

In 1975, Ottawa spent $7.6 billion on goods and services and employed over 300,000 persons. So where the government puts its offices and where it buys its paper clips can have an important regional effect, as is shown by frequent disputes over the location of military bases, the decision to build the new mint in Winnipeg, and the controversy over putting a service facility for Air Canada in Winnipeg. Quebec clearly loses out in federal employment, though with the large increase in federal offices in Hull this appears to be changing. In 1974, the federal payroll provided $155 per person in Quebec, and $255 in Ontario. Nova Scotia had the highest per capita spending on federal employment; the western provinces did badly. They are hurt even more by federal procurement policies which are heavily concentrated in Ontario and Quebec.

Ever since Confederation, a central federal role has been the promotion of economic development through a vast array of subsidies, loans, and other devices. Best known is the work of the Department of Regional Economic Expansion, which is explicitly designed to help poorer regions, both through direct assistance to the provinces and subsidies to business. The effectiveness of these grants is hotly disputed; some argue that they provide few jobs but many windfall benefits to business often located outside the poor regions, and even outside Canada. About a third of DREE funds have been spent in Quebec, and half in the Atlantic provinces. But DREE spending represents only a small part of all federal assistance to industry. In 1974–75 DREE spent $70 million assisting industry, while a group of programs operated by the Department of Industry, Trade and Commerce spent $160 million. Ontario and B.C. reaped the largest benefit from these. Quebec received somewhat less than the average, and the Prairies very little. Subsidies to agriculture cost $360 million. They were concentrated proportionately in the Prairie provinces, but also provided surprisingly large benefits to Ontario and Quebec (which together received 60 per cent of the total spending).

Thus Quebec gains from many programs, but it also contributes a large share of federal revenue. In most recent years the net result has come close to balancing. Quebec is not a big winner, but nor is it a loser. Some of the western provinces seem to have greater cause for grievance if attention is restricted to federal taxing and spending programs. Different calculations may well indicate somewhat smaller or larger gains for Quebec, but they are not likely to produce any dramatic changes in the overall picture. The important point is that this narrowly defined balance sheet does not conclusively answer the basic question about the value of federalism to Quebec or to any other region. To the extent that Quebec is a net beneficiary, however, independence—if it did not strengthen the Quebec economy—would leave the taxpayer bearing a heavier burden than he does now.

REGIONAL EFFECTS OF FEDERAL ECONOMIC POLICIES

Why are the Maritimes, and to a lesser extent Quebec, have-not provinces in the first place? Is it a result of other federal policies whose impacts on economic development are not demonstrated in government budgets? Do these broader policies help create the inequalities which are only partly compensated for by the federal spending we have just examined?

Ontario's contribution to the battle of the balance sheets suggests that federal stabilization and structural policies bring no special favours to any province or region. But Rodrigue Tremblay, in company with many other Quebec economists in recent years, disagrees. In his presentation of Quebec's *Accounts* he emphasized the view that the federal government has been depressing the level of economic activity in Quebec. It has, said Tremblay, drawn funds out of the province and used them to finance economic development in other regions of Canada. He also endorsed the opinion of many economists in the Maritimes and Quebec who argue that these areas are the first to suffer when Ottawa applies its fiscal brakes and are the last to benefit from any effort to stimulate the economy. A judgment on these matters must figure in any overall balance sheet of Confederation.

The nub of Tremblay's position is that Ottawa has in effect different fiscal policies in each region, and that by running a surplus in Quebec it has been choking Quebec's economy. He adds two refinements to the basic argument. First, "it is the job creation categories of expenditures are essentially expenditures on wages, expenditures on investment and purchases from businesses." By contrast, unemployment insurance pay-outs were high, but they do not have the same expansionary impact. Tremblay's second point: individuals and corporations in Quebec have been net savers, but their savings have largely financed capital formation outside the province:

> ... from 1961 to 1975, the net export of savings, in 1975 dollars, is estimated at some 8.7 billion dollars. . . . Quebecers have been trying for some time to understand the financial manipulations by which savings have left Quebec; the major agent in these transactions was no doubt the Federal Government for the entire period from 1961 to 1975.
> ... in addition to being able to use its fiscal power to withdraw enormous amounts of savings from Quebec, the Federal Government also acts through financial instruments [presumably banks and insurance companies?] and regularly seeks, in the forms of borrowings, large amounts of voluntary savings from Quebecers.

Although the federal rejoinder convincingly demonstrated that the Quebec data did not establish what was claimed for them (namely, that the province was a net exporter of capital), it also acknowledged that the necessary data are not currently available: hence it could criticize but not correct the Tremblay-Lévesque thesis. Missing from the Quebec *Accounts*, said Ottawa, are the balance of merchandise trade, and the flows of interest and dividends between Quebec and the outside. No reliable estimate of these is available. Without them capital flows are indeterminate and it cannot be established that Quebecers have financed economic development elsewhere in Canada, nor (on the contrary) that Quebec's growth has been fuelled by savings generated in other provinces.

From here on, uncertainties mount. The sums in dispute are modest relative to the total level of demand in the Quebec economy. Consequently, the overall expansionary or restrictive impact of federal taxation and spending policies can scarcely be decisive in determining Quebec's economic health. The regional effects of federal fiscal policies are almost certainly outweighed by more direct government intervention in the economy. For Tremblay, these modes of intervention have also hobbled Quebec's economic performance:

> By its economic policies in the areas of money, exchange, commerce, transport, energy, agriculture and immigration, the Federal Government is in a position to influence economic activity in Quebec and in other parts of Canada. These policies, from railway policies and the St. Lawrence Seaway to the Canada–U.S. auto pact, have systematically produced their principal effects outside of Quebec. The result is a general tendency for industrial and economic concentration in Ontario.

This claim will no doubt receive further documentation in the future; Mr. Tremblay has said that studies are under way, and will be made public, on transportation, textiles, wheat, and the petro-chemical industry.

The Quebec position is particularly interesting because it runs counter to the standard interpretation of the impact of national economic policies. The classic works in Canadian political economy tend to lump together Quebec and Ontario as beneficiaries of these policies, and to portray the West and the Atlantic regions as hinterland areas which shoulder the costs of the tariff and national transportation policies. For some time, however, it has been clear that many Quebec economists have regarded Ontario as the major beneficiary of federal action intended to expand and protect a secondary manufacturing sector in Canada. While Quebec industries have also relied on tariff protection—indeed, to an even greater extent than has been the case with manufacturing industries in Ontario—they have tended to be those where technological innovation is weak and wages comparatively low. The development of the more desirable forms of industrial activity, it is claimed, has been stimulated in Ontario by the federal government"s procurement policies, by the activities of the Department of Industry, Trade and Commerce, and generally by the selective use of the more discretionary instruments of economic policy. The latter include those directed to the stimulation of individual enterprises rather than the more general policies of a regulatory nature, such as the tariff. For example, the St. Lawrence Seaway, by permitting access to ports in the Upper Great Lakes, allows shipping to bypass Montreal and the Atlantic ports.

Is this a valid interpretation of the regional effect of national economic policies? The most that can be said at present is that it merits enquiry. In the meantime, we should note that if Quebec's complaints about national policies are justified, they undoubtedly also hold with added force for the other eight provinces. Even if Quebec's indictment fails because of insufficient evidence, the issues it raises are the perennial ones of Canadian political economy. In voicing its own complaints Quebec has perhaps unwittingly added weight to the long-standing claims of Canada's hinterland areas. What is not yet apparent is whether or not these claims may be advanced against Quebec too, as part of Canada's industrial axis.

The issue may be slightly rephrased. What the Quebec government now claims, on the basis of its *Economic Accounts*, is that Quebec is part of the Canadian hinterland which is the economic tributary of Ontario (or rather of Toronto-Niagara, since the north and east of Ontario are very obviously part of the hinterland). Perhaps the portrayal is inaccurate. Even so, its emphasis on the supposed burdens of economic union, as shouldered by the hinterland areas, should disquiet those who believe Canada is an harmonious economic whole.

GAINS AND LOSSES FROM ECONOMIC INTEGRATION

Economic integration means the reduction or elimination of barriers to the free movement of goods, person, capital, and so forth. It encourages economic specialization by region, so that each area produces what it is best equipped to do. It provides economies of scale since in a larger market firms can use larger production units. Hence integration promotes efficiency in the use of economic resources and permits increases in aggregate production. The growth in output thus achieved constitutes a clear gain. Most economists argue that these benefits while not strictly quantifiable are very large. All other things being equal, it is much better to be part of a market of 23 million than one of 6 million.

It would be pure chance, however, if all regions in an economic union benefited proportionately to their population (or to the income levels they would otherwise have); and some regions may actually incur a net loss. This would be most likely to happen in the case of a region which could dicker more advantageously with other potential trading partners if it were on its own. Its possibilities for doing so, however, depend on the political mood and the economic circumstances of other nations, and on the resources (including labour) which the region in question can draw on to beef up its own economic performance. A consequence is that *the distribution of the benefits of integration between regions in an economic union is indeterminate*. Arguments on the matter lie more within the sphere of political controversy than of economic analysis.

To put the same point another way: we do know that there are economic benefits to be reaped from integration, but there is no sure way of knowing which regions do the reaping. All that can be said with confidence is that those regions that gain most are in principle able to transfer some of the benefits to other regions and still be better off than they were before. In so saying, however, we are no longer addressing ourselves to the question of who benefits from integration as such, but are considering what redistributive mechanisms can be brought into play in the form of public services or deliberate policies of regional development.

What about the effects of integration in Canada? Quebec, which has never seriously questioned its economic association with the rest of Canada, presumably finds its integration within the Canadian market beneficial. There are some dissenters: Rodrigue Tremblay, before he became a PQ minister, proposed that an independent Quebec join with the United States in a common market. This would, however, involve vast and presumably painful adjustments in the structure of the Quebec economy. Evidently most Quebecers, including the PQ government, are happy to have the protection of the Canadian tariff to secure privileged access to markets in other provinces. Figures recently released by the Ontario government (based mainly on Statistics Canada data) indicate that in 1974, 177,000 Quebecers owed their jobs to sales of manufactured goods in other provinces (as compared with 123,000 workers in other provinces who owed their jobs to sales of manufactures in the Quebec market). Of course, what such figures cannot show is whether these jobs would have existed in the absence of the tariff; nor can they tell us whether total Canadian employment opportunities would have been much reduced with less protectionist policies, and if so, which regions would have been mainly affected.

The Maritimes and the West have much less reason than Quebec to suppose that economic integration with the rest of Canada brings them any significant benefit. They have not succeeded in building up large manufacturing industries, and those manufactures which they do produce depend less on the Canadian market than those of central

Canada. Attempts have been made to estimate the number of jobs created in each region from the sale of manufactured goods in other parts of Canada; as a percentage of total employment (1974) they are: Atlantic Provinces, 2.4 per cent, Quebec, 7.1 per cent, Ontario, 6.2 per cent, Prairies, 1.8 per cent, and British Columbia, 2.1 per cent.

Thus recent data confirm the conventional image of the West and the Maritimes as hinterland to the industrial axis of Canada, located in Ontario and Quebec. As hinterland areas, which produce a small range of standardized and largely unprocessed commodities, they are vulnerable to changing economic conditions in Canadian and world markets. Even minor fluctuations in economic activity elsewhere are likely to be reflected with exaggerated effect in primary-producing areas. There is, then, very little reason to suppose that these areas gain significantly, or at all, from being economically integrated with the rest of Canada, the more so as they must pay higher prices for their manufactured goods. Hence, for them, *the sole economic attraction of Confederation must be in the capability and the readiness of the federal government to underwrite their losses when times are bad, and to help them diversify and thus stabilize their economies, and to make sure that their residents have the same level of public services as does central Canada.*

By contrast Quebec, or the PQ on its behalf, has convinced itself that the federal government is superfluous and indeed injurious. Quebec relies on the tariff and the access to Canadian markets which it secures; but it now wants a treaty-like arrangement to guarantee the continued existence of such a form of an economic association. In all other respects it wishes to manage its own economic affairs. This objective is evidently so important that to secure it the PQ appears willing to see Quebec forgo federally-provided services and payments to individuals, as well as equalization and other intergovernmental transfers.

The preceding discussion has concentrated on the advantages of an integrated common market to each of the component regions. Another perspective would hold, however, that integration will benefit all *individuals* even if it does not benefit all regions. The reasoning here is that in the free movement of people among regions which is part of a common market, individuals are able to move to areas like Toronto, Calgary, or Vancouver, which provide the highest wages and best jobs. The problem is that lack of skills and other factors may well inhibit the free movement of population. The cultural impediments to the migration of French Canadians—and the cultural costs of doing so—are immense, although the history of French-Canadian emigration to the United States and elsewhere shows that in the past many have been forced to trade their culture for economic opportunity. Recent governments in Quebec have shown that they are determined to prevent this happening again.

The final economic argument for independence asks not how federal policies have affected Quebec, but rather how much greater freedom of action the province would have if it were on its own. Even if Quebec believed that on balance it had benefited from federal policies, it could still argue, "We could do it better." Indeed, in recent years it has sought much greater leverage over its own economy both to stimulate growth and to provide new opportunities for French Canadians.

In the Quebec view, Ottawa has been unsympathetic to these initiatives and has failed, both for ideological and political reasons, to develop an effective industrial strategy of its own. Quebec leaders have argued that federal economic priorities differed from theirs. An obvious example was the location of Mirabel airport, which at Ottawa's insistence was built northwest of Montreal despite Quebec's protests that a new airport would do much more to stimulate the province's economy if located east of the city. Ottawa's control over a large share of taxes and its jurisdiction in matters such as banking, external trade, transportation, communications, and nuclear power all place limits on what the Quebec government can do on its own. The PQ's conclusion: Quebec needs independence to gain control over all these levers of economic policy; it wants no more of the frustrations involved in having to bargain continually with Ottawa.

Such frustrations, and the anti-Ottawa sentiments associated with them, are not felt by Quebec alone. Similar attitudes are expressed in varying degrees by Canada's other provinces. Alberta chafes at federal controls over oil prices and exports. These controls limit its ability to plan its industrial development and to use its resources for its own benefit. British Columbia, as a province based on resource-exploitation, takes a similarly hands-off attitude. Ontario, which is the most obvious beneficiary of national economic policies and accordingly supports Ottawa's power to direct the economy, is nonetheless irritated by federal interference in the administration of provincial programs and is actively involved in promoting its own economic development. Saskatchewan, which generally declares in favour of strong central government, objects to federal backing of the potash firms which have brought the province to the Supreme Court over its regulation of the industry. Even those provinces which would go bankrupt without federal transfer payments complain that Ottawa's policies do not reflect their needs, and they resent their fiscal dependency. In short, there is widespread lack of confidence in the federal government as an agency to direct the development of Canada's economy to the benefit of all its regions. Quebec under the PQ articulates this feeling in its most extreme form but the general sentiment is shared. In some respects, it is equally or more acute in the West because of its weak representation in cabinet and because—in the case of Alberta and British Columbia—these provinces feel doubly exploited. Not only are they being gouged (as they see it) by Ottawa's tariff and transportation policies, but as provinces which are wealthy in spite of national policies they must foot part of the bill for fiscal transfers between regions.

Not all provincial complaints against the economic effects of Confederation are directed against the federal government, or against government at all: the activities of Canada's major corporations are often thought to favour Ontario at the expense of other provinces. The banks, railways, and resource firms are singled out as discouraging balanced growth in all of Canada's regions, and transferring wealth from the hinterland to the centre. Indeed, this was the chief theme of the Western Economic Opportunities Conference in 1973, a regional federal-provincial meeting called by the Liberal government in an effort to mend its fences after its 1972 election setback. At this conference the four western provinces presented joint statements of their claims and grievances. These statements mirror Quebec's complaints as voiced by the PQ: the banks take western savings and use them to promote industrial development in the east, the railways stultify the industrial development of all but the St. Lawrence valley, and so forth. Of course there is a difference: the western provinces smart under the dominance of eastern finance and industry; Quebec's nationalists object to English control of their economy. In both cases, though, the federal government and the business elite of Bay and St. James Streets are seen to be in close alliance, each working through the other.

It is scarcely surprising that in a federation the provinces should voice the interests of their regions. What we have come to observe more and more in Canada, however, is that regional considerations tend to overshadow other factors bearing on policy formation. Political disputes are seen to occur between regions rather than between classes, between rural and urban dwellers, between age-groups, and so forth. To some extent regional conflict even overrides differences between ethnic and linguistic groupings. When this happens, the fairness of the federal system is judged not by whether it promotes the growth of the whole country and benefits the mythical "average" Canadian, but rather by whether it works to the advantage of each section seen separately. In keeping with this mood, and actively promoting it, the provincial governments frequently seek to augment their powers in order to pursue their own priorities, to engage in province-building as distinct from overall Canada-building. In this Quebec is the most advanced of the provinces, but it is by no means alone.

It is difficult to know how far Canada has proceeded towards the regionalization of political loyalties. *Which government, in each part of Canada, has primary claim to the people's affection, confidence and support?* When a Canadian says "us" who does he include? This issue overwhelms all argument about the economic benefits of Confederation; and even the most scrupulous attempts at dispassionate analysis on this subject are likely to be coloured by political loyalties. As a result, scholarly enquiry on the economics of federalism will remain partisan. As we have seen, a comprehensive balance sheet must go far beyond the detailing of federal taxing and spending. But the more it is extended the more complex and contentious the problems of theory, method, and data become. Any discussion of the subject must rest on a host of assumptions, hunches, estimates, and guesses—all of them influenced by the basic preferences of the analyst. Hence the results of each accounting are likely to look much as expected or hoped for at the outset.

The statistical broadsides are unlikely to persuade any of the partisans to change their views. Each side can make telling arguments, but any complete balance sheet would have to take into account all three levels of analysis we have considered. So far all contributions to the debate have focused on only one level at a time. At the most obvious level, there are the services provided by the central (or federal) government, including fiscal transfers to the provinces. Inevitably such services will be unequally distributed between regions, and it accords both with social justice and with political expediency that the wealthier regions should share their advantages with the poorer. At the second level, there is the distributive and redistributive aspect of federal structural and stabilization policies which have a bearing on the type and level of economic activity within each of the major regions. At the third level, there are the diversion and creation of trade flows associated with economic integration which, though they augment aggregate welfare, are unlikely to distribute the benefits of economic union in equal measure among the participating regions.

The difficulty of analysing the economics of federalism virtually rules out agreement on any one balance sheet. But even if we could measure benefits and costs precisely, and it appeared that federalism had incurred a net loss for Quebec, it does not necessarily follow that independence would set things right. First, as we have argued, important constraints on Quebec's freedom of action would remain, even without association. Second, the economic turmoil and uncertainty attendant on separation itself, involving the possible flight of capital, disruption of Canadian markets, and social conflict could all impose a sharp decrease in living standards from which it might take many years to recover. In this sense the practical consequences of independence could well outweigh any theoretical benefits. Similarly, the PQ's implication that "we can have the cake and eat it too" by enjoying the economic advantages of greater independence while retaining the virtures of the integrated Canadian market is at least problematic. The close links between Ontario and Quebec might lead the former to swallow its pride and accept association, but few other provinces would have the same incentive. It is most unlikely that the complex relationships which now constitute the Canadian economy would long survive the disruption and rethinking that would follow.

The alternative to separatism, if there is one, is to try to meet the economic grievances of Quebec and other areas within Confederation. In attempting to do so, two main directions are open. The first is to devolve upon the provinces many of the economic powers now in federal hands, as both Quebec and (to a lesser extent) other provinces have demanded. However, not much can be done along these lines, if Ottawa is to retain its role as the agent of compensation and redistribution, counteracting the adverse regional effects of other national policies and of the sheer existence of a common market. If Quebec is willing to forgo the transfer payments and regional development assistance, the same is not true of those provinces which are more fiscally dependent on Ottawa. Even for Ottawa to be the policeman of the Canadian common market—preventing the erection of non-tariff barriers to trade between the regions and ensuring the free flow of capital and labour—requires that it possess extensive powers, ideally more extensive in some respects than it possesses now.

These limitations on the possible transfer of powers to the provinces suggest that much of the needed accommodation of regional grievances will have to occur through the refashioning of national policies so that the benefits of economic union are more equally distributed among regions. This may involve the modification of decision-making procedures so as to bring the provincial governments more fully into joint decision-making processes. In effect, the federal government may have to share the exercise of its powers, if not actually to endorse the reallocation of jurisdiction, in such areas as transportation, immigration, agriculture, banking and monetary affairs, and trade and commerce.

In thinking about the redress of regional economic grievances it will be important to stress, in opposition to the prevalent dualistic thinking in Quebec, that political relationships in Canada involve more than just Quebec and "English" Canada. The recurrent crisis in Confederation, though again brought to the fore by the PQ election victory, calls into question the whole range of political and economic links between all of Canada's regions. Change in one set of relationships will inevitably alter all of the others, and the tenuous balance built up explicitly and implicitly over many years will now be subject to critical assessment by all regions. The grand questions of Canadian political economy which have engaged the interests of scholars and have been the stuff of Canadian political debate remain with us, only in more acute form than in the past.

NOTE ON SOURCES

This chapter draws on the balance sheets prepared by Quebec, Ontario, and Ottawa, as well as on several more general sources. For Quebec, see *Comptes économiques du Québec, Revenus et Dépenses* (Québec, 1977) and *Presentation of the Economic Accounts of Québec 1961–1975* by Mr. Rodrigue Tremblay, Ministry of Industry and Commerce, March 25, 1977 (mimeo). For Ontario, see *Ontario Budget 1977* (Toronto, 1977), Budget Paper B, and *Interprovincial Trade Flows, Employment and the Tariff in Canada*, Supplementary Material to the 1977 Ontario Budget (Toronto, 1977). For Ottawa, see Co-ordination Group, Federal-Provincial Relations Office, "Preliminary Observations on the Economic Accounts of Quebec" (Ottawa, 5 April 1977, mimeo). An early attempt at distributing federal taxing and spending by region is found in House of Commons, Sessional Paper 108K, 6 Nov. 1964, prepared by the Department of Finance. Other relevant studies include Richard Simeon, "The Regional Distribution of the Benefits of Confederation; A Preliminary Analysis," paper presented to the Executive Development Seminar, Public Service Commission of Canada, December 1976; Economic Council of Canada, *Living Together: A Study of Regional Disparities* (Ottawa, 1977); W. Irwin Gillespie and Richard Kerr, "The Impact of Regional Economic Expansion Policies on the Distribution of Income in Canada," Discussion paper no 85, Economic Council of Canada (Ottawa, 1977); A. E. Safarian, *Canadian Federalism and Economic Integration*, Constitutional Study prepared for the Government of Canada (Ottawa, 1974); Irene Banks, "The Provincial Distribution of Federal Government Expenditures 1972–3, 1973–4 and 1974–5," Discussion paper no. 81, Economic Council of Canada (Ottawa, 1977).

Legal Aspects of Quebec's Claim for Independence

JOHN CLAYDON and JOHN D. WHYTE

Does Quebec have a legal right to independence, or to some lesser form of additional political power? If so, under what conditions? These are the basic questions in any evaluation from a legal perspective of the present Parti Québécois claims.

To answer these questions requires consideration of two different legal orders: the international legal order, which governs relations between states and establishes rules binding on them; and Canada's constitutional system. While these are distinct, they are not totally divorced from each other. For example, in deciding whether, under international law, Quebec has a right to establish itself as an independent political entity, one very important factor is Quebec's position within the Canadian federal system.

Their interaction on the question of independence may be summarized in this way: If international law gives Quebec the right to independence, a constitutional proscription against secession does not change the legal position and does not prevent Quebec from seeking the aid of the international community to implement the right. But we conclude from our preliminary analysis of the relevant criteria that Quebec has not made the case under international law for entitlement to political independence in the face of opposition from Canada. However, the international legal system would probably defer to an independence outcome if it were achieved within the Canadian constitutional system. But again we conclude that the Canadian constitution does not permit a province to secede except with the consent of the rest of the Canadian community, which would have to take the form of the House and Senate agreeing to the terms of independence and to the required amendment.

THE LESSONS OF INTERNATIONAL LAW

Two separate but related doctrines of international law are relevant to Quebec's claim for independence.[1] First, the doctrine of self-determination helps to decide whether an entity in Quebec's position is entitled to break away from another state to form an independent political community, and to invoke the support of the world community in the endeavour. Second, the doctrine of recognition governs how a newly independent entity may participate in the institutions of the international community and relate to its individual members. In deciding whether or not to grant admission to international society, with the resulting political and economic benefits, international decision-makers will take into account whether the new entity has the right to its independent existence. In other words, self-determination is important for recognition, as the nonrecognition of Rhodesia demonstrates. Canada might oppose independence but not be willing to prevent it by force. In this case Quebec's claim to acceptance in the international community might not be fully granted, at least in the short term, unless Quebec met the international criteria for self-determination.

Self-determination is also important because the judgments about whether it applies to the Quebec case may influence both support for and opposition to independence itself. Quebecers have not yet expressed a preference for political independence; the opportunity for choice will be provided by the promised referendum. In the meantime, the proponents of independence assert the right of self-determination to convince the people of Quebec and the rest of Canada that Quebec's independence would have authoritative support. Simply persuading people that they have a right can be a key element in influencing them to advance it and others not to oppose it.

Self-determination is the political and legal concept which stimulated the breakup of great empires during this century. In the post-World War II period decolonization, resulting in the emergence of a plethora of newly independent states in Africa and Asia, has been one of the major forces in the international political system. Although few colonial territories remain, appeals to self-determination are made with increasing frequency on behalf of groups seeking to establish some form of political power (not always independence) over a defined territory. The numerous examples include: Bengalis (Pakistan); Ibos (Nigeria); Basques, Catalans (Spain); Scots and Welsh (Great Britain); Mizos, Nagas (India); Eritreans (Ethiopia); Kurds (Iraq); Walloons (Belgium). The Quebec claim must be viewed as part of a global phenomenon, but it does not stand alone even within Canada: the Dene people of the Northwest Territories have also invoked self-determination as a basis for obtaining autonomy in charting their destiny as a distinctive group.

This freedom to decide a people's future is the essence of self-determination. The objective is control over the processes by which political decisions are made in a defined territory. Self-determination thus underpins claims to secure majority government (South Africa and Rhodesia are cases in point) as well as claims to establish new entities. Political control is important for securing all the values which individuals seek. This relationship between self-determination and the advancement of human dignity is expressed, either explicitly or implicitly, in all the sources of international law which refer to self-determination.

The "right" to self-determination in international law is undisputed. It is referred to in the Charter and resolutions of the United Nations, deferred to and implemented in the practice of states forming customary international law, explicitly guaranteed in treaties to which a large number of states are parties, and has been recognized by the International Court of Justice in two recent decisions dealing with the status of Namibia (South-West Africa) and the Western Sahara.

Principles of law in any legal system usually exist in pairs of opposites. In contraposition to the principle of self-determination is the principle of the sovereignty and territorial integrity of states. Like self-determination, this principle is supported by weighty legal authority and justified by its efficacy in promoting the well-being of the people. It is used to argue that an entity recognized as a state by the international community is free to choose and develop its own political, economic, and cultural systems without outside interference. The principle is invoked by states to counter a claim for secession by a part of their territory. They would try to insulate the matter from international concern by claiming that it is one of "domestic jurisdiction" or "internal affairs." Of course, at the moment Canada, not Quebec, is recognized as a state by the international community.

It is also important to emphasize that both principles are tempered by two other fundamental principles of international law. The first is the protection of human rights. The second is that when a state unilaterally uses force not in the exercise of self-defence, it may not rely on the territorial integrity principle to prevent the international community from imposing sanctions.

Since the claim for political independence advanced on behalf of

Quebec concerns the right of part of an established and recognized state to secede, assessment must focus on how the international legal system has, in response to other such claims, applied the principles of self-determination and territorial integrity. Has the choice been made by genuinely comparing the implications for all the people directly concerned and for the stability and well-being of the international system in general? Or has the scope of self-determination been confined by defining the "self" so restrictively that the claim of Quebec would be *ipso facto* inadmissible?

There is considerable authority for the proposition that the right of self-determination applies exclusively to colonial situations. For the purpose of self-determination, the Quebec-Canada relationship cannot be termed colonial according to international law. Quebec is physically joined to Canada, shares Canada's political power, and the relationship cannot be termed one of dominance and subjugation. Many scholars who are prepared to concede the existence of a right of self-determination argue that it is restricted to colonial contexts; they find support in some of the legal sources which cumulatively establish the existence of the right. For instance, the 1960 United Nations General Assembly Declaration on the Granting of Independence to Colonial Countries and Peoples, after referring to the right of self-determination, stipulates that:

> any attempt aimed at the partial or total disruption of the national unity and the territorial integrity of a country is incompatible with the purposes and principles of the Charter of the United Nations.

A similar provision is found in the 1970 General Assembly Declaration on Friendly Relations. Individual states are also reluctant to acquiesce in their own dismemberment and fear the precedent of supporting a secessionist claim elsewhere. Thus very few countries supported the Biafran attempt to secede from Nigeria between 1967 and 1970, despite the intensity of the Biafran effort and the tragic consequences stemming from the forceful Nigerian opposition. The United Nations, reflecting the policies of its member states, even intervened militarily to prevent the secession of Katanga from the Congo in the 1960s. U Thant, former secretary-general of the United Nations, stated that "the United Nations has never accepted and does not accept and I do not believe it will ever accept the principle of secession of a part of its Member State."

More recent practice and explicit legal formulations do not, however, support the absolute restriction of self-determination to colonial territories. When East Pakistan broke away to establish the independent state of Bangladesh in late 1971, in spite of the brutal attempt by Pakistan to prevent it, the international community recognized this act of self-determination. Moreover, the common article 1 of the 1966 Covenants on Civil and Political Rights and Social, Economic and Cultural Rights provides that "all peoples have the right of self-determination" (in French, "tous les peuples ont le droit de disposer d'eux-mêmes"). Although lawyers may argue about the legal effect of resolutions of the United Nations, these Covenants are treaties and are therefore binding on all parties. In 1976 Canada became a party to both Covenants. As a distinguished Canadian scholar has pointed out, the argument that self-determination is restricted to colonial settings "is tantamount to saying that, while all peoples have the right to self-determination, only colonial countries are peoples."[2] In a recent study, Dr. Lung-chu Chen of Yale Law School demonstrates that the legislative history of article 1 confirms that " 'peoples' was meant to refer to peoples in all countries and territories, whether independent, trust, or non-self-governing."

The Helsinki Declaration of 1975, which was signed by Canada along with the United States and thirty-three European countries, refers to the right of "peoples" to self-determination, clearly without restricting it to colonies. The Declaration also refers to the competition between self-determination and integrity, for the signatories stipulated that they would respect the "right to self-determination, acting at all times in conformity with the purposes and principles of the Charter of the United Nations and with the relevant norms of international law, including those relating to territorial integrity of states." There is no indication of how to decide which rival is to be preferrred. While the Helsinki Declaration was not intended to be legally binding, it declares existing law on this point and supports the interpretation advanced above. The document is rapidly becoming a potent source of customary international law through increasing invocation. It has been used, for example, by the United States to criticize Soviet treatment of dissidents.

In general, international law suggests that in colonial situations, self-determination usually prevails. Noncolonial situations are more ambiguous, but the presumption usually lies with the maintenance of integrity. In the former case, "territorial integrity" almost never wins; in the latter, it usually does not lose.

In order to evaluate the *péquiste* claim, it is, then, necessary to ascertain whether Quebec constitutes a "self" for the purpose of self-

determination. Put differently, for the purpose of making the determination about independence or continued territorial unity, is the
appropriate "self" Quebec, or is it Canada as a whole? This task forces
us to examine the basic policies underlying both territorial integrity
and self-determination as affected by the other two relevant principles
(human rights, maintenance of world order). Because of the presumption against secession, independence will be given priority only if it is
likely to significantly enhance the well-being of the people directly
concerned, while not threatening world community interests. A formidable case for independence must be made. There is no easy way of
arriving at the answer, no one decisive factor. But a series of questions
may suggest the criteria for making the choice. Which result would be
most likely to discourage international violence and to enhance human
rights? Would the claimant to independence be an economically and
politically viable member of the world community? Do the people live
in a common geographic area? Do they share a common awareness as a
people? Are there separate ethnic identities? Have these identifications
become politically salient? Has there been significant integration in
economic, political, and other spheres over a long period of time? If
secession were to be honoured, what would be the consequences for the
remaining part of Canada? What additional benefits would accrue to
the people of the seceding unit?

Independence would have little effect on the world community.
There is no reason to expect that an independent Quebec would violate
international norms for the protection of the human rights of citizens,
aliens, or ethnic minorities. Nor would Quebec be dependent on other
states for its economic survival. An independent Quebec would be a
relatively advanced state with a population, economic potential, and
international capacity much greater than those of many existing members of the international community. There is no serious expectation of
large-scale violence, with all its tragic consequences for human rights
and its tendency to encourage external intervention. On the other
hand, Canada as it presently exists is a valued member of the international community; it has played a notable role in promoting world
order and human rights. Thus independence would not be justified by
any benefits to the world community. The crucial factors, then, are the
comparative effects of secession and continued unity on the overall
value positions of the individuals who make up the two communities. It
is possible to make only general observations on these factors. Many are
necessarily speculative, and more detailed information is provided in
other chapters in this volume.

Quebec possesses clear boundaries (despite the dispute with Newfoundland over the Quebec-Labrador boundary) and a distinctive ethnic base, notwithstanding the presence of co-ethnics elsewhere in Canada and of minorities in Quebec. Most Quebecers are French-speaking, therefore possessing that element of ethnicity that was so prominent in the European "national" movements of the second half of the nineteenth century. There is no doubt about Quebec's existence as an ethnically distinct territorially-based society..

On the other hand, Quebec is not geographically separate from the rest of Canada. This relationship of physical contiguity is similar to the Katanga-Congo and Biafra-Nigeria relationships, and in those cases secession was denied. East and West Pakistan, whose breakup was accepted, were separated geographically by one thousand miles.

If a fair referendum held in the near future reflects a demand for political independence which is opposed by the people elsewhere in Canada (preferably also manifested through a referendum), it would be important to know the degree of support expressed for each outcome. It is clear that there will be opposition within Quebec, if only from English-speaking and other minorities. Concern for minorities was an important factor in the denial by international decision-makers of the Greek Cypriot majority aspiration to merge with Greece. But while in the Cypriot case there was fear for the rights of the Turkish minority under the probable new arrangement, there are no grounds for believing that an independent Quebec would pose a similar threat to minorities. Nevertheless, the presence of minorities opposed to independence will not help the Quebec claim.

A bare majority in favour of independence would necessarily reflect the opposition of a significant proportion of French-speaking people, and would obviously demonstrate a degree of commitment to a Quebec "self" different from that reflected by an overwhelming majority vote. There exists a strong feeling, especially among young Quebecers, of Quebec's nationhood. Rejection of independence would mean a strong sense of personal deprivation for them. But this psychological impact is not the only one to be considered. There are many French-speaking Quebecers whose primary political loyalties have been shaped by their involvement in the institutions and political culture of Canada and who share awareness of a common Canadian citizenship, the loss of which would be important for them. Substantial minority opposition coupled with less than a strong consensus on the part of the French-speaking people, together with an overwhelming commitment on the part of the people in the rest of Canada to maintain unity, would not help the claim to independence.

Quebec's independence would produce serious problems for the remainder of Canada, which would not receive any obvious benefits in return. Participation as a unit in a federal state for more than a hundred years has created a complex web of relationships in every sphere of human activity. Economic arrangements, both private and public, will have to be reordered. Though it may be possible to work out some form of economic association with the remainder of Canada, there would still be serious dislocations. Even if linked with economic association, which a great many Canadians outside Quebec now oppose, independence is likely to produce at least a short-term loss of domestic and foreign confidence in Canada, with possibly severe economic effects.

In any event, long-term economic stability in the context of economic association could be achieved only if the relationship could not be altered or terminated without Canada's consent, and it is not all certain that an independent Quebec would be prepared to make such a commitment. Even if it would be, because of Quebec's status of political independence Canada would face serious difficulties in enforcing such a treaty commitment if Quebec were to decide to disregard it, and Quebec would have at its disposal an array of international legal arguments that might convince a third-party decision-maker—for example, an international arbitral tribunal or court—to sanction the departure from the commitment.

Whether or not economic association can be expected to emerge as a component of the new relationship, there will be other problems, including: partitioning national assets and debts; allocating between Canada and Quebec rights and obligations now governing the relationships between Canada and other states; defending a geographically bifurcated Canada; preserving the richness of biculturalism and multiculturalism in a Canada without Quebec; and generally, maintaining national unity in the face of compelling north-south economic, cultural, and geographic links.

Although disengagement and reassociation might be ultimately worked out, it is important to note that the major recent claims to secession, whether successful or not, have been advanced in cases where long-standing integration, as in Canada, did not exist. Pakistan, for instance, had been a state for little more than twenty years when the Bengalis seceded. Biafra had been part of an independent Nigeria and Katanga part of an independent Congo for even shorter periods of time. And the independence of East Pakistan did not result in the geographic partition of the remaining unit.

Granted the negative impact for the emergent Canada, can it be argued that it is overwhelmingly overridden by the benefits—political, economic, cultural—which an independent Quebec would provide for its people? Under the standards of international law, independence is not to be viewed mystically as an end in itself, but rather must be assessed in terms of what it can do for the people affected by it.

Politically, a small and relatively compact state may be better placed to provide humane and participatory government. Smallness may reduce the feeling of individual alienation from distant, bureaucratic, impersonal government and may give people a more important role in influencing decisions which affect them. On the other hand, bigness has its own advantages in providing the resources conducive to producing conditions of human dignity, such as security and education. But inability to secure independently the welfare of their people is leading even large states more and more to establish transnational links.

Quebec, however, enjoys, as a province, many of the advantages of smallness, as well as other political powers linked with independence: control over much of the domestic decision-making process, and participation in the international community. As part of Canada, Quebec enjoys considerable autonomy. The civil law, education, social services, and many aspects of economic activity are regulated by Quebec City, not Ottawa. Quebec participates in international conferences, enters into a wide variety of transnational agreements with private and governmental entities abroad, and even maintains official representation in other countries. In addition to these autonomous powers, Quebec also has representation, roughly equivalent to the proportion of its population to that of Canada as a whole, in such federal institutions as the Supreme Court of Canada, the civil service, the armed forces, Parliament, and the cabinet, though past inadequacies, especially in the military and civil service, are important contributions to present alienation. Thus the political gains stemming from independence are limited.

There has been much debate about whether, and to what extent, Quebec would gain economically from independence. The Parti Québécois leadership has argued that the federal government has systematically impeded the economic development of Quebec. While it is not possible to assess these complex issues in this chapter (indeed, it may be questioned whether they can be assessed adequately at all), a few general observations may be made. First, the fact that there can be any genuine disagreement is significant. In the case of Bangladesh, the evidence of economic disparity between the two parts of Pakistan was overwhelming. The East Pakistanis, soon to become independent, comprised 55 per cent of the total population, yet almost 80 per cent of Pakistan's budget was spent in West Pakistan. Although most of

Pakistan's manufacturing industry was located in the West, 70 per cent of its development funds were spent there as well, in spite of that region's 100 per cent greater per capita income. It has not been alleged that Quebec suffers so dramatically. On the other hand, some commentators have suggested that independence would hurt Quebecers economically.

But would political independence have long-term economic advantages for Quebec if accompanied by an arrangement for economic association with the rest of Canada on terms favourable to Quebec? Control over movement of labour, imports and exports, the money supply, fiscal policy, and investment within Quebec and abroad can be expected to provide an independent Quebec with greater freedom to pursue its own social and economic goals than it has in the Canadian federation, although it does have considerable powers now over such matters as immigration (particularly with the help of language legislation), taxation, regulation of corporations, foreign ownership (as demonstrated dramatically by Saskatchewan's initiative to "nationalize" parts of the potash industry), and so on. It must be emphasized that all states are involved in the interdependent global economic system, and for this reason will not in any event be able to solve problems of inflation and unemployment through reliance on exclusive control of domestic economic instruments. And in order to achieve the economic advantages which many Quebecers perceive as dependent on continued economic association, exclusive control in such areas as tariffs and fiscal and monetary matters will have to be surrendered to some extent. The very fact of association is incompatible with total freedom.

An independent Quebec would have to bear a much greater financial burden than at present for such matters as defence and foreign affairs. With the probable loss of some Canadian and foreign investment, there would at least in the short run be fewer financial resources to meet these and other needs. In sum, the expected economic gains from independence are limited, even assuming the establishment of an economic link favourable to Quebec.

Concern of the French-speaking people of Quebec for their cultural survival in North America is valid. It is shared with other ethnic minorities in North America and in many other parts of the world. The tremendous recent resurgence of ethnic identities reflects a renewed recognition that the values inherent in distinctive cultures are more than ever essential to human dignity at a time of rapid social change and development of an increasingly technological and uniformity-producing global environment. But is an independent Quebec essential for cultural well-being? The recent Quebec legislation on language indicates that the government of Quebec can do much to protect the French language within the federation. Education is a provincial matter, as are areas of personal law which may be culturally rooted. Thus the Canadian constitution permits Quebec great scope to pursue its own policies in cultural affairs. Moreover, the cultural affiliation of an individual may not always be coterminous with his other allegiances. People identify with different units for a variety of purposes. A person may identify as a Québécois but may wish to affiliate primarily with Canada for economic purposes. And Quebec has recognized that cultural destiny transcends political boundaries by forging links with "la francophonie," a loose international comunity of French-speaking entities. The Canadian federation has proved to be flexible enough to accommodate this provincial incursion into external affairs.

Contemporary trends toward establishing political units both more and less inclusive than the nation-state, manifested in greater regionalism among states and within states, are not necessarily incompatible. Thus it is possible for the British government to participate in the European Economic Community and also to contemplate the devolution of decision-making competence in certain areas to a Scottish Assembly. The multiple identifications of people can be reconciled without ignoring the reality of the continuing primary position of the state as the major unit in the international system and the most important focal point of loyalties. The trend toward more inclusive units stems in part from the increasing realization that, in an interdependent world, people's needs in such areas as security, the economy, and the environment cannot be met through the instrumentality of the state unit alone. Hence trans-state institutions and links can be expected to increase. At the same time, disadvantages of the state form of organization stemming from "bigness" can be expected to result in claims for greater regionalism or autonomy within the state, especially in developed, industrialized countries. Hence one perceptive commentator foresees some states, including France, the United States, and the Soviet Union, eventually moving toward greater internal power-sharing in the form of greater autonomy for subnational groups.[3]

Canada is also moving toward more autonomy. There has been much discussion about rewriting the Canadian constitution, in part to meet a widespread demand for decentralization. While Quebec will not be the only claimant, it is likely that Quebec will be a major beneficiary, and that the result will be a further strengthening of Quebec's control over decisions affecting the specific concerns which have been articulated by the Parti Québécois government.

Our assessment is that most of the concerns of those who seek independence for Quebec can be satisfied within the evolving Canadian confederation. Even if independence would produce political, economic, and cultural gains for the people of an independent Quebec, the available evidence does not suggest that they would be great enough, especially when compared with the negative consequences for the remainder of Canada, to support undermining the territorial integrity principle through dismemberment of Canada. Such evidence must be overwhelming in view of the legal presumption against political independence through secession in noncolonial contexts. In the case of Bangladesh, on the other hand, the major factors supporting independence included the following: widespread deprivation of human rights, amounting to outright massacres, perpetrated against a *majority* of Pakistanis; a thousand miles of physical separation between the two parts of Pakistan; clear gross economic exploitation of East Pakistan by West Pakistan; a choice of political destiny expressed by the vote of a *majority* of Pakistanis. The Quebec-Canada relationship and its position in the global context are markedly different from the East and West Pakistan situation, and, indeed, from the situation of other post-independence cases. Therefore, close comparisons are risky. It is nevertheless significant that none of the features of the Pakistan situation is found in the Quebec-Canada relationship.

Political independence is not the exclusive outcome of self-determination. Free association and integration with another state have been recognized in international law as other possible alternatives. The invocation of self-determination by distinctive and territorially based groups all over the world in support of claims for autonomy within the state suggests that in a world without traditional colonialism there will be increasing need for the application of the principle to achieve outcomes below the independence threshold, preferably by a negotiated settlement between the groups directly affected, and this may provide a model for Canada. In many of these cases considerations of world order and human rights will dictate the honouring of this form of self-determination. The significance of the competing principle of territorial integrity fades in comparison. Even without such considerations behind it, self-determination would achieve greater prominence, and territorial integrity less, for it is power-sharing, not fragmentation, that is involved. The choice is not absolutely one or the other. However, Quebec already has much power, and this new self-determination does not amount to the political independence claimed by the Parti Québécois leadership. The people of Quebec may yet perceive, together with other Canadians elsewhere, that the Canadian state is in their common interest.

THE LESSON OF CANADIAN CONSTITUTIONAL LAW

The current Canadian constitution, mainly the British North America Act of 1867, is a more flexible document than many people recognize. First, in section 92(1), it gives the provinces power to amend their own constitutions, except that they may not alter the nature of the office of the lieutenant-governor. Second, the allocation of legislative powers to the central government and to the provincial governments, even after 110 years of discussion and elaboration, is not clearly and precisely settled. For example, we do not know for sure whether, even under the present constitutional arrangement, the provinces have the power to regulate cable television systems, or whether the provinces may develop their own policies and programs to restrain anticompetitive practices, just as they can regulate the securities industry. Nor is it clear that the ownership of lands, mines, minerals, and royalties which, under the BNA Act, is given to the provinces, cannot support a wide range of provincial legislation which identifies and promotes provincial economic policies, even those that affect interprovincial and international markets.

In short, the power to affect both cultural and economic activities within the province is still very wide and it is certainly possible that that capacity will be recognized and expanded by courts and legislators in the years ahead. If there is a judicial and legislative will to honour the relatively high degree of provincial autonomy that, in our view, the BNA Act recognizes, then some of the aspirations for autonomy which Quebec and most other provinces now hold can be met without raising the question of constitutional amendment. The relevant constitutional law for this sort of change will flow from the application of existing standards and will not be that which pertains to rearranging the constitutional structure.

However, for two reasons one cannot be overly sanguine about this approach. In the first place the sort of amendment of the provincial constitution which section 92(1) of the BNA Act allows does not reach the basic political goal of the Quebec independence movement because it does not permit alterations in the relationship between Quebec and the rest of Canada. In any event the limitation, in this amending power, that the office of the lieutenant governor may not be altered, is considerable. This limitation entrenches the form and many procedural aspects of provincial government, and important aspects of the relationship of the province with the central government.

Second, Quebec may simply wish to be free of federal regulation over a wide variety of matters which involve the people of Quebec. Some of these are broadcasting, medical and scientific research, defence, unemployment, and postal services. Furthermore, the government of Quebec may not wish to tolerate the limitation on its economic regulatory power that comes from federal authority to regulate directly interprovincial markets. In other words, under the present constitutional arrangement, Quebec's ability to deal directly with the place of Quebec's industry in the North American and world market, although not insubstantial, is in many respects subject to an overriding federal jurisdiction.

Third, apart from the power held by Quebec and the central government under the present constitutional arrangement, the government and people of Quebec may wish to dissociate Quebec from Canada for symbolic reasons and arguments based on functional accommodation do not answer that claim.

Therefore, it is necessary to consider what constitutional law says about reordering constitutional power in some more formal way. We must, in short, look at the law of constitutional amendment. There are at least three levels of amendment which could be involved in a move by Quebec to increase its legislative and executive power.

These levels are: constitutional amendment in the allocation of legislative powers so that all the provinces are granted greater power and the central government has correspondingly less; amendment which provides for Quebec specifically to enjoy greater legislative power but continues to subject the other provinces to the allocation of powers found in our current constitutional arrangement; and constitutional amendment which formalizes Quebec's leaving Confederation to become a juridically independent state.

The first form of constitutional amendment which might come into play is that necessary to alter the powers held by the provinces and the central government. The kind of changes which might be agreed to by the eleven governments of Canada and which might ameliorate the demands by Quebec for greater autonomy are recognition of greater provincial rights to regulate broadcasting, to participate in making international agreements, and to regulate the extraction and marketing of natural resources even to the point of affecting in substantial ways interprovincial trade and international trade policies. Quebec might also wish a greater role in transportation, federally regulated industry, and other matters.

The appropriate amending procedure for this kind of general alteration in the allocation of powers has been a political issue for the last quarter century. Legislative, executive, and judicial independence has not come quickly for Canada, the last of these being achieved only since the end of World War II. Even now Canada is not formally a self-governing country in that constitutional amendment requires the approval of the British Parliament. Canadians have sought for years to locate the power to amend the BNA Act within Canada. But it has not been possible to frame a request to the British Parliament because none of the governments in Canada has been willing to consent to such a request unless the patriation amendment is accompanied by a formula for future amendments.

Hence the method for amending the allocation of powers is not formalized. It depends on constitutional convention, a recognized source of our constitutional law. The convention is that amendment requires a joint address of the Canadian House of Commons and Senate to Britain. It is assumed that this approval will be automatic. In respect of matters directly affecting federal-provincial relations the rule is that all eleven governments in Canada must agree before Britain is petitioned. This latter position is expressed in the federal white paper, *The Amendment of the Constitution of Canada*:

> The fourth general principle is that the Canadian Parliament will not request an amendment directly affecting federal-provincial relationships without prior consultation and agreement with the provinces. This principle did not emerge as early as others but since 1907, and particularly since 1930, has gained increasing recognition and acceptance. . . .
>
> There have been five instances—in 1907, 1940, 1951, 1960 and 1964—of federal consultation with all provinces on matters of direct concern to all of them. There has been only one instance up to the present time in which an amendment was sought after consultation with only those provinces directly affected by it. This was the amendment of 1930, which transferred to the Western provinces natural resources that had been under the control of the federal government since their admission to Confederation.

It will be noted that there have been two amendment procedures: one employing unanimous consent and one involving only bilateral agreement. The former is, however, clearly the one which applies to amendments altering the allocation of legislative power generally. It is beyond doubt that this convention of unanimity, although not inscribed in an authoritative document, represents a binding constitutional norm and that any attempt to alter the allocation of powers between the provinces and the federal government which did not follow the convention would be unconstitutional.

This raises the issue of whether a revised amending formula, departing from unanimity, is likely to be agreed upon in the near future. Over the past two years, the prime minister has been attempting to obtain consent from the provinces about an amending formula, but with little success.[4] For Quebec, however, this amendment debate is irrelevant simply because the Parti Québécois government not only rejects the idea of the constitutional position of Quebec being changed in lock step with that of the other provinces, but rejects the modest reform of merely making a change in the allocation of legislative power.

It is largely because of the view held by the current government in Quebec, that the amendment debate is beside the point, that we conclude that the real issue presented by Quebec's move to autonomy is not how to bring about constitutional amendments which make generally applicable changes in the allocation of legislative powers. Rather the issue is how constitutionally Quebec's position as a part of Canada can be uniquely altered, or terminated.

The two possible courses of change, the special allocation of powers to Quebec, and the constitutional recognition of Quebec separating itself from the rest of Canada, pose a common problem. Clearly it is only the latter which is sought by the Parti Québécois. But both policy choices, although hardly equivalent, present similar constitutional issues.

Secession is not a concept recognized in the BNA Act or in any other form of constitutional norm such as precedent or convention. Special status for Quebec is, however, clearly recognized in the BNA Act in relation to, among other things, language rights, education rights, and legislative uniformity. Clearly the recognition, in the BNA Act, that Quebec for some purposes and in some matters stands in a unique relationship to the Canadian Confederation does not support a claim that Quebec has the right unilaterally to amend the constitution to create further special powers or to formalize an act of secession. The recognition in the BNA Act of Quebec's status within Confederation *is* a matter for constitutional amendment.

Since the constitution speaks only about admission of "other parts of British North America" and not about parting from Canada, any act of leaving, just as much as any increase to Quebec's power within Confederation, must be treated as a matter of constitutional amendment. In respect of the special status option it is clear that Quebec and the rest of Canada will continue to function as a political unit, with altered terms of relationship. The need for constitutional recognition of the new arrangement, that is, constitutional amendment, is unquestioned. As for secession it could be said that the proper inference to draw from constitutional silence is that there is no barrier to unilateral withdrawal from Confederation. We reject this line of reasoning. The joining together of several political units into one state creates a political arrangement to which each of the parts contributes and from which each of the parts benefits. It is in the knowledge of the nature of the new state that the parts make their commitment to join. This is as true at the time of initial confederation as when new provinces are added. The coming together as a federal state creates expectations about what values may be enhanced and what interests may be pursued at a national level. When one province seeks to leave the union the pattern of union is fundamentally altered and the expectations about the country must undergo change. These observations point to the position that secession is not a matter of choice for one province but is a matter of constitutional amendment. In light of what we argue is the proper method for effecting an amendment it should be emphasized that Confederation creates a new political unit with discrete values and interests and it is primarily those, not regional interests, which are at stake at the point of secession.

Having identified both courses of action as requiring constitutional amendment, the second question remains: must the procedure for amendment which requires unanimous consent be followed in making amendments which alter the relationship between one province and the rest of Canada?

This question in turn involves an examination of how we discover constitutional rules. One method is to look to prior conduct in similar situations. For instance, this is the way in which we know something of the constitutional law pertaining to the powers of the governor general to dissolve Parliament. That there is also a great deal of uncertainty about these powers is in part a result of the lack of general acceptance of some of the acts of the governors general in this country and in Australia.

The method of discerning from prior conduct is the source of the amending convention that we do have. But the context out of which that experience flows is the limited one of amendments of general application and as a result the case for its applicability in the case of bilateral amendment is not strong. The basis for the present convention is that changes "directly affecting federal-provincial relations" alter by way of enhancement or diminution the powers of the provinces. Amendment recognizing special status for, or the secession of, Quebec will affect provincial interests but will not effect a general alteration of provincial powers.

When constitutional text and historical precedent are silent, the next source by which we discover new constitutional "rules" is to ask what arrangement corresponds most closely with the structures and values entrenched in the constitutional document—in this case the BNA Act, as it has evolved. This source of constitutional law does make it possible logically to infer some conclusion about a proper amending procedure for special treatment or secession of one province. First, the allocation of powers in sections 91 and 92 are not merely lists of powers, disclosing no values or overriding goals. Clearly the federal government was given power to enhance national economic viability and likewise the provinces were precluded from engaging in activities which would frustrate national economic development. The constitutional allocation of power speaks to national economic growth by limiting provincial power to create barriers to trade. That is to say, there is a proscription against falsities in the market: no false demands may be created by the protection of local producers, no false revenues through creating exclusive routes or markets, no false investment through the creation of regulation free zones for goods moving in interprovincial trade. The point of the Privy Council decision in *Winner*[5] is precisely that those who are willing to participate in national and international markets and who are willing to make a stronger and more unified economic unit are to be free, to a large degree, from provincial regulation.

In addition to these economic goals, the federal government is given jurisdiction to make laws for "the Peace, Order and good Government of Canada." The precise effect of these words is unknown but they do indicate that when there are questions of fundamental importance to the future of Canadian society, the federal government has the competence to act unilaterally.

Finally, the allocation, in the text, of interconnecting works such as railways, canals, and telegraph systems to the federal government, although not originally perceived in terms of authority to enhance the sense of national community, has, in the last half century, acquired that meaning. This allocation originally served as part of the package of powers which clearly demonstrated a preference for federal jurisdiction in matters and arrangements which develop national economic strength. Since Confederation, however, this power has been used (in conjunction with other federal powers) to support a federal claim for jurisdiction over aeronautics and broadcasting. These fields of activity are important in developing a national identity and economy. As to broadcasting, there is no doubt that, to the extent that we see ourselves as a separate and unique nation, this view is powerfully enhanced by what is produced on radio and television. Broadcasting plays a significant role in creating and preserving our cultural self-awareness. To this extent then, Canadian cultural and symbolic interests are within federal jurisdiction, but are not exclusively federal.

These centralist aspects in the constitution suggest that the interests shared in common by all parts of Canada that would be affected by a constitutional change in the status of Quebec are explicitly or implicitly given to the federal government to protect. If the government of Canada wished to negotiate with Quebec for a special status for Quebec or for Quebec's separation, then an agreement between the government of Canada (approved, of course, in a Joint Address of the House of Commons and Senate) and the government of Quebec would be sufficient to bring about a legitimate constitutional revision. Under the present regime for constitutional amendment this means that the British Parliament ought to enact amendments to the BNA Act which would recognize special status or separation for Quebec if the request to do so comes from Quebec and from the central government, and is the product of negotiated agreement between the governments of those two political units. The federal government, in making a special status or a secession agreement, may want to consult with the provinces or with Canadians generally through a national referendum. But it is not obliged, under constitutional law, to do the former and may not be obliged to do the latter. More important, the interests of the provinces in the Quebec settlement do not imply a requirement for obtaining unanimous provincial consent. They are represented, according to our perception of the constitutional mandates, through the promotion of Canadian or national interests by the federal government.

There is, of course, a certain irony in this position. The desire for autonomy represented by the policies of the Quebec government is, as we have noted, not unique to Quebec. Many, if not all, other Canadian provinces wish for recognition of greater provincial power. Yet the amending procedure which we consider to be appropriate flows from a reading of centralist notions in the BNA Act and a de-emphasis of very real provincial concerns about the impact on provincial fields of jurisdiction of Quebec's changed constitutional status. We do not wish to minimize the legitimacy of either the quest for the decentralization of power or the general provincial interest in Quebec's status within Confederation but we do think that the large scale interruptions which will result from a separate Quebec or a Quebec with special powers will be in areas over which the federal government has primary competence. If the federal government is satisfied that the values underlying its jurisdiction are sufficiently protected (or not compromised beyond a tolerable level) then Quebec should not have to negotiate terms of settlement with nine provincial governments.[6]

However, our conclusions about what the constitution currently requires are based on inferences not yet crystallized in law. If so, it is necessary to look again at the question of how constitutional norms are formed. When there is an absence of clear authority in the constitutional document, in precedent, or in inferential reasoning we are forced to look elsewhere. At the root of any country's constitutional system are the community's basic shared expectations about values and powers. Normally the chief moulder of these expectations is the constitutional document itself or constitutional conventions. Since we have already concluded that the proper inference to draw from the express language of the BNA Act is that the sort of constitutional amendment being considered may be implemented by agreement between Quebec and Ottawa, it is not strictly necessary to consider the question of community expectations about the process for making legitimate changes in our relationship with Quebec.

Evidence of contemporary expectations is so scanty and inconclusive that conclusions must necessarily be tentative. We start with the observation that it is not by accident that the national debate is largely being carried to the Canadian public by Prime Minister Trudeau and Premier Lévesque. The prime minister, even if he were not a Quebecer holding a long-standing commitment to a specific conception of Quebec within Confederation, would inevitably assume the mantle of protagonist putting forward the virtues of one country embracing two cultures. The interests which all parts of Canada have in preserving Canada with Quebec are best represented in the advocacy of the country's prime minister. The reason for this is that the counterforce to separation is the identification and articulation of those values which can be maintained only by minimizing our differences and asserting our common aspirations. These are values which are, as we have explained, embodied in large part in the BNA Act.

It follows that just as the central government must be the primary advocate, it is also the primary negotiator in establishing the terms of accommodation. At the point of accommodation of the competing interests of Quebec's independence and Canada's present integrity, regional interests which are not also federal interests cannot be vindicated regardless of cost. In other words regional and provincial interests may be defended by the federal negotiators but the nature of the conflict which secession creates is that they are not, as such, the focus of the debate and to grant provinces veto power to protect them would be to assign an incorrect role for these interests. They enter into the negotiation as part of the overall pattern of national interests.

On the other hand it can be argued that the separation of Quebec from Canada represents a disintegration of Confederation that affects provincial interests and provincial jurisdiction at least as profoundly as the reallocation of legislative powers. If this contention is right, Canadians might feel that all the governments of Canada should participate in the separation settlement, or at least be formally consulted. However, we believe that the more logical inference to draw from the loss of national integrity is that it ought to be resisted by the government vested with the responsibility for protecting those values and institutions which comprise national integrity. If the country is seen to be in danger then "country" values and "country" interests should be advanced and not regional interests and claims.

Finally, at the most basic level of community expectations, it might be urged that perceptions of the country held by individual Canadian citizens should not be forced into a radical readjustment through bilateral governmental action without a prior systematic consultation with the population. In short, it could be argued that the precondition to negotiations leading to Quebec's separation is a national referendum on the question of whether Quebec should be allowed to sever its constitutional ties with the rest of Canada. This is, at least, a plausible constitutional requirement that serves to condition the basic position that it is at the federal level that there is power to consent, or not, to Quebec's separation.

In arguing for a special rule we are not suggesting that a secession or special status amendment will never require the application of a general amending rule. For instance, if the BNA Act were amended so as to patriate the constitution and entrench an amending formula, the new formula would apply to all future amendments, even those involving one province only, unless there were a provision in the formula for special amending procedures in particular cases. A new entrenched amending procedure would necessarily have been accepted by all eleven governments and if that acceptance had been given even though there were no special provisions for some classes of amendment then no province could claim that the prepatriation position should prevail. This would be the position even if the agreed formula was that the federal government and all provinces must give consent. It is for this reason Quebec will not likely accede to patriation or to the simple formula for future amendment.

Since it is unlikely that patriation or entrenchment of an amending formula will happen before the question of secession is resolved we have been primarily concerned with the question of requirements for amendment under the current constitutional arrangement..

We conclude that a requirement of both international law and constitutional law is the consent of Canada to any move by Quebec to change its relationship with the rest of Canada, whether involving greater autonomy within Confederation or actual secession, before such a change attains legality.

We also conclude that Canadian federalism is a dynamic process which is capable of producing change, reflecting new interests, and dealing with new needs. If our constitution is read in the spirit of these capacities it will be possible to arrive at standards and mechanisms that will allow Canada to make the kinds of adjustments in our federal system which are required by circumstances, good judgment, and generosity.

NOTES

1. In writing this section we have drawn heavily on an article by one of the authors, J. Claydon, "The Transnational Protection of Ethnic Minorities: A Tentative Framework for Inquiry," *Canadian Yearbook of International Law*, XIII(1975), 25–60, as well as on two excellent specialized studies: L. Chen, "Self-Determination as a Human Right," in Reisman and Weston, eds., *Toward World Order and Human Dignity* (1976) pp. 198–261; V. Nanda, "Self-Determination in International Law," *American Journal of International Law*, 66 (1972), 321–36.

2. J. Humphrey, "The International Law of Human Rights in the Middle Twentieth Century," in M. Bos, ed., *The Present State of International Law* (Deventer, Netherlands, 1973), p. 103.

3. R. Falk, *A Study of Future Worlds* (New York, 1975), p. 214.

4. See letters from the Prime Minister to Premiers of the provinces, dated 19 April 1975 and 31 March 1976, Appendix, H. C. Debates (30th Parl., 1st Sess., 9 April 1976), 12695–12705; and letter setting out revised position, tabled in the House of Commons on 25 Jan. 1977, H.C. Debates (30th Parl. 2d Sess., 24 Jan. 1977), 2277.

5. *Attorney General of Ontario v. Winner* (1954), A.C. 541 (J.C.P.C.).

6. W. R. Lederman argues the contrary position. See "Constitutional Amendment and Constitutional Change for Canada" (paper delivered at a joint seminar held by the Canadian Bar Association and the Faculty of Law, Dalhousie University, Halifax, N.S., 19 March 1977).

Securing Human Rights in a Renewed Confederation

W. R. LEDERMAN

In December 1948 the General Assembly of the United Nations endorsed a noble document entitled "The Universal Declaration of Human Rights" which, in its first paragraph, speaks of "recognition of the inherent dignity and of the equal and inalienable rights of all members of the human family," and asserts this to be "the foundation of freedom, justice and peace in the world." This was not intended to deny that persons and groups differ in many of their interests, beliefs, and inherent characteristics; such denial would be hopelessly simplistic. Rather these opening words and the rest of the "Declaration" do affirm that human diversity in all its variety nevertheless rests on an essential foundation of common humanity for every person. This sense of common humanity should evoke mutual and reciprocal respect between persons and groups of persons in spite of the extent to which they differ one from another. The effective and just organization of society depends in the end on such sympathy and empathy between human individuals.

But we live in a world where there is a scarcity of good things, both tangible and intangible, including what may be described as opportunities for personal self-fulfilment. This scarcity means that every available person cannot simply do as he wishes or have what he wants without limit. We have to have processes or systems for sharing what is available, and this is the root of the need for constitutions, and for the government and legal systems that stem from constitutions. In the complex modern world we see that people must often look to governments and courts operating under the rule of law to create and maintain social conditions in which they may satisfy to a reasonable degree their basic needs and desires. Because of the relative scarcity of the good things of life, this is always a process of compromises between conflicting interests and claims, compromises that fall short of perfect satisfaction of those interests or claims. In terms of this analysis we come to a relative and pragmatic definition of justice. Practical justice means that the overall scarcity shortfall should be kept to the unavoidable minimum, and that the limited opportunities for self-fulfilment available should be distributed fairly among the people. One must add that what use people make of their opportunities is not the gift of a government or a law. What they may then accomplish is rather a matter of personal choice and effort. The last thing people want is that there should be a law telling them what to do or not to do at every turn. To be assured of reasonably broad areas of personal option and opportunity, our society needs enough law, but not too much law; always a delicate balance.

These are very lofty and general sentiments, but what is their bearing on present problems of Canadian unity? Simply this. Among the most important and fundamental of human rights are those concerning the use of language, and for the average person this mainly means rights, options, and opportunities to use one's mother tongue. I believe it is fair to say that the present crisis issues of Canadian unity are in the main language-related; and that the course of Canadian history has been such that these issues concern the assured use of the English language or the French language or both of them in education, in government, in business and industry, and in radio and television broadcasting. That list is not exhaustive, of course, as language is all-pervasive in significance and social impact. All communication between persons, and within and between groups of persons, depends on language. All organized activities of whatever kind can only go forward on the basis of the spoken and written word. A person's mother tongue is fundamental to his thinking and feeling, to his development and self-fulfilment, and to his relations with others. No wonder the area is so sensitive for both anglophones and francophones. And no wonder that, so far as law touches language use at all, it usually does so in terms of legally sanctioned rights and legally protected freedoms. Legal prohibitions are rare and should be carefully justified and limited when they are used.

The purpose of this paper is to bring to bear on present language-related issues critical to the unity of Canada the juristic learning and analysis that has been developed concerning fundamental human rights and freedoms generally. In so doing, I hope to make three points: these issues are very complex juristically, and over-simplification of them is foolish and dangerous; compromises of some sort between English and French language groups in Canada (and indeed in North America) on terms fair to both are inevitable and necessary, whatever the political or constitutional future of Canada may be; fresh linguistic compromises that should be appropriate and effective to keep Quebec within a genuinely revised and renewed Canadian federal union are indeed possible and available.

The starting point for juristic consideration of language rights is surely to examine the nature of freedom of expression itself, whatever the language or languages that may be the means of expression at a particular time or place. As a basic human liberty, freedom of expression is part of our historically inherited English public law. Moreover, it is declared in statutory form by the Parliament of Canada in the Canadian Bill of Rights of 1960, and declared also in statutory form by the National Assembly of Quebec in the Quebec Charter of Human Rights and Freedoms of 1975. Finally, this liberty or freedom is also proclaimed in the International Convention on Civil and Political Rights of the United Nations, which is binding on Canada, having been ratified as an international obligation by Canada in 1976, with the consent and approval of the provinces.

What then is the juridical nature of a freedom or liberty such as freedom of expression? In answer, I quote from what I said on this point when writing in the Canadian Bar Review in 1959 on the Canadian Bill of Rights.

> The concept of liberties or freedoms in a duly precise scheme of legal terminology is the concept of residual areas of option and opportunity for human activity *free of specific legal regulation*. In such areas of conduct there are neither affirmative legal prescriptions nor legal prohibitions—a man is at liberty to act or do nothing as he chooses, free of obligatory instruction by the law either way. Now to call these areas or classes of conduct residual is by no means to disparage them, far from it. Indeed, in a democratic country they are large and important areas, and one of the principal things a Bill of Rights attempts to do is to safeguard their essential boundaries. Only a relatively small portion of the total of actual or potential human activity is regulated in detail by specific legal duties, whether positive or negative, and life would be intolerable if this were not so. Indeed, just here lies one of the differences between democracy and dictatorship, for under a dictatorship there is in a sense too much law. The point is rather aptly made by the saying that, in a democratic country what is not forbidden is permitted, whereas in a totalitarian one what is not forbidden is compulsory. . . .
>
> To speak generally, this means that when you have defined the extent of specific legal regulation in terms of existing duties, *ipso facto* you have

drawn the outside boundaries of the areas of liberty or freedom. To delineate the unregulated area you must first define the regulated area, to do which is strictly a legal matter. So, in this residual sense the extent of liberty or freedom in some given respect is a matter of legal definition and properly has its place in the working concepts of the lawyer or jurist. For example, . . . the law forbids the uttering of defamatory, seditious or obscene words, and there specific legal prohibition stops. At the boundary so marked freedom of expression starts, and now the law takes no hand at all except to stop riots or other breaches of the peace. Beyond this boundary the law does not tell a man what to say or what not to say, nor does it compel anyone else to listen to him or to assist him to be heard by publishing in some way what he has said. So far as the law is concerned, he is on his own, and the factors and pressures involved in his choices and efforts concerning self-expression are extra-legal ones.

This residual and unspecified character of liberties or freedoms in relation to specific legal obligation is critical when we come to consider the relation of public legislative power to liberties or freedoms. Freedom of expression, for example, is not a single simple thing that may be granted by some legislature in one operation—it is potentially as various, far-reaching and unpredictable as the capacity of the human mind.

Nevertheless, as indicated, though very wide freedom of expression—freedom of language use—is a basic value of society, it cannot be allowed to operate without limit. Considerations of decency, public order, and private reputation also provide principles of equivalent generality that conflict and compete with freedom of expression, and which deserve to be given some effect in spite of and at the expense of the latter. So the law provides that, by way of exception, one is not free to utter obscene or seditious words, or words that falsely damage the good reputation of another person. Here we see the need for and the inevitability of compromise between competing and conflicting values of which I spoke earlier. Both legislators framing statutes and judges interpreting existing laws have to establish such compromises at reasonable equilibrium points between the values in competition. Nevertheless, the importance of freedom of expression means that the limitations on it should be few and as closely defined as possible. The presumption should run in favour of freedom of expression.

The need for compromise, however, is not peculiar to freedom of expression, it is general in relation to the whole range of proper values and goals of our society. For example, the United Nations declarations of rights speak of the right to work, but they also speak of the right to form and join trade unions and of the right of the latter to organize strikes. Our labour relations laws must somehow compromise the conflicting values involved here. If labour laws provide, as they often do, for a legal strike by a recognized union after efforts at bargaining in good faith have broken down, then, at that point, the right to work gives way to the right to strike. We find that this need for compromise is also generalized in the key United Nations documents on human rights and freedoms. For example, Article 29 of the United Nations Declaration of 1948 is as follows:

> 1. Everyone has duties to the community in which alone the free and full development of his personality is possible.
>
> 2. In the exercise of his rights and freedoms, everyone shall be subject only to such limitations as are determined by law solely for the purpose of securing due recognition and respect for the rights and freedoms of others and of meeting the just requirements of morality, public order and the general welfare in a democratic society.
>
> 3. These rights and freedoms may in no case be exercised contrary to the purposes and principles of the United Nations.

Compromise, then, as in the labour law example, itself requires much detailed law-making and interpretation by legislatures and courts or other tribunals. But jurisprudentially there is another reason why such detail is needed, which can be illustrated by another example from the United Nations Declaration. In general terms it tells us that there shall be no arbitrary arrest and that every person charged with a criminal offence is entitled to the presumption of innocence and to a fair trial by an independent and impartial tribunal. That is about all it says. That is fine, but actually to deliver justice in these terms to the citizens requires hundreds of pages of laws about detailed criminal procedure and thousands of pages of judicial interpretation of them. It requires also elaborate and expensive official institutions and systems, including police forces, departments of justice, courts, and penitentiaries. All these linkages are necessary for the effective implementation of general values expressed in very succinct and general terms. A failure in the linkages at any point may well result in denial of justice to the ultimate consumer, the human individual subject to charges or making claims. To quote from the McRuer Report of 1969 on Civil Rights:

> Highly abstract principles do have great importance in themselves simply as directive principles concerning the goals and ideals of a society. Although it is true that general declarations of principles mean little unless worked out on a massive scale in precise detail, we must appreciate the general implications of what it is we are doing in precise detail.

Particular detailed rules cannot be properly understood or applied as parts of a reasonable scheme or system unless we pursue as far as possible the general implications involved in them. Only then can we bring order and purpose to the mass of detail in our laws. . . .

. . . The point is that general principles and their detailed implications are all part of a legal or constitutional system. They are complementary one to the other. The general controls the mind in dealing with the particular. There is necessarily a constant interaction between the more general and the more particular in a living legal process, always conceding that it is beyond man's capacity to be ultimately general or finally particular in creating standards. The upper and lower limits of abstraction are relative, not absolute, for legal and constitutional purposes.

So far, in speaking of freedom of expression and language issues related thereto, I have said nothing of the problems posed by the fact that different communities and groups have different languages, and that relatively few persons are bilingual or multilingual. But of course this is frequently the situation, and here we encounter further conflicting values and interests in relation to freedom of expression; which means further need for compromises by appropriate and rather detailed laws. Nevertheless, I do maintain that these compromises should endeavour to accomplish their purposes with as little derogation from the master principle of freedom of expression as possible in the circumstances.

In any event, in Canada the course of our history has determined that our problems in this respect primarily concern the assured use of the English language or the French language or both of them, in education, parliamentary bodies, courts, government documents, public administration, business and industry, and so on. This is complicated by the fact that francophones are very much in the majority in the Province of Quebec, whereas anglophones are very much in the majority in the other provinces of Canada and in the United States. In these circumstances, the Bourassa government and the present Lévesque government of Quebec have felt compelled to take special legislative measures to protect the ongoing viability of the French language, culture, and way of life in Quebec. Moreover, the current movement for the political independence of Quebec has the same objective.

Consideration and analysis of these issues may usefully be undertaken at this point in relation to two sets of laws of the Province of Quebec, one actual and one proposed. In 1975 Quebec moved into the main stream of human rights legislation in the western world by enacting as a statute the Charter of Human Rights and Freedoms. On April 28 of this year (1977) the Charter of the French Language in Quebec was introduced into the current session of the Quebec National Assembly as Bill 1. Extensive hearings were held on the bill and on July 12 the Quebec government reintroduced the Language Charter as Bill 101. Bill 101 contains the amendments to Bill 1 that the Quebec government is willing to make as a result of the hearings, and so is very likely the form in which the Charter of the French Language will soon become law.

If Bill 101 is read in relation to the Quebec Charter of Human Rights and Freedoms, my view is that the two may well be inconsistent in important respects. If so, which has priority and thus overriding effect? The Quebec Charter of Human Rights, in section 52, states that its essential provisions "prevail over any provision of any subsequent act which may be inconsistent therewith unless such act expressly states that it applies despite the Charter." Bill 1, the original proposed language law, did expressly state (in section 172) that it applied despite the Charter of Human Rights, but in this respect the Parti Québécois government has changed its position. It has dropped section 172 from Bill 101, thus leaving the Charter of Human Rights with priority over the forthcoming language law, in the event of inconsistency between them. It is encouraging at this juncture in Canadian affairs that the Quebec government has thus recognized the primacy of the essential values of a democratic society. Nevertheless, by way of contrast, we find that Bill 101 maintains the severe restrictions of the previous Bill 1 on rights of access to the minority anglophone school system of Quebec. No doubt the Quebec government considers there is no conflict between Bill 101 and the Quebec Charter of Human Rights and Freedoms, in this respect as well as in others. They may well be wrong about this. Let us consider the issue in relation to access to the historic anglophone school system, which is all that space permits in this short essay.

The Quebec Charter of Human Rights and Freedoms asserts in section 3 that every person possesses the fundamental right to freedom of expression, and in section 10 asserts further that every person should enjoy that right "without distinction, exclusion or preference based on race, colour, sex, civil status, religion, political convictions, language, ethnic or national origin or social condition." Articles 26 and 27 of the International Covenant on Civil and Political Rights of 1966 are to the same effect, though they are more explicit, and thus reinforce the Quebec Charter.

Article 26

All persons are equal before the law and are entitled without any discrimination to the equal protection of the law. In this respect, the law shall prohibit any discrimination and guarantee to all persons equal and effective protection against discrimination on any ground such as race, colour, sex, language, religion, political or other opinion, national or social origin, property, birth or other status.

Article 27

In those States in which ethnic, religious or linguistic minorities exist, persons belonging to such minorities shall not be denied the right, in community with the other members of their group, to enjoy their own culture, to profess and practise their own religion, or to use their own language.

As noted, Canada, with the concurrence of Quebec and the other provinces, has ratified this convention, article 50 of which specifies that it "shall extend to all parts of federal states without any limitations or exceptions." Our task now is to apply the foregoing general analysis concerning freedom of expression to the educational rights of linguistic minorities in Quebec and the other provinces of Canada. The issue may at some point be taken before the courts in these terms, so that, in exploring it here and giving my own views, I am looking at considerations the judges might well take into account in deciding such a case.

In the first place I feel full sympathy for the concept of the French language as the priority language in Quebec; that Quebec must be the homeland of French language and culture in North America. Nevertheless, the large anglophone minority in Quebec has historic rights to the use of the English language that should be allowed greater freedom and accorded greater recognition than we find in the proposed Charter of the French Language in Quebec. In the matter of education, leaving aside transitional provisions, parents will not be permitted to send their children to schools where the language of instruction is English unless one parent at least was himself or herself previously educated in Quebec in the anglophone school system of the province. In effect this gravely inhibits the immigration of anglophones to Quebec because it means, after the Charter of the French Language becomes law, that any anglophones who immigrate cannot send their children to a school system centred on their own language and culture, though historically that school system has existed and presently exists in Quebec. It seems to me, to adopt the words of Article 27 of the International Covenant on Civil Rights, that this does deny to anglophones who go to Quebec to live the fundamental right to enjoy their own culture and use their own language, whatever their reasons for immigration may be, and thus is in breach of Article 27.

In my view, the right to attend the anglophone school system in Quebec should obtain for any children whose mother-tongue is English, wherever the family comes from in the English-speaking world and whenever they come. At least Bill 22 of the Bourassa government did in effect allow this, though the statute had other shortcomings. I do not believe that there would be any threat to the full and effective priority of the French language in Quebec if the proposed Charter of the French Language were altered to accord rights of access to the English school system of Quebec in the terms I have just advocated. To do this would meet the standards in this respect of the Quebec Charter of Human Rights and Freedoms and of Article 27 of the International Covenant on Civil and Political Rights to which Quebec has subscribed as a part of Canada. In my view failure to make this change would be to fall seriously short of those standards. At the level of rights of immigration alone, to bar anglophone immigration to Quebec indirectly but effectively by restricting access to the historic anglophone school system would be obnoxious even if Quebec were politically a separate state. It is all the more obnoxious when Quebec is a province of Canada. It is not necessary to go this far to assure the priority of the French language and the security of the French culture in Quebec. The fundamental freedom that underlies my reasoning here is freedom of expression itself, and it is wrong to infringe on that freedom any further than is necessary for the reasonable protection of relevant competing interests and claims of the same order and level of importance.

On the other hand, since English-speaking persons are the minority linguistic group in Quebec, I think it is reasonable for the proposed Quebec Language Charter to require that children in the anglophone school system should, by virtue of instruction there, become fully proficient in French as their second language. This is a proper compromise between the competing requirements of the two linguistic groups for freedom of expression, in the circumstances that obtain in the Province of Quebec.

I am well aware that Canadian francophones in both Manitoba and Ontario were deprived of rights to education in French at the end of the last century and in the early years of this one. These denials of rights were wrong, and I do not defend or condone them, but they did occur generations ago. We should not now dwell unduly on past injustices, because things have changed. The situation is moving in favour of francophone minorities in most if not all of the nine anglophone Canadian provinces, especially in Ontario and New Brunswick. For example, in recent years in Ontario, a complete francophone school system, publicly financed, has become available to the French-speaking residents of the province, with two bilingual universities at the apex of the system. These francophone rights in Ontario are not yet expressed and assured in a straightforward way in legislation, as they should be. Ontario and other provinces of course have the same obligations to respect the historic minority educational rights of their francophone residents as those that I have asserted belong to the anglophone minority residents of Quebec. If the English-speaking provinces were to enact more and better legislation about this, and devote more resources to francophone school systems and also to teaching the French language to anglophone children, French Quebecers might well read such developments as assurance that they do not need to seek political independence for Quebec to protect the French language and culture. They might indeed conclude that they are better off within Canada in this respect. I acknowledge of course that the efforts of the federal Parliament and government under the Official Languages Act of Canada should likewise be persuasive and conducive to the same end, though it is beyond the scope of this paper to discuss them.

In conclusion, I return to the fundamental right of freedom of expression itself. As the root of opportunities for self-fulfilment this has both its individual aspects and its community or collective aspects. In both aspects, the standards involved need to be expressed in statutes, constitutions, judicial decisions, and international treaties. When conflicting claims and interests arise in the area, as they inevitably do, compromises must be established that keep infringement of the basic freedom itself to a minimum. Securing freedom of expression (and other basic human rights) in a renewed Canadian Confederation requires sophisticated efforts on the part of our parliaments, our governments, and our courts. If we can succeed with these efforts, the unity of Canada will endure. I am both very anxious and very hopeful.

J'ai le goût du Québec
but I Like Canada:
Reflections of an Ambivalent Man

JOHN MEISEL

This chapter differs from its predecessors in two ways. It does not focus on any one aspect of the book's theme but attempts to take an overall view of our current situation, and it unabashedly contains the personal, subjective views of an individual participant in Canada's national drama. I feel the way I sometimes do when finding myself alone at dawn in the wilderness, or after all the guests leave as the sunny summer afternoon turns sad, the shadows lengthen, and I am confronted with the imperatives of the human condition. Moments like these sharpen one's awareness of the ultimate isolation of the individual despite his dependence on natural and human forces. They make one realize the need not only to perceive things as they really are but also to respond to them with wisdom and decency. What I am trying to do here is what many Canadians are doing, consciously or otherwise: to establish for themselves where they stand, as individuals, in face of the vast, possibly tragic forces challenging the future of our country.

An almost infinite number of issues affect relations between French and English-speaking Canadians. To sort them out requires a brutal discarding of all those aspects, no matter how vital they may seem at times, which do not relate to the absolutely central, enduring features of the problem. Three points stand out; the rest is peripheral.

1. What really matters in the lives of individuals and groups is the nature of the links between them rather than their form. In marriage, for instance, it is the substance of the relationship, and not the formal structure and legal content of the contract which is everything. The most important aspect of the coexistence of French and English Canadians is not whether politically they cohabit a unitary state, a federal or confederal monarchy or republic, a loose or tight union, but the quality of their relationship.

2. The way people interact is influenced by many factors, not least by the formal structures in which interaction occurs. Therefore the organizational, constitutional, or contractual forms regulating human ties cannot be overlooked. But it is important to resist the temptation of allowing them to grow into goals in their own right.

3. Both the forms and the structure of the relationship depend, at least in the Canadian case, on the cost-benefit analysis made respectively by Quebecers and the rest of the country. There is no question that both Quebec and the rest of Canada have the capacity to go it alone as separate states. The possibility of their choosing this path will depend on whether the politically effective leaders on each side believe that the benefits outweigh the costs. In converting the decision into a crude cost-benefit analysis we must think of much more than mere economic or material benefits. The psychic, cultural, social, and political dimensions are equally important.

If the Quebec leadership decides that remaining in Canada is too "costly" in relation to the advantages, compared with what they expect from a separate existence, or if English Canadians become convinced that the burdens of sharing a country with Quebec are greater than the benefits, then a break is inevitable. The calculations are being conducted at this very moment and will gain in momentum and relevance with the approaching referendum or, more likely, referenda. Disaster threatens if Quebec decides that the attractions of independence outweigh the costs while English Canadians decide that the costs to them of Quebec's leaving are unacceptable.

The first of these three observations leads one to hope that, if secession does occur, it is carried through as painlessly as possible for both sides, so that the subsequent relations between the two language groups could be close, friendly, and mutually rewarding, despite the political divorce. Since the impetus for separation is almost certainly very much greater on the French than on the English side, at least insofar as organized opinion and political mobilization are concerned, this means that the onus will lie on English Canada to respect the outcome of the deciding referendum and to respond to it with tolerance and goodwill—so as to ensure the quality of post-separation ties. This response may be more than English Canada can muster and may, furthermore, be opposed on tactical grounds.

Quebecers voting in the plebiscite may well include in their cost-benefit calculus the ease or difficulty of the separation itself. Those who do not feel very strongly for or against independence might make their choice on the basis of the cost of the divorce procedure. If the latter is low, why not try breaking away? If it is likely to be high, why bother risking losses, unpleasantness, and hassles? Indeed, there are those among English Canadians who advocate extremely harsh separation terms enumerated well in advance, designed to prevent a "yes" referendum vote by portraying the independentist leaders as irresponsible gamblers ready to plunge their countrymen into a disastrously expensive and hate-generating adventure.

This course, like its opposite, also involves risks. It might backfire or simply fail to provoke the anticipated response. In either case, post-separation contacts between French and English would likely be minimal and extremely hostile, depriving both groups of the contribution they can mutually make to one another regardless of the political ties between them.

Since too conciliatory a stance vis-à-vis Quebec might bring about separation and too unyielding a line might endanger the future of Canada, what should we do? We must for the present assume that Quebecers have so far failed to express a clear-cut wish to separate. Until such time as they do, we ought to pursue a policy of preserving the Canadian framework, albeit under substantially new, yet to be developed, conditions. But if at any time, now or later, the terms of independence have to be negotiated, then considerations of strategy and tactics must take second place to those of fairness and justice.

But beyond the question of strategy lies a deeper one. Why should Canada remain a country comprising both French and English-speaking people, and including Quebec as well as the other provinces? I believe it should for both national and personal reasons. Quite apart from the acute dislocation and hardship which would be experienced by virtually all Canadians in the event of separation, I am convinced that despite Canada's many failings, the political, social, and economic institutions which have evolved in this country as the result of the presence of two cultures are worth preserving. Canada is a better country than it would have been if Quebec had not been a part of it; and it will be a less desirable country if Quebec removes itself. I also believe that, despite the unquestionable penalties francophones have paid for being part of a predominantly English-speaking country, Quebec is also a better place today than it would have been had it not been a part of Canada. The association of diverse traditions, values, styles, and experiences makes for a richer, more varied, more open, and, in the final analysis, more creative society than is otherwise likely. I therefore reach a positive cost-benefit analysis: for both the province and the country there are very many more mutual benefits to be had from Quebec-in-Canada than there are drawbacks. This will be even more so as Quebec moves to assert control over its own cultural and economic life, so that the relationship can be one of equals, rather than of strength and weakness, which has been too frequently the case in the past.

From the purely personal viewpoint, the balance is even more favourable. In my own work in universities, as both teacher and re-searcher, in professional associations, in government inquiries, and as a contributor to the CBC, not to mention my private interests, I have enjoyed forming serious and lasting friendships with Quebecers. The Canadian practice of creating boards and committees made up of anglophones and francophones has allowed me to work with a large number of the latter. I have found many of these friendships incalcul-ably enriching. The cultural diversity has deepened my own percept-tion of life and of myself. While these friendships would no doubt endure (although the decline of organizational incentives for personal encounters would unavoidably have some effect), I fear that future generations of francophones and anglophones would be much less likely to benefit from one another's proximity if Quebec separates. There are for me, therefore, strong personal reasons for preferring a Canada in which Quebec and the rest of us have strong institutional ties. The point made here may appear idiosyncratic and highly elitist. It is true that the enriching experiences I have enjoyed result from a series of lucky and exceptional circumstances, and for this reason they may be seen as of little relevance to the country as a whole. This would be wrong. While it has not been given, as yet, to a large number of Canadians to benefit from institutionally inspired close ties with fellow citizens of the other major ethnic group, this is in part the result of the lingering two solitudes. It is one of the tragedies of our country that so few of its people have had this kind of opportunty. But one of the emerging consequences of bilingual policies has been that the number exposed to the exhilaration of living in a mixed society has grown, particularly in eastern Canada.

The foregoing assessment of the benefits of a continuing Canada is predicated on the assumption that Quebec's association with the rest of the country is compatible with the attainment of its own goals. If I thought that the survival of Quebec culture were impossible within a Canadian framework, that the majority of Quebecers would not feel fully at home in Canada, as Quebecers and Canadians, then I would not hesitate to advocate independence for Quebec. We must therefore ask ourselves whether it can achieve these goals without major national surgery. The answer is only mildly encouraging: it is possible but not certain. Much will depend on how both sides react to the need for change, at governmental, corporate, organizational, and personal levels.

This challenge has a further dimension: given its population, its far-flung territory, the structure of world and North American economic life, can Quebec attain its goals at all, in Canada or alone? Again, the answer must be equivocal.

There is much speculation nowadays about the extent to which any state—even the giants—can be thought of as being independent. What does independence mean under currently prevailing conditions? It is always relative, eluding the grasp of all seeking to clutch it. For Quebec to strive for independence is to seek *relatively* greater scope for decision-making unrestrained by the federal and the other provincial governments. But it is a nice question whether the constraints of inescapable interdependence imposed by world conditions would be reduced or exacerbated by separation from Canada.

It is not easy to combine the establishment of national independence, social democracy, and a high level of personal freedom, in a world of growing interdependence, multinational giants, voracious capitalism, and unceasing onslaughts on individual freedom. To do so within a radically new political framework adds problems and increases the number of obstacles even while it may remove others. But if the goals can be attained at all, they are more easily achieved in collaboration with groups, individuals, and governments who see themselves as allies rather than foes or uninterested spectators.

This was brought home dramatically by René Lévesque's January 1977 speech to the Economic Club of New York. It was vicariously humiliating to see this excellent man seeking the confidence and support of a basically hostile audience, for regardless of the outward trappings of proud independence, the role he played was that of an impotent suppliant. The energies expended on this exercise would have borne so much more fruit had they been directed towards English Canada. Here, despite much incomprehension, there *is* support for the aspirations of Quebec and it is not unthinkable that new investment policies could be generated jointly by public and private initiatives in several jurisdictions benefiting the Canadian and Quebec economies. The insistence on the exclusion of all Canadian insignia and the banning of federal officials from the head table, and afterwards the blaming of the icy New York reception of the speech on an English-

Canadian fifth column shows how belittling such nationalist gestures can become.

This incident is not in itself important—we can expect much petulance and pettiness on both sides—but it provides an admirable curtain-raiser to our discussion of some of the problems the separation raises for Quebec itself. Although some Quebecers tend to dismiss the argument as mere English rhetoric, the Canadian state does provide a potentially much more powerful shield for Quebec culture in North America and the world than an independent Quebec could. Because of much that has happened in the past, many Quebec intellectuals underestimate the extent and power of forces in English Canada strongly disposed to champion the flowering of Quebec culture and a Quebec nation. The Quebec media have in this respect not served their public well. Like their English counterparts, they tend to report French-English tensions and misunderstandings and to pass over harmonious, collaborative episodes indicating that French Canada is valued and understood by large numbers of anglophones.

Many actions of the Pearson and Trudeau governments and of several provinces and, more important, innumerable instances of deep interest on the part of voluntary associations, attest to the presence in Canada, outside Quebec, of strong champions of Quebec's goals. Public concern is not easily aroused in a democracy, particularly in one basking in relative affluence. So it was not until after 15 November 1976, and perhaps not even until after Premier Lévesque's New York speech, that English Canada started to mobilize in earnest for "Operation Survival." But it is remarkable how intense is the concern in English Canada about what must be done to cope with the current situation. And for many the problem is not simply one of saving a united Canada but also of assuring that the goals of French Canadians and Quebecers are met. There is hardly an association or professional group of my acquaintance which has not in the last few months launched some sort of program designed to deal with our impending crisis and its consequences for both linguistic groups. The current reaction to the situation created by the PQ victory may be among the most significant "nation-building" experiences English Canada has undergone since Confederation. The media and the pervasive associational network are mobilizing and alerting us to think about a national problem in Canadian (not imperial, West European, or North American) terms, and very often imposing the conclusion that our concern for the future must find expression in action forging new solutions to neglected problems.

For a Quebec government or for Quebec entrepreneurs, in whatever endeavour, it is more promising to seek outside help in terms of investment, skills, and even markets within this inherently friendly world than to seek support among a basically unconcerned milieu of strangers. There is, in other words, much capital—psychic and otherwise—ready for Quebec to draw upon in English Canada; such support is unlikely to be found elsewhere, even from France.

One factor arguing against the successful attainment of the Parti Québécois' goals is thus the indifference to Quebec to be found outside Canada, as compared to the sympathy that exists inside the country. But Canada, as everyone knows, also has its bigots who hate Quebec and who will seek to punish any efforts to destroy the country. And herein lies a second factor weakening the argument that a separate Quebec could attain the goals of its present government. It has consistently argued that an independent Quebec would continue to maintain close economic ties with what remains of Canada. This argument assumes that English Canada would agree to such arrangements. Here again many Quebecers have failed to understand the mentality of people outside their province. Struck by the *relatively* lower level of English-Canadian nationalism, compared with that in Quebec, many have assumed that there is *no* nationalism at all among the English-speaking population. This is patently wrong. And there is a possibility, or even a probability, that feelings would run extremely high among many individuals against a Quebec perceived as the destroyer of their country. Quebec leaders make subtle distinctions between "separation" and "independence" and have argued that they are not interested in destroying Canada but these reassurances strike many, both within and outside Quebec, as being semantic or merely opportunistic. The departure of Quebec from Canada would be deeply wounding to the vast majority of anglophones and might result in bitter animosity, making any kind of economic alliance or agreement exceedingly difficult, even if it were to the clear material advantage of provinces like Ontario or the Maritimes.

The third factor casting doubt on whether Quebec can best achieve its goals by separating from Canada arises from the fragility of all democratic systems. Democratic institutions can easily deteriorate into totalitarianism. No country—rich or poor, developed or underdeveloped— is immune from this tendency. Quebec is undergoing so rapid and major a transformation—a bloodless revolution—that its democratic goals may be jeopardized by the felt need, in the face of acute stress, to have recourse to undemocratic means. Quebec is not alone in this position in Canada but the evolution of its values and social institutions, the profound cleavages between francophones and anglophones, the exigencies of upcoming problems in an atmosphere of aroused expectations, all may make it difficult for the present regime to prevent a drift towards a freedom-destructive *dirigisme* and the abrogation of certain critical human rights.

This tendency may be exacerbated by the not uncommon post-revolutionary pattern of the first group of leaders being ultimately swept away by a second, less moderate wave. One must not forget that the Parti Québécois emerged as an alliance of widely disparate groups, both left and right, united under the strongly democratic and charismatic leadership of René Lévesque. Although the latter has the support of a number of exceptionally able and responsible colleagues there is always the question of whether the moderates will survive the inevitable setbacks and disappointments of the new regime.

A few straws in the wind indicate that the temptation will be very strong to bend the normal democratic procedures and safeguards so as to further the purposes of the independentist movement. Parts of the White Paper on language and the subsequent Bills 1 and 101, and the reaction to them in certain quarters in Quebec, are disquieting. The Quebec press, with some notable exceptions, has not always played the vigilant role one could have wished for, when the party and government favoured by its journalists deserved to be checked and possibly exposed. These potential weaknesses and stress points in the democratic fabric are not unique to Quebec. After all, it was the federal government which invoked the War Measures Act in 1970. But these strains show that even individuals committed to a genuine democratization of the political game may succumb to temptation born of frustration. How much greater the danger when acute and potentially successful opposition appears to threaten the achievement of the government's most cherished goals?

While there is certainly no clear-cut indication that the substantive goals of the Parti Québécois government could not be achieved in an independent Quebec state, there are grounds for anxiety on that score. This being the case, we must ask ourselves whether the goals of Quebec's leadership could be achieved in a "new" Canada.

Considered abstractly, changes *could* be brought about which would permit Canada to survive as a political unit, albeit in a fundamentally different guise from its present one, and Quebec to flourish in the new Canada. But this would require the effective decision-makers on both sides to work together to develop the necessary changes.

Despite the unsettling consequences of radical change inside

Canada, these are almost certain to be less severe than the disruption of outright separation. The political climate in and outside Quebec would therefore be comparatively more conducive to the solving of cultural and economic problems. The shock experienced by English Canadians at the possible breakup of the country, and the realization by francophones of the potential dangers of such an event, might quite possibly create a climate conducive to the renewal of the political and cultural partnership. To recognize that this development is theoretically possible is not, however, to forecast it. We are confronted with two questions: Is it too late? Can English Canada rise to the occasion? My answers are "probably yes" to the first and "probably no" to the second. But pessimism should not prevent efforts being made towards the achievement of even improbable goals. On the contrary, the probability of failure implies a possibility of success and this situation can act as a spur towards a new political creativity.

That such an effort is not entirely quixotic is indicated by what has been happening in English Canada in the wake of the PQ victory. I have already alluded to the unprecedented expression of concern for the future outside Quebec, taking a surprisingly open-minded and action-oriented form. The most encouraging aspect of this turn of events is not so much its scope, which is impressive enough, as its context: the agitation is chiefly occurring not at the governmental level but among private individuals and institutions who, in the final analysis, provide both the incentives for and the limits on what governments do. In this sense a new climate of opinion—one which the politicians may not as yet have fully perceived—is providing grounds for radical reappraisal of Canada's nature and of the political structures that may be needed in the future. A new spirit seems to be abroad, providing an impetus and a new ambience for the solution of Canada's national problem.

Three tasks need to be achieved. First, English Canada must transform itself so as to create a country in which French-speaking Quebecers feel genuinely at home. Second, new political initiatives are required, enabling Ottawa to share with the provincial capitals the role of seat of government for citizens in each province. The federal government in other words, must cease to be the alien "they" which it has increasingly become and discover a renewed legitimacy among all groups. Third, the transformation of Canada along the lines suggested here must be made visible among the Quebec majority which is still uncommitted to independence and also among the elites currently bent on creating an independent Quebec state.

The first task requires the continuation of past and present policies making the Ottawa area and the federal government as hospitable to francophones as they are to anglophones. It implies that provincial governments and local authorities, particularly in Ontario and New Brunswick but elsewhere as well, provide services to French-speaking citizens in education, the administration of justice, and in other spheres. It means an end to the myriad irritants which have been inflicted on French Canadians by English-Canadian thoughtlessness, whether at the official level (as in the Department of Transport or within Air Canada) or in the private sector (among corporations, voluntary associations, and ordinary citizens). This was difficult enough, even in the heyday of the Royal Commission on Bilingualism and Biculturalism, but it is becoming much more so now that the PQ government is pursuing many policies unpalatable to English Canadians both inside and outside Quebec. Nevertheless, irritation and backlash, no matter how understandable, must be seen in the context of the changing nature of the Canadian state. To retard or stop efforts to make this country a congenial place for francophones is to further reduce the likelihood of Canada's survival.

Official bilingualism, despite the hostility it has aroused, remains one of the necessary conditions. The prime minister and his cabinet have in the eleventh hour decided to explain Ottawa's language policy to the country, particularly to those areas where it has been misunderstood or distorted. There is, of course, nothing wrong with this idea, but the exercise would have been easier had it been undertaken a lot earlier. More important, the manner in which the federal case is now put is dangerous. Ottawa insists, in its efforts to defuse opposition to the federal language program, that there never was any intention to force French down the throats of anglophones who do not wish to learn or use it. This is in a sense correct (and also a little disingenuous); the Official Languages Act is only concerned with the use of French and English by the federal government and the availability of the two official languages to citizens dealing with ths government. But this emphasis overlooks two critical points.

If francophones are to feel that Canada is their home, it is imperative that in a variety of situations and in public and even some private places throughout Canada they should be able to operate with ease in their own language. Some knowledge of French must be evident throughout the country and the teaching of French as a second language cannot be left to chance and drift. It must receive much greater support from the federal government and the provinces which are ultimately responsible for it. A lot of lip and little service has been devoted to this critical aspect: the statistics show that the teaching of French in schools has declined lamentably in such key regions as Ontario. If this is to be reversed (and some small remedial action is admittedly now being launched) then an honest and massive effort needs to be made to persuade the public of both the intrinsic and the political advantages of widespread knowledge of both languages. This may be difficult when Quebec is making determined moves towards unilingualism but it should not be beyond the capacity of anglophones throughout the land to perceive that the institutional defences needed to protect the English language in North America, including Quebec, differ fundamentally from what needs to be done to protect and propagate the use of French.

There is another, equally important aspect of the bilingual question. I noted earlier how rewarding it is personally for anglophones to be thrust into close contact with francophones, and how few have had the opportunity. If such benefits are to be enjoyed by increasing numbers of people from all walks of life, it is essential that they have at least a passive knowledge of both official languages. It is no longer tolerable or possible for Canada-wide organizations and associations to conduct their business in English only, always expecting the francophones to be the ones to adapt. If the advantages of living in a culturally mixed society are to be shared by more than a small elite, then the schools throughout Canada must teach the second language effectively. Any Canadian who aspires to a leadership role in national life, whether in public or private organizations, must, if the country survives, be able to understand both languages. For a youngster to be educated in only one language is to some extent to lower her or his occupational and social mobility, or to impose a difficult process of acquiring the second language during adulthood.

Linguistic aspects, though critical, are only part of the problem. It is unnecessary to add anything here to what others have said about the economic inequalities between French and English, and the plight of the French minorities throughout English Canada. Curiously, what has often been neglected in public discussion is the political dimension. The federal government and the provinces have not been unaware of the political nature of Canada's problem, but they have been unable to respond to it. It is significant, in this context, that even the sensitive Royal Commission on Bilingualism and Biculturalism shied away from addressing the central issue—the political aspects of its mandate.

There has been widespread recognition of the need to redistribute the powers of the federal and the provincial governments, to increase provincial autonomy. This is necessary to meet the demands of Quebec and of the other provinces as well, particularly Alberta, British Columbia, and Ontario. Although Ottawa has been grudging in relinquishing its powers in areas coveted by the provinces (with respect to communications, for instance, and some economic matters), it has recently displayed a more open attitude and some willingness to consider a substantial revision of the constitution. But it has been anything but forthcoming or explicit in indicating what it had in mind. This is not a helpful stance and there is widespread agreement in the provincial capitals that a devolution of the federal power is necessary. There is less consensus that Quebec should enjoy special status in a new federation but the idea continues to receive support in English Canada. There is much to be said for this possibility.

What has usually been ignored or at least played down by advocates of decentralization is the clear need, if the federal system is to work at all, for the central government to retain fairly substantial powers. But in a community aggressively seeking regional and/or ethnic autonomy, there will be little or no disposition to forgo any significant powers claimed by an "alien" central government. The Ottawa government is perceived by many people, and by the governments of several provinces, as a force to be distrusted and even fought.

It is therefore unlikely that the central government in a new Canadian federation would be accorded adequate powers unless something fairly drastic were done to enhance the legitimacy and acceptance of Ottawa. One means of achieving this would be to "provincialize" some central political institutions. Certain mechanisms at the federal level should incorporate representatives or spokesmen or nominees of provincial governments. Federal institutions composed in this way would thus quite frankly act as brokers of distinct regional and ethnic interests and the decisions of such bodies, while applicable nationally, would result from the reconciliation of various provincial interests. This would enhance the identification of the provinces and perhaps certain groups, like the Dene nation, with the central government and would give Ottawa greater acceptance throughout the country. Federal policies would more likely respond to regional interests; but also the regional interests represented in Ottawa would begin to perceive the national dimensions to be their concerns. The resulting policy process might be messy, but it would at least reflect the interests to be reconciled.

It is probably too early to be specific about the mechanisms and institutions which make likely candidates for this sort of transformation. "Provincializing" the Senate and the Supreme Court is the obvious place to begin. Provincial governments (and possibly some groups occupying very special status—the Inuit, for instance) might nominate or elect members to the Senate which would thus become something of a provincial Trojan horse in the federal camp. Likewise, the Supreme Court of Canada which, among other things, is the final arbiter in constitutional disputes affecting the powers of Ottawa and the provinces, could include provincial nominees. In addition, an ever growing number of matters is being decided in this country by independent regulatory, administrative, and even quasi-judicial agencies not directly responsible to Parliament but exercising broad powers. Some, like the CRTC and the Canadian Transport Commission, are within federal jurisdiction, but deal with matters vital to provincial development; others, like the National Energy Board, operate in areas where the provinces share constitutional responsibility. In both cases, there are good reasons for shaping their structure and membership so as to provide closer ties to provincial governments.

The popularity and credibility of the federal government could be increased by other institutional changes. Canadian parties and the party system, for example, have increasingly failed to provide adequate national representation. The virtual exclusion of the Conservatives in Quebec and of the Liberals on the prairies is a strong threat to unity. The adoption of a modified system of proportional representation in federal elections might, by relating seats won more closely to votes, alleviate this problem and so enhance the credibility of Parliament.

These possible changes are much more radical than is apparent at first glance. They could alter the fundamental nature of our political system. Nevertheless, I believe that our circumstances require that they be considered as real alternatives to present arrangements. In exploring their consequences we need to consider not only their potential effects on Canadian unity but also their impact on the operation of the whole political system.

In this context it is almost inevitable that the "provincialization" of federal political institutions would fundamentally modify the parliamentary system and the party system. For if provincial representation were to be genuinely built into federal institutions by provincial nominees in the Upper House then the latter would have to enjoy powers substantially equal to those of the House of Commons. Anything else would smack of tokenism and would be self-defeating. A provincially sensitive Senate would thus establish true bicameralism in federal politics, in which the representation and complexion of the two chambers would inevitably reflect two quite different and probably noncongruent definitions of constituency interests. This would make the convention of cabinet responsibility to the legislature nearly unworkable and would very likely also lead to an attenuation of party discipline. A new relationship between the executive and the legislature (and between the two chambers) would emerge, changing some essential features of the current system.

One's first reaction is to decry such a transformation of our cherished cabinet and parliamentary system. It would deprive us of institutions and conventions which are supposed not only to assure cohesive policy-making but which are also responsible, presenting the electors with party choices that enable them to judge the past performance of governments and to predict what each party will do if elected. To abandon our current institutions could, in short, plunge Canada into the chaotic logrolling world of the congressional system. But how realistic is our conventional pride in the parliamentary system, and how accurate our comparison of the performance of the American and Canadian governments?

This is hardly the place in which to develop answers to these questions. But already serious and responsible politicians and scholars have become sceptical of the capacity of Parliament to function effectively. The runaway expansion of government, the incapacity of the federal government to reduce the size of the public service, and to hold down its expenditures even to the guidelines it has set for the rest of the country, and the inability to control both inflation and the growth of unemployment have given rise to doubts about how effective the system really is. As for its being responsible and responsive, the scathing attack of the Trudeau Liberals on the Conservatives' proposal for government-imposed restraints on wage and price raises during the 1974 election, followed by a Liberal imposition of wage and price controls, makes a mockery of the democratic rhetoric, just as does the presence of the notoriously francophobic one-time Conservative Jack Horner in the Liberal cabinet. Finally, with all its obvious inconsistencies and lack of cohesive policy-making, the American system has produced a governmental structure considerably more open than ours and one which has coped better than we have with both inflation and unemployment.

We need to take a realistic look at whether the institutions we have come to accept as inviolate really do serve the purposes we ascribe to them or in fact stand in our way. In doing so we need to remember that our political institutions are in any event undergoing considerable change. Parliament's importance has been declining for some time as the result of the increasing influence of interest groups, particularly with respect to the civil service; the growing importance of federal-provincial conferences and of executive federalism; and more recently because of the government's interest in the tripartite consideration of economic problems by representatives of labour, management, and the government. We may be moving from an essentially parliamentary system to a new form of corporatism. Modification of the parliamentary system by the "provincialization" of federal institutions may therefore not be as startling as it may seem at first.

Some of the changes mentioned above, as well as others, might lead to the evolution of a new political system combining useful features of parliamentary, congressional, German, and Scandinavian practices. Motivated by the need to avoid disaster and to fashion a new community, we might succeed in creating political institutions suited to the unique circumstances imposed both by the regionally and ethnically divided nature of Canada and the demands of a post-industrial society.

I have stressed the need to re-establish the legitimacy of the federal government, because our opportunities here have received less attention than any others. But this does not diminish the urgency of making all francophones feel completely at home in Canada and assuring that Quebecers do not suffer economically as the result of the Canadian connection.

The final imperative if Canada is to survive is to demonstrate to a reasonably large majority of prospective voters in the Quebec referendum that it is in the interests of Quebec to reject the independentist option espoused by the PQ. This will be exceedingly difficult, first, because it is unlikely that English Canada will be prepared to make needed changes, and second, because of the difficulty of presenting the federalist argument to the Quebec public. The PQ government will not only phrase the referendum so as to maximize the chances of receiving a mandate for separation but it will of course do everything in its power to prevent the federalist option from being advocated effectively. In this effort it has the zealous, enthusiastic, and passionate support of the francophones vast majority of Quebec intellectuals, artists, and other moulders of opinion. It is not always easy in the present climate for Quebec francophones to argue a federalist case and yet it is they, rather than the anglophones, who must do so if it is to meet with any response.

The opponents of independence have one trump which could help them turn the trick. It is related to the nature of the referendum itself. The PQ strategy of *étapisme*—seeking power first on the basis of the promise of a referendum—is a double-edged sword. It brought the PQ victory by enabling it to dampen the independence issue in the election campaign and to permit the polarization of opinion with respect to the record of the Bourassa government rather than in relation to independence. But whereas in the election the promise of a referendum fragmented the opponents of independence, the referendum itself will unify them. This means that to win, the government will have to convert a substantial number of Quebecers who, as current polls indicate, have as yet shown little enthusiasm for the cause.

Everything will depend on the phrasing of the question, the performance of the PQ government, and the imagination and behaviour of English Canada. My reading of events and their causes does not lead to great optimism. Ottawa's response has so far been neither imaginative nor politic. Some of the provinces have done a little better but their record is at best uneven. There are, on the other hand, some things which stand between us and unrelieved gloom. Chief among these is the still amorphous state of public opinion in Quebec. Another is the extent, viability, and openness of a startling number of concerned groups and individuals in English Canada who are attempting to come to grips with events and to essay new solutions. If these efforts bear fruit, and if they goad governments into appropriately daring action, then a much stronger and better Canada may emerge from the present crisis.

It is easy, in the face of the constitutional and political crisis, to overlook the extraordinary prospect before us, should we succeed in working out our present problems: we will have undergone a collective experience of the sort which in the long run cements ties among people, enters their national and group consciousness, and later facilitates further joint efforts and common enterprises.

There is also the promise of a more equal collaboration between French and English Canada. The atmosphere in Quebec now is vibrant, expectant, innovative, bursting with the desire to try new ways of dealing with its problems. This climate is reminiscent of the early CCF era in Saskatchewan under Tommy Douglas. It has enabled the Lévesque government to commit itself to planning and to controlling the economy, and to experiment with new social policies and democratic procedures. The first PQ government is impressive and there is a possibility that its élan and reformist zeal may stimulate political debate and innovation in the rest of the country. There is therefore a chance that a new political climate and style may emerge from the trauma of the present crisis, giving the country a collective task and ideal, leading it towards the sort of politics for which it has tantalizingly shown promise but which it has so far never quite managed to attain.